Wills & Trusts Kit

FOR

DUMMIES®

Wills & Trusts Kit FOR DUMMIES®

by Aaron Larson
Attorney-at-Law

Wiley Publishing, Inc.

Wills & Trusts Kit For Dummies®

Published by
Wiley Publishing, Inc.
111 River St.
Hoboken, NJ 07030-5774
www.wiley.com

WILEY

About the Author

Aaron Larson is an attorney practicing law in Ann Arbor, Michigan, where he lives with his wife and daughter. After graduating from the University of Michigan Law School, Aaron started practice as a quintessential small town lawyer, providing legal services that included estate planning, probate, and guardianship services. He subsequently worked for the Institute of Continuing Legal Education in Ann Arbor, Michigan, where he developed professional education programs for lawyers in areas including estate planning, litigation, and family law. His present legal practice focuses on civil appeals. He operates the ExpertLaw Web site (`www.expertlaw.com`), offering free legal information and assistance to consumers, as well as resources for legal professionals.

Dedication

To my wife Laura and our wonderful daughter Emma.

Author's Acknowledgments

I would like to thank the following people for their invaluable contributions to this book.

- My editor, Kelly Ewing, for her many valuable suggestions.
- My agent, Barb Doyen.
- My acquisitions editor, Michael Lewis, for bringing me into this project.
- My technical reviewer, Joseph Maguire, who has helped keep the presentation of legal issues in this book clear, simple, and accurate.

Publisher's Acknowledgments

We're proud of this book; please send us your comments through our Dummies online registration form located at www.dummies.com/register/.

Some of the people who helped bring this book to market include the following:

Acquisitions, Editorial, and Media Development

Project Editor: Kelly Ewing

Acquisitions Editor: Michael Lewis

Editorial Program Coordinator:
Erin Calligan Mooney

General Reviewer: Joseph Maguire

Associate Project Manager: Jenny Swisher

Assistant Producer: Kit Malone

Quality Assurance: Shawn Patrick

Senior Editorial Manager: Jennifer Ehrlich

Editorial Supervisor and Reprint Editor:
Carmen Krikorian

Editorial Assistant: Joe Niesen

Cover Photos: Steve Owens

Cartoons: Rich Tennant
(www.the5thwave.com)

Composition Services

Project Coordinator: Erin Smith

Layout and Graphics: Carl Byers,
Reuben W. Davis, Melissa K. Jester
Christine Williams

Proofreaders: Melissa Bronnenberg,
John Greenough, Linda Seifert

Indexer: Potomac Indexing, LLC

Special Help: Cynthia Davis-Hubler

Publishing and Editorial for Consumer Dummies

> **Diane Graves Steele,** Vice President and Publisher, Consumer Dummies

> **Joyce Pepple,** Acquisitions Director, Consumer Dummies

> **Kristin A. Cocks,** Product Development Director, Consumer Dummies

> **Michael Spring,** Vice President and Publisher, Travel

> **Kelly Regan,** Editorial Director, Travel

Publishing for Technology Dummies

> **Andy Cummings,** Vice President and Publisher, Dummies Technology/General User

Composition Services

> **Gerry Fahey,** Vice President of Production Services

> **Debbie Stailey,** Director of Composition Services

Contents at a Glance

Table of Contents

Part IV: Carrying Out the Intent of Your Will and Trust....................... 193

Introduction

Congratulations. Simply by opening this book you have put yourself a step ahead of most people. Yes, it's tough to think about what will happen to your family after you die, but confronting these issues is part of taking care of your family.

My goal in writing this book is to give you the information and resources you need to create an estate plan. This book includes do-it-yourself tools to help you draft your own estate planning documents.

But don't go thinking that this book will help you only if you want to create your own will and trust. It's much broader in focus. I want you to be comfortable with estate planning documents, but also to recognize when you'll benefit from professional estate planning services.

I am of the strong opinion that everybody needs an estate plan, and especially a will. With this book, anybody can create a simple will, even if it serves just as a stopgap before hiring a professional.

About This Book

Wills and Trusts Kit For Dummies is written in language that is easy to understand. It covers the basic issues in planning your estate, but also delves into the details and complications you can encounter in choosing your estate plan and creating a will or trust.

You probably won't read this book and conclude, "This is easy," but you'll probably conclude, "I can do this." If not, or if you realize that you simply don't want to plan your own estate, that's fine, too. You'll be an educated consumer when you hire a professional to draft your estate plan.

Everybody needs an estate plan, so I'll immodestly claim that anybody who doesn't have an estate plan will benefit from reading this book. You'll also benefit if your estate plan is out-of-date, and you're not sure whether or how to update your plan.

A Special Note for Residents of Louisiana

If you've been shopping around for books on drafting your own will, you've probably found that most of them say, "This book is valid for all states except Louisiana." You see this warning for two reasons:

- ✔ Louisiana's laws governing the execution of a will are more complicated than those of other states, and a mistake can invalidate your will.

- ✔ More importantly, Louisiana's unique forced heirship laws will trump inconsistent bequests in your will, and you're severely limited in your ability to deviate from the state's mandatory bequests.

Even if you create an otherwise valid will, without a good understanding of forced heirship laws, a court may end up largely disregarding your will or allocating your estate in a way that bears little resemblance to what you directed.

It's beyond the scope of this book to give you the state-specific understanding you need to be sure that a Louisiana court will uphold your will. I thus reluctantly urge residents of Louisiana to have their wills drafted by a legal professional.

Conventions Used in This Book

Whenever you see a word in *italics,* I'm either introducing a new term or using it for emphasis. Likewise, all Web addresses appear in `monofont` type.

What You're Not to Read

Throughout the book, I include sidebars that contain information and anecdotes that expand on the topics discussed in the chapters. You'll easily spot the sidebars by their gray background color. The sidebars can be amusing and informative, but there's nothing in them that you have to read to understand the material in this book. If you're pressed for time, skip over the sidebars. If you find the time to read them later, they'll still be there.

Foolish Assumptions

When writing this book, I had to make a few assumptions about you, the reader. If you meet any of these qualifications, you can find what you need in this book:

- ✔ You don't know much about estate planning and want to get a comprehensive understanding of what is involved.

- ✔ You have a small to average estate and want to create your own estate plan composed of a will and possibly a living trust.

- ✔ You have a large estate and want to do the basics of your estate plan yourself while getting professional assistance with specialized trusts and tax planning.

- ✔ You have absolutely no desire to plan your own estate, but want to know how the estate planning and probate processes work and want to know what you're doing when you hire an estate planning professional to create your estate plan.

I also assumed that you have a computer and can use it to print the worksheets from the accompanying CD to create your own estate planning documents. (You don't have a computer? Then I'm assuming you have a friend who can print the forms for you.)

How This Book Is Organized

This book is organized into six parts that guide you through the estate planning process and specific estate planning documents. I include some stories and anecdotes to help you understand the concepts I discuss.

Part 1: Getting Started with Your Will or Trust

This part explains why you need to plan your estate, the dangers of failing to do so, and the many benefits you get from completing your estate plan. I also cover some of the most important aspects of estate planning, and some of the biggest mistakes people make. You find out when you should get help from an estate planning professional, what professionals can do for you, and how to work with them.

Part II: Everything You Need to Know about Wills

This part helps you understand the central role of your will in your estate plan and the importance of keeping your will up-to-date. You also find out what you need to know about probate court.

In addition, you discover common landmines that can disrupt your estate plan and what you can do to avoid will contests.

Part III: Trust Me! How Trusts Work

If you're considering using a trust for your estate plan, it's important to know exactly what trusts are and what they can do for you. You've heard of a revocable living trust, but what about other types of trust. How can trusts help you avoid estate taxes? This part has all the answers.

Part IV: Carrying Out the Intent of Your Will and Trust

After you figure out the basics of your estate plan, you still have a bit more work to do. You need to take a look at how your retirement and life insurance plans figure into your estate and the special issues that can arise from your real estate holdings. You also need a plan for your personal and financial care in case of illness or disability. This part addresses those topics and more.

Part V: The Part of Tens

This part contains lists to help you with common estate planning issues and traps. I describe mistakes people often make when planning their wills and highlight situations where you may benefit from having a trust. I also tell you how to avoid traps that may increase your estate taxes.

Part VI: The Appendixes

This part contains supplemental information to help you complete your estate plan. Appendix A describes state law signing requirements for wills.

Appendix B summarizes state estate and inheritance taxes. Appendix C is a form that you can use to help gather information for your estate plan. Appendix D lists the forms provided on the accompanying CD.

About the CD

The CD accompanying this book includes forms and worksheets for creating your estate planning documents. You can print them and mark them up by hand or fill them in on your computer and use them to produce your final documents. See Appendix D for a lot more information about the CD and the forms it contains.

Icons Used In This Book

In the margins of the pages of this book, you'll find little pictures, called icons. These icons call your attention to important points about estate planning and help you avoid mistakes:

When you see the Tip icon, you find hints and suggestions to help you with your estate plan.

The Warning icon flags a potential trap or pitfall that you may encounter and helps you avoid costly mistakes.

The Remember icon highlights important actions to take and elements of your estate plan that you truly should not forget.

The Louisiana icon flags unusual aspects of that state's laws, which make it very difficult to draft your own will.

This icon lets you know that you can find a form on the accompanying CD corresponding to the estate planning document or process described in the passage you're reading.

Where to Go from Here

You don't have to start at the beginning of this book and read straight through if you don't want to. This book is designed so that you can look at a topic you're interested in and flip straight to that discussion. However, if you're new to estate planning, consider reading through this book to get an overview of what's involved.

- ✔ If you're about to do something dangerous and need an estate plan "yesterday," you need a will so start with Chapter 7.

- ✔ If you're concerned about how much of your estate will get eaten up by taxes, the news (good and bad) is in Chapter 6.

- ✔ If you have young children and want to be sure that they're taken care of, proceed to Chapter 5 for some quick guidance.

- ✔ If you have a will or trust already, Chapters 9 and 13 cover how to update your estate plan and amend or replace wills and trusts.

Part I

Getting Started with Your Will or Trust

"The instructions for the Will say we should name a guardian whose personality is consistent with our children. I'm not sure we know anyone with a Godzilla/Batman/Barney personality."

In this part . . .

This part explains why you need to plan your estate and the dangers of failing to do so. You find out the process of planning your estate, the tools you can use, and when you need to get help from a professional estate planner. You also discover the process of gathering information about your heirs and assets and planning your bequests. You discover how to plan for special family and personal circumstances, including the care of your children, and avoiding taxes.

Chapter 1

Ensuring That Your Last Wishes Are Honored

. . . .

In This Chapter

▶ Understanding the estate planning process

▶ Creating your estate plan

▶ Getting help when you need it

▶ Making your wishes known

▶ Avoiding common estate planning pitfalls

. . . .

*Y*ou've worked hard all your life, have accumulated some assets, and have bought a copy of this book. You're ready to plan your estate.

My best guess? You're not excited about planning your estate. You have already figured out that you have a lot of work to do. You must also think about unpleasant things, including your death, the possibility of your incapacity, and how your family will cope without you.

What's the primary purpose of an estate plan? Taking care of your loved ones after you're gone. Why plan your estate now? Because the sooner you start, the more certain you can be that your plan will take care of your family's needs in the way that you want.

As you proceed with this process, you'll probably find out your estate planning needs aren't as complicated as you thought. You may discover that all you need is a will, perhaps backed up by a simple living trust. You may discover that your needs are more complicated and enlist the help of an estate planning professional. Yet even then, your understanding of the estate planning process and tools will help you communicate your needs and choose your best options.

Having an estate plan also provides a great deal of comfort. You'll be able to plan for your family's financial needs. And after your death or incapacity, your loved ones won't have to fret about what you would have wanted them to do. They'll know your actual wishes.

The Good, the Bad, and the Ugly: What Can Happen When You Don't Plan Your Estate

Simply put, if you don't plan your estate, the government has an estate plan in store for you. Your state's laws of *intestate succession* will apply, and the state will decide who inherits your assets, usually your spouse and children. But that's not all:

- ✔ In the event of your incapacity, a court may appoint people to make decisions for you regarding your personal and medical care and the management of your money. A stranger may end up deciding where you live, what medical treatment you receive, and perhaps even whether you really need $20 for a haircut.

- ✔ If you have minor children, a court will have to decide who will care for them, but will not have the benefit of your input.

- ✔ The business you spent a lifetime building may end up failing or in the hands of a court-appointed receiver.

Planning your estate isn't a one-time task. Changes in your life circumstances can dramatically alter both your wishes for your estate, and whether your original estate plan even remains viable.

Sometimes it seems like your life doesn't change much, so you may be wondering what sort of changes I am talking about. Consider the following:

- ✔ Your estate will probably grow substantially over the course of your life, although it may also shrink.

- ✔ You may marry, divorce, separate, have or adopt a child, or experience a death in your family.

- ✔ Your children will grow up and establish their own households.

- ✔ You may move between states, buy and sell property, or start your own business.

- ✔ Your designated trustee or personal representative may no longer be available, or your relationship with that person may change.

- ✔ Laws may change. In fact, they will. You can expect a new estate tax bill to be working its way through Congress within the next year or two, and it won't be the last.

In all probability, you'll update your estate plan several times during your life, and on occasion you may even start over from scratch.

If you don't update your estate, over time your estate plan may become largely ineffective. When that happens, you're not much better off than you were before you created the outdated estate plan.

Reaping the Benefits of Planning Your Estate

The biggest advantage of planning your estate is that your wishes will be respected, both while you're alive and after your death.

Your estate plan helps you in several ways:

- ✔ Incapacity planning helps ensure that you receive the type of medical care and treatment you want, that your assets are managed according to your own wishes, and that your end-of-life decisions are respected.
- ✔ Your will and trust ensure that your assets are distributed to the heirs you choose, under terms and conditions you define.
- ✔ Your business succession plan helps ensure that your business doesn't fail following your incapacity or death, and that control of your business passes to a suitable successor.

When you don't plan your estate, your incapacity plan will be defined by a court, and your estate will be carved up according to state law. The result may be far different from what you desire.

Planning for your care while you're alive

In addition to planning for the distribution of your assets after you die, a complete estate plan looks at what will happen to your estate if an accident or illness leaves you unable to properly care for yourself.

Your incapacity plan includes your durable power of attorney, healthcare proxy, and living will:

- ✔ Your durable power of attorney appoints an attorney-in-fact who can make financial decisions for you if you become incapacitated.
- ✔ Your healthcare proxy appoints a healthcare advocate who can help you make medical decisions if you're unable to make or communicate those decisions yourself.
- ✔ Your living will describes what care you want to receive, and don't want to receive, during the final days of your life.

If you don't appoint people to help with your medical and financial needs, your family may have to go to court to have somebody appointed to make decisions for you. Your loved ones will face unnecessary burdens and confusion:

- ✔ Your family will have to go to court to have somebody appointed to manage your personal and financial needs, at a time when they're already under stress due to your incapacity.

- ✔ The court won't know who you'd prefer to assist with your medical and financial decisions, and may appoint somebody who you would find unacceptable.

- ✔ Your helpers won't know your wishes or the limits you'd impose on their choices if you were able to communicate them. They'll have to try to guess what you would have wanted.

The impact of these choices may be profound. Whatever your plans, with a court-appointed guardian supervising your medical care, you're more likely to undergo more intrusive medical care and to spend your last days in a hospital or nursing home. (Chapter 14 discusses incapacity planning in more detail.)

Ensuring that your assets go where you want

When you plan your estate, you pick your heirs and decide how much you want to leave to them. Although state laws do restrict your ability to disinherit certain heirs, especially your spouse, for the most part you can leave your money to family, friends, schools and charities, or anybody else you choose.

In defining your bequests, you may choose to simply distribute your assets to your heirs upon your death. But you may also choose to be very creative in how you distribute your assets.

- ✔ You can defer your bequests to a later date (for example, "When my son turns 25").

- ✔ You can mete out your gifts in installments (for example, "$20,000 to my daughter upon her 18th birthday, $20,000 on her 23rd birthday, and $60,000 upon her 30th birthday").

- ✔ You can impose conditions on your bequests, requiring your heirs to satisfy those conditions before they receive the inheritance (for example, "$50,000 to my son upon his graduation from college").

If you don't plan your estate, the state will make all those choices for you. Your estate will go to your heirs according to your state's laws of intestate succession, described later in this chapter in the section "Realizing What Happens If You Don't Have an Estate Plan." If you have minor children, the probate court may appoint a conservator to look after their assets until they turn 18. But any adult heir will immediately receive their legally defined inheritance. Your wish to support your alma mater or to give to charity? Forget it.

The only way to be sure that your assets are distributed the way you want is to plan your estate. (Chapters 3 and 4 detail the process of collecting information about your assets and planning your bequests.)

Looking Out for Common Pitfalls

Everybody makes mistakes, but some mistakes get made a lot. Actions that may seem like they'll simplify your estate may in fact make it more complicated, burden your ability to use and enjoy your own assets, or increase the tax burden to your estate and heirs.

At the same time, once you understand the common pitfalls, most are pretty easy to avoid. You can avoid some mistakes simply by planning your estate now, rather than putting it off until your health starts to fail. (For more discussion of common estate planning mistakes, see Chapters 8 and 18.)

Benefits and dangers of jointly titling real estate, property, and bank accounts

A common shortcut to estate planning involves adding your desired heir to the title of your real estate, financial account, or other titled asset. You can choose between a number of different types of joint ownership, discussed in Chapter 17. In all likelihood, when you add somebody as an owner, you'll create a *joint tenancy with right of survivorship,* meaning that they automatically inherit your share if you die before them.

Some huge risks can arise from joint ownership of a home. Take a common example, where you add your child to the deed as a joint tenant:

- ✔ Your son gets divorced, and his wife asks the divorce court to award him half of "his share" of your house.
- ✔ Your son may decide that the home is "more than you can handle" and ask a court to force the sale of the property.
- ✔ Your son decides to move in. It's his home too, isn't it?
- ✔ Your son suffers financial problems or doesn't pay his taxes, and his creditors or the IRS try to collect against "his share."

Also, adding a joint owner can increase that person's capital gains tax exposure when the property is eventually sold.

Other issues may also arise:

- ✔ What happens if you can no longer afford to support your home, or are no longer physically able to care for it, but your child won't agree to a sale?

- ✔ What happens if you want to refinance your mortgage to improve the property, get a better interest rate, or withdraw equity from your home, but your child refuses to cooperate?

- ✔ What if you want to sell your house and move into a smaller home or condo, but your child wants to keep "the family home?"

- ✔ What happens if you have to move into a long-term care facility?

When you give up your full ownership interest, you run the risk that your children will suddenly decide that they know what is best for you, and prevent you from making perfectly reasonable decisions relating to your own home.

Similar issues arise with joint ownership of bank accounts. As the law presumes that both you and your joint account holder have equal rights to the money, your co-account holder may empty the account. His creditors may try to garnish the account to satisfy his debts. If it truly is a joint account, with both of you contributing toward the balance, the IRS will still try to include the entire account balance in your taxable estate, and your child will have to prove to the IRS that he contributed part of the money and that his contribution should not be taxed.

Possible alternatives to joint ownership include the use of a living trust, or transfer-on-death titles and accounts. (Part III discusses living trusts. For discussion of joint ownership of real estate, see Chapter 17.)

Benefits and dangers of life estates

You own your home, and you want your children to inherit your home. So how about a life estate? In a *life estate,* you retain the right to use and control your home for the rest of your life, and you provide for your ownership of your home to pass to specific people upon your death. You're called the *life tenant,* and the people who eventually receive your home are your *remaindermen.* Although I'm speaking in terms of your marital home, you can create a life estate for other property as well, which is called a *retained life estate.*

In a typical arrangement, once you create a life estate, you retain the exclusive right to the use and possession of your home. You pay the day-to-day expenses of your home, including routine maintenance, homeowner's insurance, and property taxes. You pay the interest on the mortgage, but your remaindermen pay the portion of the mortgage payment that goes to the principal balance.

"My children wouldn't do that to me"

You probably have thought at one time or another that your offspring would never do any of these awful scenarios to you. While other people may have children who will abuse joint ownership or empty a joint bank account, your children would never do such a thing. You know what? You're probably right. The worst abuses happen in exceptional cases, and most children try to respect their parents' wishes. But not all the problems arise from malice.

Your child may encounter financial troubles. It's easy to "borrow" a car payment or a house payment from your joint bank account. Maybe your child even repays the loan the first time or two. But then she finds herself having borrowed two or three payments. Then four. And before she even appreciates what she's doing, she's "borrowed" far more of your money than

she can realistically pay back. Do you sue your child? Call the police? The odds are that you won't. You'll suffer a strain in your relationship and have a less comfortable retirement than you had previously expected.

On the flipside, your child may be far more concerned with your financial stability than you are. Every time you make a purchase, your child may be demanding to know what you spent "all that money on" and "did you really need it." I recently encountered a case where a child emptied out her mother's joint bank account, not because her mother was spending inappropriately but because the daughter was afraid she *might*. She didn't approve of her mother's new boyfriend and was concerned that her mother might make excessive gifts.

As a life tenant, you face the same type of dependence upon the goodwill and cooperation of your remaindermen as you do with joint ownership (see preceding section). You need your remaindermen's consent to refinance or sell your home, and difficulties can arise if you become unable to pay the home's ongoing expenses.

A life estate may also appeal to you if you have children from a prior marriage who you wish to eventually inherit your home, but want your current spouse to be able to live in your home following your death. You can provide in your estate plan for your spouse to receive a life estate in your home, with your children as the remaindermen. But consider the consequences:

- ✔ Say that you're considerably older than your spouse. You die at age 82, and your spouse is 63. At this time, your children are nearing retirement age. If your spouse lives for another 20 years, your children will be elderly by the time they inherit your home. By then, they may have little need for an inheritance.

- ✔ Your spouse may neglect the property, causing your children to have to pay insurance, taxes, and repairs and possibly having to take your spouse to court.

✔ You may create acrimony between your spouse and your children, who see your spouse as standing in the way of "their inheritance."

✔ Your spouse may remarry. Do you want to subsidize your spouse's new family?

An alternative? Keep your house in a trust for five to ten years, or whatever other time period you desire, and let your spouse have full use and enjoyment of it during that period. Then have your trust convey your house to your children.

Danger of subjecting an asset to Medicaid spend-down rules

Medicare is a federal health insurance program that provides payment for certain hospital and medical expenses for people aged 65 and older. But as you age, you face a huge potential expense that Medicare doesn't ordinarily cover: long-term care.

If you're wealthy enough, lucky enough, or hold sufficient long-term care insurance, you may not need to worry about the cost of your long-term care. But most people, even those with some insurance, can face significant financial hardship from the high cost of residential care.

This is where Medicaid comes in. Medicaid is an additional federal program that covers medical costs, including the cost of long-term care, if you're financially unable to pay for that care yourself.

But before you can qualify for Medicaid, *spend-down rules* apply. If you have too much income or too many assets, you won't qualify for Medicaid until your income or assets are spent down to a qualifying level. The goal here is to make you pay for your own care before the government takes over, while still protecting you and your family from becoming impoverished by the costs of long-term care. Note that spend-down rules don't require that your assets be spent on your medical care, but you do face restrictions on how you can spend your excess money without affecting your qualification for Medicaid.

What if you give your assets away instead of spending them? Can you qualify for Medicaid? That's where *look back rules* kick in. When you apply for Medicaid benefits to pay for long-term care, the government examines your financial transactions over the past five years to determine whether you've transferred assets out of your estate. If you have, the government will impose a penalty period before you can qualify for Medicaid benefits. Any gifts, including payment of tuition for an adult child, charitable donations, and even Christmas presents, can trigger a penalty period for long-term care benefits.

You benefit from a modest Medicaid exemption for income and savings. But you may benefit from a large exemption in the form of your home. If you're in a nursing home but are expected to return to your own home, your home is exempt from the spend-down rules. Note that if you stay in a nursing home for six months or longer, Medicaid assumes that you won't return home. Also, if you're married, as long as your spouse remains in your home, it's exempt from spend-down rules.

So how do you accidentally lose your exemptions? Usually in one of two ways:

✔ You don't understand the exemptions and believe that the government will take your house no matter what. You transfer title to an heir, probably your children. Your home is no longer yours, and the government will apply spend-down rules to its fair market value.

✔ You aren't even thinking about Medicaid. You decide that the easiest way to leave your home to your heirs is to add them to the title, giving them outright ownership. The transfer of an interest in your home for less than fair market value during the look-back period can trigger spend-down rules or penalties.

Traditionally, people often used life estates to try to avoid Medicaid spend-down rules. The value of a life estate isn't counted toward your assets when you apply for Medicaid benefits. But states are eager to recover Medicaid expenses and are increasingly imposing liens against the property a Medicaid recipient has placed into a life estate.

One more thing to consider: Even when an exemption applies during your lifetime, the state may seek to recoup its costs by imposing a lien against your property after your death.

Your best approach is to engage in estate planning long before you end up in long-term care. If you plan for your long-term care needs and implement an asset protection strategy before the Medicaid look-back period begins, you can minimize the effect of spend-down rules and recoupment policies on your estate.

If you believe you or your spouse will require Medicaid benefits later in life, you can consult a lawyer who specializes in Medicaid planning. Your lawyer can help you create a strategy to minimize the effects of Medicaid's spend-down and look-back rules, as well as helping you avoid or minimize liens Medicaid may attempt to assert against your estate after you die.

Potential for increased tax exposure

Most people won't pay federal estate tax. The current estate tax exemption is $2 million, and the estate tax is scheduled to be totally repealed in 2010.

But the law repealing estate taxes is scheduled to expire at the end of 2010. Most people expect that Congress will pass a new law sometime in 2009 that restores an estate tax, but with an exemption set somewhere between $1.5 million and $4 million.

The estate tax is substantial. Above the exemption, the current estate tax rate is 45 percent. If your estate is large enough to pay estate taxes and you do no advance planning, the government may turn out to be your biggest beneficiary.

Realizing What Happens If You Don't Have an Estate Plan

Are there drawbacks to not planning your estate? Yes, and some of them are *big*.

If you have a large estate, you will maximize your estate tax liability (see the preceding section). But in addition to the possibility that you'll increase the government's cut, you have two huge reasons to have an estate plan:

- ✔ If you don't plan your estate, the government will decide who inherits your assets.
- ✔ If you don't designate a custodian for your minor children, the state will pick somebody for you.

You may enjoy many smaller benefits as well, including picking the person who will administer your estate and providing instructions for your funeral and memorial service. If you don't draft a will, others will make those choices for you.

Following the laws of intestate succession

If you don't make an estate plan for yourself, the state has already made one for you. State *laws of intestate succession* define who inherits the property of people who die without a will. Typically, your surviving spouse will receive half of your estate, with the remainder divided between your children. If you have no surviving spouse or children, your estate is distributed by formula to other surviving members of your family.

In some cases, the state's plan for your assets may be very similar to your own. In others, it will be wildly different. But the only way to be certain that your estate is distributed the way you want is to create an estate plan.

Even if you plan your estate, intestate succession laws may apply to some of your assets in the following situations:

✔ You forget to include an asset in your estate plan.

✔ You direct an asset to an heir through your living trust, but forget to transfer ownership of the asset into your trust.

✔ After all of your bequests are made, you'll almost certainly have something left over in your estate, even if just a small amount of cash or your clothing and personal effects.

You should include a *residuary clause* in your will, describing how any assets left in your estate are to be distributed after all specific bequests have been made. That way, all your assets will be distributed consistent with your own wishes, and not through choices the state makes for you.

Determining the custodian of your minor children

Although uncommon, tragedy can strike your family and kill both you and your spouse. Families tend to travel together, so a terrible car accident or plane crash could leave your children as orphans.

If you draft a will, you may designate custodians for your minor children. You can pick people you trust to care for your children and raise them in a manner you approve. If you want, you can designate one person to care for your children, and another person to manage their money.

Although courts aren't bound by your designation, judges usually defer to a parent's wishes. But if you don't make a choice, the judge will pick somebody for you. That person or persons could be

✔ Your in-laws, who were abusive to your spouse throughout her childhood

✔ Your sister, whose husband was adamantly opposed to caring for your children until he learned about their Social Security survivor's benefits

✔ Your cousin, who has never been able to manage money but will now be responsible for overseeing your children's inheritance

Granted, often the court will make a good decision and pick somebody who will provide excellent care for your children. But why take the chance?

Even if you're divorced from the other parent, you can designate a guardian. That way, you don't have to update your will if something happens to their other parent. If you have custody of your children and have serious concerns about the other parent's ability to properly care for them if something happens to you,

you can include with your will an explanation of why you'd prefer somebody else to take custody of your children. Although courts will almost always give custody to a surviving parent, as that's typically what the law requires, you will at least make the court aware of your concerns.

Issues you may face in providing for your children and dependents are discussed in Chapter 5.

Creating Your Will or Trust

If you're reading this book, you're probably considering drafting your own estate plan. If you don't expect to owe estate taxes, don't want to disinherit your spouse or child, and have the time to work through the process, you should be able to do it yourself. But if you lack the time or inclination, have a very large estate, are disinheriting an heir, are the owner of a business, or have a complicated plan for the distribution of your estate, you'll almost certainly benefit from professional estate planning services.

Whatever you decide, your understanding of the estate planning process will help you. It's essential to planning your own estate, but it will also help you understand your own needs and communicate your wishes to an estate planning professional.

Deciding who should create it

As you embark upon the estate planning process, you need to ask yourself, are you able to plan your entire estate yourself? You may discover that

- ✔ You're capable, but don't have sufficient time or interest to go through the process of planning your estate.
- ✔ You can plan the bulk of your estate, but require some specialized estate planning services that should be performed by a lawyer.
- ✔ Whether due to the size and complexity of your estate, or your own discomfort with the process, you should hire a professional to plan your estate.

There's absolutely nothing wrong with getting help with your estate plan. Most lawyers I know don't plan their own estates. It's not a matter of ability, as most are capable of figuring out what they would need to do. It's a matter of getting things done quickly, and getting the benefit of an expert's advice and knowledge.

Although you may cringe at the thought of paying money to a lawyer, remember that your time is valuable. How many hours of your time do you want to spend learning the intricacies of estate tax law or business succession, when an experienced estate planning lawyer will be able to do a better job in a fraction of the time, by dint of experience? And if you make a mistake, the increased capital gains tax, income tax, and estate tax exposure will probably dwarf the cost of professional estate planning services.

For more guidance on working with estate planning professionals and figuring out when you need an expert, see Chapter 2.

The state of Louisiana has chosen to make it very difficult to draft your own will. The steps you must take to execute a valid will are the most complicated in the nation. But that's not all. The state's *forced heirship laws* mandate minimum bequests to certain heirs and restrict your right to reduce their bequests or disinherit them. You can create what by all appearances is a valid, properly executed will, yet still have the state restructure your bequests to your heirs. Pretty much everybody in Louisiana, including most lawyers, should have a professional draft their will.

Understanding the process

Planning your estate can be a big job, but it's something you can handle. Approach the process step-by-step:

1. **Gather your facts.**

   Take stock of your personal situation, including where you live, who lives with you, your extended family, and other potential heirs, including friends and charities.

   Take a thorough look at your assets, determining what you own, how you own it, and what it's worth. Also review your debts, including what you owe and who you owe it to.

   This process is covered in Chapter 3.

2. **Determine your estate planning needs.**

   Ask yourself the following questions:

   - You need a will, but do you also need a living trust?

   - Do you want to use other trusts, to delay or structure inheritances, or to protect your heirs?

   - Will your estate owe estate taxes? How complex does your estate planning strategy need to be? Do you also need a gifting strategy, to transfer wealth to your heirs during your lifetime?

- Do you own your own business? What sort of business succession plan do you need?

- What other special circumstances do you need to address? For example, do you have children from a prior relationship? Do you want to disinherit an heir?

- Who will serve as your helpers? Your *personal representative* manages your estate in probate court, pays your bills and taxes, and oversees your funeral and burial arrangements. Your *trustee* manages, controls, and distributes assets held in your trust. Your minor children need a *custodian* to take care of them if something happens to you, and perhaps a second person to take care of their money.

- If you're creating a trust, what property do you want to put into your trust?

- How will you leave your assets to your heirs? Will they receive their inheritances immediately, or will they be held in trust until some point in time in the future? Will any of your gifts be conditional, with your heirs only receiving their inheritance when a condition (such as college graduation) is met?

- How will your estate pay its bills and expenses? Do you have enough money available to pay your debts and taxes, pay for the administration of your estate and trust, and cover funeral expenses? Should you carry some life insurance to cover those costs?

This process is described in Chapter 4.

3. **Prepare your will and living trust, making sure that you address all your major assets, including those with sentimental value.**

For some assets, you'll want to designate contingent beneficiaries, in case an heir dies before you do or declines an inheritance.

You will also include a residuary clause, directing how any assets left in your estate will be distributed after all your specific gifts have been made.

For guidance on drafting your will, see Part II of this book. Trusts are covered in Part III.

4. **Execute your estate planning documents to give them legal effect, obtaining proper witness signatures and notarization.**

You can execute your documents as you complete them or, if you prefer, as you complete each document. Guidance for executing your will is provided in Chapter 7 and Appendix A. Instruction for executing your trust is found in Chapter 11.

5. Lather, rinse, repeat.

You'll review your estate plan on a regular basis, perhaps annually (and not less than once every few years), to make sure that it still suits your needs.

You'll also review your estate plan when you experience major changes in your life, including moving to another state, marriage, divorce, separation, childbirth or adoption, significant change in your financial situation, or the death of an heir.

For information on reviewing and updating your will, see Chapter 9. Guidance for updating your revocable living trust is provided in Chapter 13.

Throughout this process, ask yourself whether it's realistic for you to plan your estate yourself. You can manage a will and living trust, but tax planning, business succession planning, more complicated trusts, or complicated plans for the distribution of your assets can change that. So can state laws, particularly if you want to leave your spouse less than the law requires, or if you live in Louisiana.

Thinking about your kids, money, life insurance, and more

You need a plan for your incapacity. That plan may include a living trust, granting the trustee authority over the trust's assets if something happens to you. But you should also prepare a durable power of attorney and healthcare proxy and should consider a living will (see Chapter 14).

If you own a business, you probably need a business succession plan. This plan has two major components. First, how do you convey your business to your heirs while minimizing capital gains taxes and estate taxes, and second, who will take control of your business and manage it if you die or become incapacitated. Without a good succession plan, you risk that your business will collapse (see Chapter 4).

Do you have retirement accounts? As with your life insurance policies, they'll typically pass to a named beneficiary instead of going through your estate. Have you considered what rollover rights your beneficiary may enjoy? Inheritance of tax-deferred retirement savings can be more valuable to an heir who can roll those savings into his own retirement accounts instead of having to immediately pay taxes (see Chapter 15).

Do you have life insurance? Take a look at who owns the policy, and who you have named as beneficiaries. Ownership will affect whether or not your insurance proceeds are included in your taxable estate. Your beneficiaries will receive the proceeds outside of probate, meaning that your beneficiary designation controls who receives the money even if your will says something else. When you review and update your will, you should also review and update your life insurance beneficiaries (see Chapter 16).

How will your estate pay its bills? Do you have enough cash assets, or investments that can be liquidated to pay the costs of your estate? Do you need to have life insurance to help cover those costs? If so, will the insurance proceeds be subject to estate taxes, and can those taxes be avoided? (See Chapter 6 on the costs of estate administration and estate taxes.)

Will your estate have to pay estate taxes? Are you unsure? If your estate will owe estate taxes you will almost always benefit from professional estate planning services. Estate taxes are so high that in the long run those services will typically pay for themselves several times over. (See Chapter 6 on estate taxes.)

How do you keep your estate planning documents safe? How can you be sure that your personal representative can find your will, or that it won't be lost or destroyed? See the suggestions on safeguarding your estate plan in Chapter 2.

Chapter 2

Making Crucial Decisions

As you begin the estate planning process, your first task is to decide how much help you need. Can you plan your entire estate yourself? Do you need help and, if so, how much? Or are you better off simply hiring a professional? Your choices will depend upon the complexity of your estate and your comfort with the estate planning process.

This chapter also explains what wills and trusts are and how they fit into your estate plan. You find out how to work with an estate planning professional, how to protect your will or trust, and who should have a copy.

Going It Alone

Some estate planning books are full of warnings that you should not attempt to plan your estate without getting help from a lawyer. I'm working from the assumption that you understand that planning your own estate may be difficult, but you intend to try. You're the only one who knows your limitations and abilities.

Are you the type who hires an accountant to prepare your 1040-EZ? Then estate planning will probably prove to be daunting. Do you eschew professionals and tax software, instead delving into tax instruction pamphlets and paper forms? Then this is probably right up your alley. Most people fall somewhere in the middle. If you're comfortable doing your own taxes, you're probably up to the job of planning your own estate.

If you're so comfortable, why haven't you done it?

Has this book been sitting on a shelf for six months, and you're just now cracking the cover for the first time? Did you eagerly start reading the day you bought this book, but weeks later have yet to start organizing to draft your will?

Perhaps you're capable, but you're procrastinating. Perhaps you're intimidated or overwhelmed. Either way, consider giving yourself a deadline to get started. If you don't meet your deadline, perhaps it's time to hire a professional.

It's never fun to open your wallet to pay an estate planning professional. Yet this book would not be complete if I did not help you understand:

✔ When planning your estate might exceed your abilities

✔ When it makes sense to have part of your estate plan created by a lawyer

✔ When your use of an estate planning professional can save you (or your estate) time and even money

There is wisdom in knowing your own limitations and recognizing when you need assistance from an estate planning professional.

Are you comfortable doing it yourself?

The first question is one that only you can answer: Are you comfortable creating your own estate plan? Drafting a will is easier than drafting a revocable living trust. Drafting a revocable living trust is easier than drafting a bypass trust. If you add enough conditions and caveats, you can make drafting pretty much any document impossibly complicated.

How complicated is your estate?

The estate planning process can be as easy or as difficult as you make it. I have seen some very complicated estate plans for small, simple estates. Factors that may complicate your estate plan include planning for a large estate and estate tax issues; business ownership; marriage, children, and remarriage; and delaying or controlling distribution of inheritances after your death.

Some factors that complicate your estate are beyond your control. Others, you create. As much as possible, try to keep it simple.

Large estates

For this chapter, when I refer to a *large estate,* I mean an estate that will incur estate taxes. If your estate is large, or you expect that your estate will be large when you die, your estate inevitably becomes more complicated. Consider estate taxes:

- ✔ If you try to avoid estate taxes by making gifts during your lifetime, you have to consider gift tax issues, as well as the impact on your heirs' taxable basis in gifts you make to them. (See Chapters 6 and 21 on estate taxes.)

- ✔ If you try to avoid estate taxes through trusts, you must select the proper trusts, make sure that they're in proper form, choose appropriate trustees, and fund your trusts. If you make errors, the consequences can be serious. For example, the assets you intend to convey by trust may be treated as part of your taxable estate, or you may accidentally trigger generation skipping taxes on top of estate taxes. (See Chapter 12 on trusts.)

- ✔ If you try to avoid estate taxes through charitable giving, you have many choices to make. Do you want to begin your charitable giving during your lifetime — for example, by using a charitable remainder trust to generate income or tax savings? Should you make charitable donations by bequest? (See Chapter 6 on estate taxes and Chapter 12 on trusts.)

 If your estate is very large — $20 million or more — good tax planning may save your estate a small fortune in taxes. But the types of estate planning tools a professional will recommend and implement will often be very complex and aggressive and may come under intense scrutiny from the IRS. Planning your estate is not realistically a do-it-yourself project.

Business assets

Do you ever wish you had a day job? If you own your own business or are a partner in a privately owned business, you have worked very hard to build your business.

- ✔ If you don't plan for estate taxes, your estate may have difficulty covering the tax bill. In some cases, your business may be sold or liquidated to cover your tax bill. (See Chapter 6 on estate taxes.)

- ✔ If you don't plan for business succession, who will manage your business when you're gone? In the event of death or disability, can your business even access its accounts to pay its bills, let alone continue its daily operations? Will your business close for want of new management? Will your heirs fight for control? (See the discussion in Chapter 4 on estate planning for your business.)

You need a management succession plan to cover not only the tax and financial aspects of business succession, but also practical issues in picking your successor and avoiding family conflict. As a business owner, even if you're capable of researching every aspect of your estate and creating your own business succession plan, I doubt that you have the time.

An estate planning lawyer can help you devise a strategy that includes succession planning and estate tax avoidance. He can balance estate taxes against capital gains taxes and often structure business stock to minimize its value to your estate, without impairing its value to your heirs.

If you own shares in a small business, you have issues beyond leaving your shares to your heirs. If you or one of your partners dies, think about the following:

- ✔ Who will inherit their shares, and will that person (or those *people*) have the right to participate in the business?

- ✔ If the business has the right to buy the shares from a deceased partner's estate, how will you determine their value? How will the business afford the shares? Will buying the shares create cash flow problems?

You and your partners should have a buy-sell agreement that addresses these issues, as well as related issues that may arise during your lifetimes.

Family issues

You may not want to believe it, but the way you treat your family in your estate plan can overshadow a lifetime of love and support. Your bequests will probably be seen as an expression of approval or disapproval, of love or rejection.

You may have very good reasons for you to give your children different inheritances or disinheriting a child. But you must do so in a manner that is legally effective, and you will probably want to do so in a way that minimizes the likelihood of a family rift.

If you're married but have children from a prior relationship, you need to consider how you will divide your estate between your spouse and children. This decision gets even more complicated if you have children with your current spouse or if you have stepchildren who will inherit your spouse's estate. If you die first, how much of your estate will go to your stepchildren instead of your children? For more discussion of estate planning issues arising from second families, please consult Chapter 4.

Although the story of Howard Hughes is fading from popular memory, you may be surprised that he died without a will. Hearing that, you will probably *not* be surprised that a decade long legal battle ensued over his $6 billion estate. The estate of a man who, at least officially, was long divorced and never had children was besieged by claims from people claiming to be his wives and children.

If you *may* have children from prior relationships or believe somebody may be tempted to falsely claim to be your child to try to grab a share of your estate, you need to anticipate that possibility in your estate plan. If a court concludes that you omitted a child from your will, that child may end up with the largest inheritance of any of your children, and perhaps any of your heirs.

Choosing a Will or Trust for Your Estate

The revocable living trust is probably the most heavily marketed estate planning tool in history. You create this trust during your lifetime and may amend or revoke it as you wish. The trust becomes irrevocable upon your death, and the trust's assets are distributed according to your instructions. For details on living trusts, see Part III of this book.

Marketing materials may leave you with the impression that everybody needs a living trust. By comparison, a will may seem ordinary. Don't be fooled. Your will is a failsafe for your estate plan. You may not need a trust, but you do need a will.

What a will can do for you

A will is the easiest tool to direct your assets to your beneficiaries. Your probate estate includes the property owned by you at the time of your death.

Your will designates the *personal representative* (executor) for your estate. If you wish, most states permit you to waive any bond that your personal representative is otherwise required to post under state law.

You can use your will to create a trust, often called a *testamentary trust,* to hold and distribute some or all of your assets. You can also provide that part of your estate, or the balance of your estate after your bequests, will go into an existing trust. A will that funds an existing trust is known as a *pour-over will.*

If you have minor children, you should designate a custodian for your children in your will. A court will review your designation and confirm that it is consistent with your children's needs, but courts usually defer to a parents' preference. You can designate the same person, or if you prefer a different person, to act as custodian of your children's assets. (For more on providing for your dependents, see Chapter 5.)

Some of your assets, such as insurance and financial accounts with designated beneficiaries, or the assets you have transferred into your living trust, are not included in your probate estate and thus are not affected by your will.

What a trust can do for you

There are many different types of trust, each of which potentially provides a different set of benefits to your estate. Potential benefits of estate planning with trusts include avoiding probate, increased privacy, avoiding taxes, succession planning for your family business, and controlling the distribution of your estate. Among the trusts you may consider

- ✔ A *revocable living trust* is an excellent tool to plan for incapacity and the distribution of your assets, but is a poor tool for avoiding estate taxes.

- ✔ *Charitable trusts* and *insurance trusts* may help you avoid estate taxes, but are not of themselves tools for distributing assets to your heirs.

- ✔ *Asset protection trusts* can help protect your financially troubled heirs from losing their inheritance to creditors.

The most popular trust is the *revocable living trust.* You transfer ownership of your assets into a trust that becomes active upon your death or legal incapacity. At that time, a trustee who you picked manages your estate consistent with instructions you included in your trust. After you die, trust assets are distributed to your heirs without going through probate. (Chapter 12 describes a wide variety of trusts commonly used in estate planning.)

Trusts give you great flexibility in planning bequests. For example, you can delay the age at which your children inherit assets, provide income and support for your heirs prior to distributing the bulk of your estate, or provide an inheritance in several installments.

You may benefit from having both

If you do not have a will to back up your trust, anything that isn't included in your trust will go through probate. Those assets will pass by the *laws of intestate succession,* meaning that the court will determine who inherits your estate and what they inherit by state law.

Even if you carefully convey ownership of your property into a living trust, you will have personal property when you die. You will have clothes in your closet, cash in your wallet, and other items of personal property that must be conveyed to your heirs. You can use a will to do that, or you can use your will to direct your remaining property into your trust.

In many cases, significant assets are never transferred into a living trust. I have even encountered a very expensive, professionally prepared estate plan where *nothing* had been transferred into the trust. The trust was a thing of beauty, but the entire estate went through probate.

The choice is thus not between a will and a living trust. Your estate plan should include a will. You may benefit from also having a trust.

Going with a Pro

When you start planning your estate you may find that you lack the time to put together the estate plan you want. You may find the process daunting or confusing. You may find it incredibly boring. Whatever your reason, if you're unable to complete your own estate plan, you should not hesitate to hire a professional.

An estate planning practice involves knowledge of a significant number of legal disciplines, including:

- ✔ Wills and trusts
- ✔ State and federal tax law
- ✔ The law of business organizations
- ✔ Medicare and Medicaid law
- ✔ Real and personal property law

In addition, estate planning requires knowledge of financial matters, including insurance and annuities, asset valuation, and retirement plans and pensions.

Nobody, not even a great estate planning lawyer, can master every aspect of estate planning. Even lawyers may employ outside professionals to assist them with complicated estates.

How lawyers and accountants can help

Lawyers and accountants can help you get a realistic view of your estate and finances. They can help you assess which estate planning tools will best serve your goals for:

- ✔ Avoiding taxes during your life
- ✔ Your business
- ✔ Your retirement
- ✔ Disability and the cost of long-term care
- ✔ Your estate and heirs

An experienced estate planning lawyer will understand the problems that can result from your estate plan and can help you identify and avoid similar problems as you plan your estate. That includes potential conflict within your family or between your heirs.

I'm not suggesting that you need or want all the services that estate planning professionals provide. But you don't have to do everything yourself. Even if you're doing the bulk of your estate plan yourself, you may find that you need some professional services to fully and properly complete your plan.

Do you save money in the long haul?

When planning your estate, you can save money in two ways:

- ✔ You can avoid the expense of hiring a professional to help you review your options, determine what estate planning tools you need, drafting your estate planning documents, and help you transfer assets into your trusts.

- ✔ You can create a strategy that helps you avoid expenses and taxes after your estate plan is created. That strategy can help you avoid capital gains taxes and gift taxes during your lifetime, as well as estate taxes to be paid after you die.

If you value your time, consider this: You're investing considerable time and energy in learning how to plan your estate, and you will invest even more in implementing your estate plan. The more complicated your estate plan, the more likely it becomes that it will require significant future revision.

When you choose between hiring a professional and planning your own estate, keep the following points in mind:

- ✔ No matter how much research you do, a good lawyer may suggest approaches to estate planning that haven't occurred to you.

- ✔ Some firms offer periodic reviews of clients' estate plans at a reasonable cost, or discount their work when updating an estate plan.

- ✔ Some firms will automatically notify you of changes in the law that affect your estate plan, reducing the risk that part of your plan will be invalid.

Also, you get two forms of insurance if you have a professional prepare your estate plan. The first is figurative: No matter how attentive you are, you have a much lower chance of error when estate planning work is performed by somebody who does it for a living. The second is literal: Your estate planning firm will carry malpractice insurance, and if a mistake occurs, your estate can attempt to recover from that policy.

An important caveat: Legal malpractice insurance is voluntary, so you need to ask whether your law firm carries insurance. If it doesn't, go elsewhere.

Pricing for estate planning services is not uniform. Some firms charge by the hour for all work, usually between $175 and $300 per hour. Some firms offer estate planning documents or sets of documents at a fixed fee, with an additional fee charged for customization. You may find a firm that will quote you a fixed fee for your entire customized estate plan.

Some law firms base their fee on the size of your estate. Be cautious, as you should be paying for legal work performed. The amount of work performed on an estate is only loosely correlated to its size. Also, pricing based on size sets up a potential conflict between you and your lawyer over what your estate is worth.

Find a law firm that provides a lot of estate planning services to people with estates similar to your own. If you go to an estate planning firm that primarily serves people who are significantly wealthier than you, you can expect to pay a premium, but you won't necessarily get a better estate plan. If you find somebody who does a bit of estate planning as a sideline, you may not get the type of advice and assistance you need. A lawyer experienced with clients like you will be better able to anticipate and serve your needs.

The most obvious short-term cost of a professional estate plan is the attorney's fee for creating and executing the plan. Over time, a professional also charges fees for updating your estate plan. These expenditures must be weighed against the value of your time. And at the end of the day, they must be evaluated against potential costs savings in the administration of your estate or trust, and the potential cost to your estate of any errors in your estate plan.

If you expect your estate to be worth more than about $1.5 million, you need to think about estate taxes. The estate tax repeal law soon expires, and it's very likely that there will be an estate tax in the future. While I can't predict the exact amount of the exemption, I expect it will be between $1.4 million and $4 million. There will be a separate lifetime gift tax exemption that I expect will remain lower than the estate tax exemption.

Uncertainty about the future of the estate tax makes it difficult to plan larger estates. Although professionals have no greater insight into the future than you, they may help you formulate an estate plan that is less likely to require substantial amendment when tax laws change.

A professional can also help you plan your estate to minimize other taxes, including taxes you may incur during your lifetime.

Working with a Professional

You've decided to hire a professional to help plan your estate. But where do you find an estate planning lawyer?

- ✔ Seek referrals from people you know who have hired estate planning lawyers.

- ✔ Contact associations of estate planning specialists. Investigate whether your county has an estate planning council and consider hiring a member. Nationally, the American College of Trust and Estate Counsel (www.actec. org) is considered to be a good source of skilled estate planning attorneys.

- ✔ Check to see whether your state bar has a certification program for estate planning lawyers and consult a member lawyer. Similarly, look for lawyers who are members of your state or county bar's estate planning committee.

- ✔ Use a state bar or ABA-approved attorney referral service.

- ✔ Check the phone book or search on the Internet.

Hiring a lawyer

Once you find some estate planning lawyers to potentially hire, you must choose between them. Did I make that sound easy?

While most lawyers can draft simple wills, there's a lot more than that to planning an estate. You want to find a lawyer who is experienced planning and settling estates similar to your own. A lawyer experienced at helping clients with similar personal and financial backgrounds is better able to anticipate your needs. A lawyer who has settled estates knows about problems that may arise in probate court and with trust administration and can use that experience to help you avoid trouble with you own estate plan.

You will want a lawyer who:

- ✔ Has considerable experience, probably ten or more years, planning estates.

- ✔ Has a practice that is primarily or exclusively devoted to estate planning and probate.

- ✔ Has an organized, professional office.

If you interview several estate planning lawyers before deciding whom to hire, you should let the lawyer know that when you schedule your meeting. You should think of the interview as an opportunity to learn about the lawyer. You should not expect any significant advice on your estate plan until after you retain your lawyer.

Meeting with your lawyer

After you hire an estate planning lawyer, the law firm will probably provide you with questionnaires and checklists to facilitate in the collection of information and to inform you of any documents you should bring with you when you meet with your lawyer to plan your estate. This information gathering process is of the kind described in Chapters 3 and 4.

Complete the forms to the best of your ability and collect the documents your lawyer requested. Make a list of your goals for your estate plan, as well as your concerns.

This meeting with your lawyer involves the review of your personal and family situation, property, and beneficiaries. During the meeting you tell your lawyer about your heirs and intended bequests, and you will discuss possible personal representatives or trustees.

Reviewing and executing the documents

After your lawyer has completed your estate plan, you must carefully review the documents. You should not be surprised if at least one revision is required.

After you approve the documents, your lawyer will arrange for you to sign them in front of witnesses and, in most cases, a notary. The danger of invalid execution is that a probate court will later invalidate your will. When a lawyer arranges this signing ceremony for the execution of your will, there is little chance that the execution won't be valid.

Take your time when you review your estate plan. This is not easy reading. Even with careful review, you can potentially overlook a mistake or omission. Errors that are often overlooked include typos, misspelled names, and the omission of a name from a list of heirs (for example, "To my children, Jane, Joe, and Jim," omitting your fourth child, Jillian).

Taking the final steps

After you sign your estate plan documents, you still have some work to do. If your estate includes a living trust, you must transfer assets into your trust. The same is true of any other trusts you create, which are to be funded during your lifetime. Your lawyer may assist with this process, and in particular with the preparation of deeds to transfer real estate.

You will need to find an appropriate storage place for your original estate planning documents. You may wish to provide a copy of your will to your executor, and a copy of your trust to your trustee.

The danger of multiple originals

Some people, including some lawyers, believe that you can help ensure that an original will is available for probate by executing more than one original copy. This advice is actually a recipe for more complicated probate.

It is possible that nobody will be aware that there is more than one original, or that nobody will bring the issue of duplicates to the attention of the probate court. But if the probate court learns of multiple originals, in most states the court will require that all originals be filed with the court. If one copy is lost, the court may presume that it was destroyed in an act of revocation, requiring your heirs to prove that you did not revoke your will.

Some lawyers will ask that you and your witnesses sign more than one copy of a trust or will, but will mark or stamp all but one as copies. This is the better approach, as there is only one original will to submit to the probate court. If the original is lost or destroyed, and your heirs have to try to probate a copy of your will, a hand-signed copy is likely to be more convincing to the court than a photocopy.

Safeguarding Your Estate Plan

Now that your estate plan is complete, you have a stack of important legal documents that must be secured and preserved. How do you protect your original trust? How do you store your will so that it is safe from theft or destruction, but available for probate?

The problem of the disappearing document

Sometimes a will or trust can't be easily located. The search for a lost document may involve

- A thorough search of your home and car. (Yes, some people keep their important personal documents in their cars. No, I'm not recommending that you do that.)
- Examination of your keys, or keys found during the search, to see whether any of them might be to a safe deposit box.
- Tracking down the lawyer who drafted your will to see whether the lawyer's office kept a copy.
- Tracking down friends or family members to try to find the witnesses to your will.

✔ Checking any will registries offered by your state or county government.

✔ Checking the probate court file from your spouse's estate, if your spouse died before you.

This process is far from foolproof. Many lost documents are never located. Sometimes the problem is not that you were careless, but that the heir who found your will or trust didn't like its terms and destroyed it.

What if your heirs can't locate your will or trust?

If your heirs can't locate your will, your estate will pass through probate, and your assets will be distributed as if you died *intestate* (without a will).

If your heirs find a copy of your will, they may submit it to probate as a lost or destroyed will. The exact procedures are different in each state. Typically, the probate court will presume that you destroyed your will in order to revoke it.

Your heirs will have to prove to the court that your lost will remains valid and the copy they possess is authentic. If possible, your witnesses will testify about their recollection of the will and your intentions. If your heirs succeed in convincing the court that you did not revoke your will and the copy is genuine, the copy of the will is probated as if it were the original.

If your heirs can't locate your trust, the first question raised is whether you had transferred ownership of any property into the trust. If you never funded your trust, its absence is of little practical consequence.

If assets were transferred into the trust and a copy of your trust is available, under most circumstances your trustee will be able to administer your trust based upon the copy. In some circumstances — and in particular if the authenticity of the copy is challenged — it may become necessary to have a probate court rule on the authenticity of the copy. If your heirs can find the trust or a copy, your assets will be probated in accord with your will or your state's laws of intestate succession.

What if an heir destroys your will or trust document?

Often the first person to find your will or trust is one of your heirs. If you have disinherited that heir or provided a smaller inheritance than would follow from your state's laws of intestate succession, the heir has an incentive to destroy your original documents. If other copies of your trust exist, the loss of the original may not have a significant effect on trust administration. But the loss of your original will may result in your estate being probated as if you died intestate (with no will).

Keep your will in a location where it is safe from destruction and take steps to help ensure that the first person with access to your will is somebody you trust.

Storing your will or trust

You have a number of options for storing your will or trust, some much better than others. I'll skip right over keeping it in a drawer or in the trunk of your car. (Because you're not going to do that. Right?) Possible storage locations include

- **A fireproof, waterproof lockbox or safe in your home.** This is a good place to store a will or trust, provided your personal representative or heirs know where the lockbox is located and can access the keys or combination.

- **A safe deposit box.** Some lawyers recommend keeping your original estate planning documents locked up in a bank vault. There are few places where your documents will be better protected from theft, accidental damage, or destruction. However, if you keep your will in your safe deposit box, you may tie up your estate for weeks while your heirs or personal representative try to gain access. Locking your original trust away in a safe deposit box is reasonable, but make sure that you give a copy to your trustee.

- **Your lawyer's office.** Many lawyers who offer estate planning services will store their clients' original documents. This can also help keep your will safe from destruction, as your lawyer has a duty to safeguard your will and to deliver it to the probate court or to your personal representative.

If you're concerned that the first person to find your estate planning documents will destroy them, despite the inconvenience it may cause, your safe deposit box may be a better option than any storage location in your home. Tell your personal representative where you have stored your will, but only share that information with friends or family members you trust.

Registration of wills and trusts

In many states, you will be able to register your will with the Secretary of State or County Clerk's office or have it stored in a vault at the probate court. The clerk at your probate court can probably describe your options for your state and county. There may be a small fee. Although on rare occasion people have tried, it is unlikely that somebody will successfully steal your will from a probate court or government office.

At times, I have seen private companies offer will storage services. The problem is, if your heirs don't know where you've registered your will, they won't be able to find it. And even if they do know, using a private company is not likely to provide any advantage over your safe deposit box, but presents the new problem that the company may go out of business.

Chapter 3

Gathering Pertinent Information

. . . .

In This Chapter

▶ Getting a big-picture look at your estate

▶ Taking an inventory of what you own

▶ Determining the value of your estate

. . . .

*A*s you prepare to plan your estate, you must assemble a great deal of information. You need to figure out what is in your estate, including both assets and debts. You must consider how your property is held, and what it's worth. You need to figure out who your heirs are, and what you want to leave to them.

Your best approach is to methodically work through your relationships and finances. This chapter should help you organize your thoughts.

A form designed to assist you in the full review of your assets and debts is provided on the accompanying CD and is included in this book as Appendix C.

Asking Yourself Some Basic Questions

"Who are you?" is a simple question, right? You're the person reading this book, who will soon be writing a will and possibly a trust. You'll stick your name at the top of it, and that's who you are.

Sure, identifying yourself in your will covers the legal formality, but consider this point as well: Your will may be your final communication to your loved ones. The way you treat your family in your will can color (or discolor) their memories of you. So when you think about who you are, think about how your will reflects your values, and how your family will react to your bequests.

"Where do you live?" is another easy question. You live in your home, right? But what if you have more than one home? If you're splitting your time between residences in different states, which state is your legal residence?

That's the state where your estate will be probated, so you need to plan your estate with that state's laws in mind. (For more discussion of issues in real estate ownership, see Chapter 17.)

If you've lived in a community property state during your marriage or are married and own real estate in a community property state, you must consider the effects of community property laws. (For more discussion of community property issues, see the section later in this chapter, "Considering Community and Jointly Owned Property.")

In most cases, the people you most want to provide for in your will are the people you live with. Typically that's your spouse and children. You may have other family members living with you, or you may be taking care of someone else's child. The manner in which you plan your estate can provide them with significant stability or may seriously disrupt their lives.

Beyond your immediate household, who else is in your family? Are there family members you help to support? Do you want to provide for them and, if so, how?

Identifying Your Assets

As you prepare to plan your estate, you need to take a comprehensive look at the following:

- ✔ What you own
- ✔ Where it's located
- ✔ How it's owned or titled

Ownership of property is more complicated than you may realize. For most of your belongings, ownership is pretty simple. You paid for it, it's in your home, and its yours.

But what if you're taking care of somebody else's property? You have certain legal rights pertaining to the property, but it isn't yours. Similarly, you may be the beneficiary of a trust. The trustee has legal authority over the trust assets, but doesn't own them. You have an interest in the trust assets as beneficiary, but you can't control them. These examples demonstrate the concepts of *legal interest* and *beneficial interest.* Your legal rights as the custodian of somebody else's property give you a legal interest in the property, but it's not yours to take. Your status as the beneficiary of a trust gives you a beneficial interest in the trust, but it's not yours to control.

Your beneficial interest in property can take one of two forms:

✔ A *present interest,* where you have an immediate right to use the property

✔ A *future interest,* where you don't have the right to use the property until some time in the future

You may have heard of a *life estate.* That's an ownership arrangement where one person, the *life tenant,* has the right to use and enjoy property. When the life estate is created, *remaindermen* are also identified. The remaindermen receive ownership of the property upon the death of the life tenant. While the life tenant survives, the remaindermen have a future interest in the property. Their right to use and enjoy the property is postponed until the death of the life tenant.

For example, consider a man who has two children from a prior marriage and who wants them to eventually inherit his home. At the same time, he wants to be sure that his new wife always has a place to live. He may create a life estate in favor of his wife, identifying his children as the remaindermen. Following his death, his wife becomes the life tenant. For the rest of her life, she enjoys the exclusive right to use and possess the home. Upon her death, his children receive ownership of the home.

Finally, your ownership interest in your property may be contingent or vested.

✔ If you have a *vested interest* in property, you have a fixed right in the property. You can sell your interest or give it away. But having a vested interest doesn't of itself mean you have a present interest. Your remainder interest in a life estate is vested, but it's still a future interest. For example, if you participate in a pension plan, you probably have to work for your employer for a certain number of years before you have a vested pension benefit. Once your pension vests, you will receive your pension even if you change employers.

✔ If you have a *contingent interest* in property, your ownership interest depends upon something that may or may not happen in the future. For example, your parents may have left you an inheritance contingent upon your graduating from college. If you never go to college, you will never receive that inheritance.

After you inventory your assets, you can determine the value of your estate. Sum up the value of your assets, subtract the value of your debts, and that's your *net worth.* You will also use your inventory to figure out which assets should be included in your will or trust, which will automatically pass to a beneficiary or joint owner, and how to structure your bequests to serve the needs of your heirs.

You can also determine how your estate will pay its debts and taxes and, for larger estates, your approximate estate tax liability. If you have a large estate, advance planning is very important. The sooner you take inventory of your assets, the sooner you can implement tax-saving strategies.

Your review of your assets should be comprehensive. When planning your estate you benefit from having a full understanding of your estate's assets and liabilities, as well as what assets need to be included in your will or trust and which will pass to co-owners by operation of law.

Real estate

If you're like most people, you own some real estate. If you're a homeowner, your home is probably your most valuable asset. You may also own vacation property, business or investment property, or other real estate. For each of your real estate holdings, take note of

- The address
- The amount you paid for the property
- The cost of improvements you have made
- The balance of any outstanding mortgages or unsatisfied liens
- Its market value

Do you own your real estate jointly with others? If your co-owners have a right of survivorship, they will inherit your share by operation of law, and the property doesn't need to be left to them in your estate plan. (See the section "Considering Community and Jointly Owned Property," later in this chapter, for more on joint ownership and community property issues.)

For a discussion of the many different types of real estate, how they may be owned, and how that can impact your estate plan, see Chapter 17.

Personal property

What other assets are in your estate? Everything in your house, for starters. Do you have a storage unit? A safe deposit box? What's inside? Most likely you own some or all of the following:

- Home furnishings
- Jewelry
- Collectibles
- Art

✔ Antiques

✔ Clothing and personal effects

Those items are all forms of tangible personal property, items you can touch and feel. You may also own intangible property, including stocks, bonds, investment accounts, and intellectual property, such as copyrights and patents. Investments are addressed more specifically later in this section.

As you inventory your personal property, your belongings break down into three general categories:

✔ Items with appreciable market value

✔ Items with little market value but high sentimental value

✔ Items of little value

You probably already know what I'm going to say, but don't underestimate sentimental value when allocating items of property between your heirs. Consider how to keep family heirlooms and other treasures within the family and how to divide them equitably between your heirs. One common approach is to make specific bequests to your heirs for your more cherished belongings and then having your heirs take turns choosing items that they want until your personal belongings have been fully distributed.

Titled personal property

Titled personal property includes cars, boats, manufactured homes, and any other item of personal property where ownership is conveyed by a title instrument. For each item of property, consider how it's owned and the amount of any outstanding loans.

If you're married, some or all of your titled property may be jointly owned. If it isn't and you want your spouse to receive the property upon your death, rather than conveying it by will or trust, you can usually add your spouse as a co-owner before your death.

For heirs other than your spouse, I suggest sticking with your will or trust. Your conveyance may trigger sales taxes. Also, adding somebody outside of your household as a co-owner of your boat or car creates a risk to you. Do you want that person to have the legal right to drive away in your car, keeping or returning it at his own convenience? If you add a co-owner to your title, he will have this right.

If you have an outstanding loan against the property, adding a co-owner will normally require the consent of the lienholder.

Savings

Your savings include your cash, savings accounts, checking accounts, money market accounts, CDs, and other liquid assets. Don't underestimate the value of your savings to your estate plan.

- ✔ Your estate will have bills to pay, including any unpaid credit-card debts, mortgages and car loans, medical bills, funeral expenses, and the costs of estate administration,

- ✔ If your savings aren't sufficient to cover your outstanding bills and the expenses of your estate, other assets will be sold to pay those expenses.

Are you short on cash? You can help plan for a cash crunch by describing in your will which assets are to be sold to pay off those debts. You can also obtain a modest life insurance policy that will provide your estate with additional liquidity.

Investments

Your investments include your stocks, bonds, mutual funds, brokerage accounts, and stock options. If your estate requires money to pay its bills or to cover the costs of administration, often these will be the first items of property you want to liquidate. Make note of each investment, where it's held, and its value.

You may be able to add a beneficiary to your investment accounts. You may also opt to add somebody as a joint owner of certain of your investments, granting her a right of survivorship. You can utilize your investments as part of a gifting strategy, giving stock shares to your heirs each year to reduce the size of your taxable estate.

Do you own a small business, or own shares in a small business? You should be thinking about a business succession plan. See Chapter 4 for advice and ideas.

Insurance policies and annuities

If you own life insurance policies or annuities, for each policy you need to take note of the following:

- ✔ The type of policy
- ✔ The owner
- ✔ The beneficiaries
- ✔ The death benefit

> ✔ The surrender value
>
> ✔ The balance of any outstanding loan
>
> ✔ The premium

You may be able to avoid estate taxes by transferring ownership of a life insurance policy to somebody else or into a trust. For more information about estate planning with life insurance, see Chapter 16.

Retirement savings

Retirement savings accounts can take many forms, including 401(k) plans, 403(b) plans, qualified stock bonus plans, profit-sharing plans, regular IRAs, Roth IRAs, SEP IRAs, and tax-sheltered annuities.

Normally, you'll designate beneficiaries for your retirement accounts. Your account will pass to your designated beneficiary without going through probate. If you're married, you will probably name your spouse as the primary beneficiary, and perhaps name your children as contingent beneficiaries.

For more information on how your retirement savings figure into your estate plan, see Chapter 15.

Pensions

If you're receiving pension benefits or will receive a pension upon retirement, your plan will define what benefit your spouse will receive after your death. You may be able to change the survivor's benefits for your pension by increasing or decreasing your contribution.

If your pension plan doesn't have survivor's benefits, consider how the loss of income is going to affect your spouse upon your death. Similarly, if you will be the spouse who is left out in the cold, how will you support yourself? You may want to consider investing in life insurance.

Considering Community and Jointly Owned Property

Where you own property may affect your estate plan. If you do nothing, your estate will have to commence *ancillary proceedings,* a fancy term for additional probate proceedings, in the states where your property is located. Those proceedings will cost money and will almost always cause delay.

You can minimize those issues by transferring ownership of those properties to a living trust during your lifetime, although you must weigh the benefits of simplified probate against transfer taxes and possible tax reassessments triggered by the transfer of title.

If you're married and have lived in a community property state for any amount of time during your marriage or own real estate in a community property state, then you probably own community property. *Community property* is property that you acquire during your marriage or that you buy with money earned during your marriage, including interest earned on investments made before your marriage. However, even in community property states, gifts and inheritances received by one spouse are regarded as separate property. Whenever you move to or from a community property state, you should review your estate plan.

Community property laws exist in Arizona, California, Idaho, Louisiana, New Mexico, Nevada, Puerto Rico, Texas, Washington State, and Wisconsin.

Under community property laws, you have the right to decide who inherits your separate property and half of your community property. If you leave community property to your spouse, your spouse enjoys a *stepped-up basis* in your share of the asset, meaning that the difference between the amount you paid for your share and its value at the time of your death is erased for tax purposes. This stepped-up basis reduces the amount of capital gains tax that may be owed if your spouse sells the property. For example, if you paid $60 for a home that is now worth $300,000, your spouse avoids capital gains taxes on a $240,000 gain — a substantial savings. However, your spouse doesn't receive a step up in basis for other jointly owned property.

If you move out of a community property state, most states have statutes that will continue to apply community property laws to the disposition of your community property. But if you sell community property while living in your new state, the asset you purchase with the proceeds of the sale will no longer be community property.

Keeping track of separate property and community property can become very difficult. If you commingle your money, combining separate assets with community assets, it can become impossible to determine where your separate property ends and community property begins. The longer your marriage, the more difficult the task.

If you reside in a community property state, live in a community property state during part of your marriage, or own real estate in a community property state, you need to understand how community property laws affect your estate plan. If you and your spouse are comfortable talking about financial issues, you can sit down and agree what portions of your estate are community property and what are separate property.

You may enter into a prenuptial agreement with your spouse, modifying how community property laws apply to assets you acquire during your marriage.

You can help avoid having to revise your living trust by including a *choice of law* clause, stating that the trust is governed by the laws of the state in which it was executed. In some cases, you can even choose to have your trust governed by a different state's laws. That way, even if you move, your trust should continue to be interpreted in the manner you intend.

Jointly owned property is another ball game. When you own property with others, one of two things may happen:

- ✔ The other person may have a *right of survivorship,* automatically inheriting your share of the property when you die.
- ✔ They have no right of survivorship, and you may leave your share to the heirs of your choice.

You don't need to include provisions in your estate plan for property where your co-owner has a right of survivorship. However, you do need to provide for other jointly owned property.

Consider how your bequests will affect your joint owners. Think about how you would you feel if your co-owner left her interest to somebody without considering the impact on you. Consider, for example, a rental house that you jointly own with your sister. You may want to negotiate a buy-sell agreement that allows either of you to purchase the other's share from her estate. That's usually far better than a bequest that translates into, "Surprise! You have a new business partner!"

If you own shares of a small business, you may be restricted in your ability to give, sell, or bequeath your shares to others. Your business partners may also have the right to purchase the shares upon your death. You should review the terms of your stock ownership, any buy-sell agreements, or other succession plan that your business has put into effect. If your business doesn't have a succession plan, sit down with your partners and create one.

Valuing Your Property

When you die, your assets are valued at their *fair market value,* the price you would expect to pay for a comparable item on the open market. Your personal representative or trustee oversees the appraisal process. In most cases, your estate is valued as of your date of death. However, if your estate decreases in value, your estate may seek to use an alternate valuation date of six months after your date of death.

For cash assets, investment accounts, and retirement savings, determining fair market value may be as simple as obtaining a bank statement or an account balance from a financial institution. As their historic values are a matter of record, your personal representative can obtain actual market values for stocks, bonds, and other investments as of the valuation date.

Other assets, such as real estate, fine art, collections, and antiquities, will need to be appraised. Your estate may also need to have an appraisal of your household items and personal effects, although often an estimate will suffice. Your estate will pay the cost of any appraisals.

After values are determined for all your assets, your executor or personal rep uses those numbers to prepare an accounting for the probate court and a tax return for your estate. Your estate's liability for gift and estate taxes is determined from the total value of your estate. Your heirs benefit from a step up in basis for their inheritances. (For more on this topic, see the section "Considering Community and Jointly Owned Property," earlier in this chapter.) Unless new legislation passes by the end of 2009, the estate tax will be entirely repealed in 2010. During that year, there will be no step up in basis on inheritances. While the estate tax repeal works primarily to the benefit of large estates, stepped-up basis can benefit almost anyone. The estate tax repeal expires at the end of 2010, so unless new legislation passes, the estate tax will return with a vengeance on New Year's Day 2011, as will stepped-up basis for inherited property.

If you expect that your estate will owe estate taxes, you can utilize a gifting strategy or other estate tax-planning techniques to transfer the value of your assets during your lifetime. If you give your assets away before they appreciate, your estate tax obligations are determined by their value at the time of your gift as opposed to the time of your death. You can also employ estate planning tools that may give your heirs a discount against market value, again potentially saving estate taxes. Although your heirs may eventually face greater capital gains tax liability, capital gains taxes are substantially lower than estate taxes. For more on estate tax planning, see Chapter 6.

Chapter 4

Planning Your Bequests

. . . .

In This Chapter

▶ Leaving your assets to your heirs

▶ Planning your estate after remarriage

▶ Keeping your business from failing

▶ Choosing a dependable personal representative and trustee

. . . .

*G*iving away your assets is easy, right? You just make a list of the people in your life who are closest to you, divide your assets between them, and you're done. Well, maybe not. You have to consider many other factors in order to be sure that your estate plan is carried out as you intend and that your beneficiaries receive the full benefit of your gifts.

This chapter helps you identify the people, institutions, charities, and other beneficiaries to whom you wish to leave bequests. It also helps you recognize special circumstances that may affect your estate plan, such as the effect of blended marriages and business succession planning. You also discover how to select a trustee or personal representative, when you should get help from an estate planning professional, and how to find and choose a lawyer, accountant, or institutional trustee.

Calculating Your Assets

In creating your estate plan, you need to figure out what assets you have and how you wish to leave them to your heirs. You inventory your various assets, including your savings, investments, retirement accounts, real estate, personal property, cars, boats, jewelry, collections, and anything else you own. You consider your debts, including asset-related debts, such as mortgages and car loans. You also consider how your property is held and whether jointly held property will pass to the joint title holder without going through probate. (Joint ownership of property is discussed in Chapter 3, and the common forms of joint ownership of real estate are discussed in Chapter 17.)

For the most part, your estate plan is written on paper and isn't locked in stone. You may change your will or revocable trusts at any time you choose. Similarly, you may change the beneficiaries on your life insurance policies, annuities, and retirement accounts. If you use irrevocable trusts in your estate plan, once you transfer assets into those trusts, you can't change your mind about your gifts.

The CD contains a form to help you keep track of your assets and plan your bequests. For your easy reference it is also available in Appendix C.

Determining Your Intended Heirs and Beneficiaries

After you create a list of assets and heirs, you can decide how to divide those assets. Consider your family, including your parents, spouse, children, grandchildren, siblings, and perhaps also aunts and uncles, cousins, nieces and nephews, or more distant relatives. Think about whether you want to make gifts to friends or other nonrelatives. You may also decide to leave bequests to charities, schools, churches, or other organizations.

Even with this list in hand, you're not quite done. You need to think about how your heirs may change over time, through birth, death, adoption, divorce, remarriage, or anything else that may happen in the future. You don't have to write your estate plan to cover every contingency, but your forethought can help you create an estate plan that needs less frequent amendment. You will also have a better picture of what types of changes in your life will necessitate the revision of your estate plan.

Your estate will have bills and expenses of its own and has to repay your outstanding debts. Your trust will also incur expenses. Make sure that you provide sufficient money for those expenses, or your gifts to your heirs may have be reduced in amount or sold so that your estate can pay those expenses.

You should include a clause in your will or trust distributing the *residuary* — anything that is left over after all specific gifts and bequests have been made. This clause will ensure that any gifts or bequests that are declined by an heir or that lapse due to the death of an heir, are properly distributed. It will also prevent the need to have a court distribute what may be a small amount of money or an asset with limited value, with court costs and legal fees potentially exceeding that value.

Individuals

After you figure out who your heirs are, you need to figure what you want to leave to them.

- ✔ How much do you want to leave to each heir?

- ✔ Do you want your heirs to inherit equally?

- ✔ Do you want your heirs to inherit immediately upon your death, or do you want to defer part or all of their inheritance to a later date?

- ✔ Do you want to make any bequests conditional, such as requiring a child to marry or graduate from college before they inherit?

- ✔ Do you want to disinherit any heirs so that they receive nothing under your will or trust?

- ✔ What do you want to happen to your bequest if your heir dies before you or declines to accept it?

If you intend to leave specific assets to your heirs, you need to remember that the value of your assets may change over time. In some cases, the asset may be sold, lost, or destroyed before your will or trust is administered. You may include language in your trust that equalizes the value of specific gifts, such that a child receiving a less valuable gift will also receive a sum of cash. You can also give heirs a percentage of your estate instead of specific dollar values to help preserve your intentions in the event that your estate grows or shrinks in size. For more discussion of these gifting techniques, see Chapter 8.

If you want to keep an asset in the family, you should designate an alternate beneficiary just in case your primary beneficiary dies. For example, if you leave your daughter your grandmother's engagement ring, do you want it to go to your son-in-law if she dies before you? Or would you prefer that it go to another child or to one of your grandchildren?

You may leave your household furnishings or other personal property to your heir without making an exhaustive list of everything you own. For example, you can leave your clothes to a specific heir or charity. Another option is to describe a mechanism by which your heirs will inherit personal property — for example, you could leave your children your furniture, but provide that they take turns selecting a piece of furniture until all of it has been distributed between them. If you provide for them to take turns selecting items, you should also either indicate who picks first or describe a technique, such as drawing a high card from a deck of cards, to determine who will be randomly selected to pick first.

To make sure that some heirs benefit from your request, you must engage in some extra estate planning. For example, your minor children will require somebody to manage their assets. One of your children may be bad with money, so you may want to create a *spendthrift trust* to prevent them from squandering an inheritance or having it taken by creditors. If you have a child or grandchild with special needs, you may need to create a *special needs trust* to allow him to benefit from your gift instead of the state taking it as reimbursement for the cost of public assistance. These trusts are discussed in Chapter 12.

You're not limited to describing your heirs by name. You may also describe your heirs by class, such as "to my children" or "to my grandchildren." Such language may help ensure that children or grandchildren born after you complete your estate plan share in an inheritance. Or, if you prefer, you can expressly exclude after-born children. You may also state whether or not you want adopted children or stepchildren to be treated as your children or provide for them separately.

State law restricts your ability to disinherit your spouse and may also restrict your ability to disinherit your minor children. You should expect that under state law, your spouse will have the legal right to an *elective share* of your estate , possibly including assets held by your living trust. If you leave your spouse less than that amount, your spouse can choose to take the elective share instead of your bequest. The consequence can significantly alter the distribution of your estate to your other heirs.

Disinheriting heirs through a trust is easier than disinheriting them through your will. If you want to disinherit a legal heir or want more information about state law restrictions on your bequests, read the discussion of those issues in Chapter 8.

Louisiana has an unusual set of laws described as *forced heirship laws,* which attempt to force you to leave certain minimum bequests to your spouse and children. Louisiana also limits the circumstances under which you can avoid the application of those laws. These laws can make it difficult to plan even a simple estate in Louisiana, unless your wishes happen to accidentally correlate with what state law requires. Although most people will benefit from discussing these laws with a lawyer, you can find a summary of Louisiana's forced heirship laws on the Web site of the law firm of Baldwin and Haspel (www.bhbmlaw.com). Click Publications and then choose the article Louisiana Forced Heirship.

Institutions or charities

You may want to leave part or all of your estate to an organization that advances the public good or supports a cause you believe in. Subject to state law restrictions on disinheriting your heirs, discussed in the preceding section of this chapter, you are free to do so. Many charities and educational institutions offer model documents you can use to leave bequests to them.

Charitable giving may also help you avoid estate taxes. A bequest to a tax-exempt organization may provide your estate with a tax deduction.

You may also consider using a *charitable remainder trust* to reduce the size of your taxable estate or to help you avoid capital gains taxes. Typically, the trust is set up to provide an income for yourself while eventually making a gift to charity. The trust may also be reversed, providing an income to a charity from an asset that will pass to your heirs upon your death. Chapter 6 discusses charitable remainder trusts.

Other bequests

It's your money, so for the most part, you can leave it to whomever you want. You can set up scholarships or memorial funds, support a public garden, or engage in other creative gifting.

You can also create a trust to benefit your pet. Pet trusts are not universally recognized as valid, although a growing number of states have passed laws making them enforceable. In states where they're not formally recognized, try to choose a trustee who will carry out your wishes even though they're not legally binding. Chapter 12 discusses pet trusts in detail.

Thinking about Your Family Circumstances

Generally speaking, the complexity of your estate plan increases with the size of your family. It's pretty easy to plan your estate when you're single. Getting married doesn't add much complication. But then you have kids, divorce, remarry, have a blended family. . . . Each new development may complicate your plans and wishes.

If you're in a domestic partnership, the odds are your state provides no inheritance rights to your partner if you die. Consistent with your wishes, you must create an estate plan that conveys assets to your partner and grants your partner authority over your estate and person in the event of incapacity. Chapter 17 discusses real estate issues affecting domestic partners.

Whenever your family circumstances change, whether by birth, death, adoption, marriage, separation, divorce, remarriage, or anything else you can think of, you need to review your estate plan to make sure that it remains consistent with your wishes and goals.

Estate Planning for Second Families

If neither you nor your spouse have children, estate planning for your second marriage is pretty simple. You simply execute new estate planning documents designating your spouse as your beneficiary. In some cases, you may want a more complicated estate plan, leaving some of your premarital assets to other friends, relatives, or charities instead of your spouse.

But if you or your spouse have children from prior relationships, things become a lot more complicated. And the complications compound if you later have children together. Here are some questions to think about:

✔ Do you wish to treat all your children equally? Including your stepchildren? Including minor children, who must be supported during their childhood and who may need assistance with college costs?

✔ Does your spouse want to treat your children equally with his own children?

✔ Is your spouse younger than you? If you leave your estate to your spouse "for life," how will your spouse's age affect when your children receive their inheritances?

✔ If your spouse survives you, will your spouse's estate plan include all your children, or will your children from your prior relationship be effectively disinherited?

You may feel 100 percent certain that your spouse "will take care of" your children and be comfortable leaving your entire estate to your spouse. Most of the time, your instincts will be correct, and your spouse will respect your wishes. But if your spouse chooses not to leave money to your children from the prior marriage or dies intestate, your children are effectively disinherited.

Start thinking about estate planning before you marry. You may find that you need a prenuptial agreement in order to keep some of your premarital assets from becoming part of your marital estate or subject to your spouse's elective share of your estate. The *elective share* is the amount your spouse may choose to inherit under state law, and your spouse may exercise that right if your will provides for a lesser inheritance.

Giving your new spouse a life estate

A common tool used in estate planning for second marriages is the *life estate*. If you own your marital home as separate property, you can make your spouse a life tenant. Your children receive title to the home upon your spouse's death. But a life estate may prove to be an imperfect tool:

✔ **If your spouse is younger than you, your children may be elderly by the time they inherit your home.** As your home is usually the most valuable asset in your estate, this delay can mean that they inherit little or nothing during the years when an inheritance would be most useful to them.

✔ **A life estate can put your spouse in conflict with your children.** Your children may believe that your spouse is neglecting the property. At times this is true, with your spouse failing to pay taxes or the principal portion of the mortgage, or failing to fix a leaky roof or other structural problem, putting your children's inheritance at risk.

✔ **A life estate may not be consistent with your own wishes.** For example, you may prefer that your home go to your children after your spouse remarries.

Even without a prenuptial agreement, you can help mitigate these issues.

✔ **If you can afford to do so, you can purchase life insurance for the benefit of your children.** Although their inheritance of your house is delayed, they immediately get the proceeds of your insurance when you die.

✔ **You can hold the house in trust and provide for your spouse to reside in the house for a fixed number of years, perhaps five or ten years.** After that period of time expires, the house is conveyed to your children.

Using trusts to hold your assets

Your living trust can be beneficial in directing your separate property to your children. You can also place some of your assets in an irrevocable trust for the benefit of your children before you remarry, but you need to be aware of gift tax consequences. (Gift and estate taxes are discussed in Chapter 6.)

A common estate planning tool for second marriages is the *bypass trust,* in which you leave a substantial bequest to your children. This gift takes advantage of your gift tax exemption, by keeping the gift out of your spouse's taxable estate. It also permits you to provide income for the support of your spouse, while directing the principal of the trust to your children.

Another common estate planning tool for second marriages is the *Qualified Terminable Interest Property (QTIP) trust,* which is often used in conjunction with a bypass trust. You can use the bypass trust up to the amount of your estate tax exemption and then use a QTIP trust for other assets, which will be treated as part of your spouse's estate, but which you may still direct to your children upon your spouse's death. These trusts are discussed in detail in Chapter 12.

Prenuptial agreements

As you enter your second marriage, you may want a prenuptial agreement, but be afraid of how your prospective spouse will react to the idea. Another common concern involves the full disclosure of your assets to your spouse. You may not want to make that type of disclosure. Yet a prenuptial agreement may provide significant estate planning advantages. You can help mitigate worries by keeping the agreement simple or, particularly if your primary interest is in your estate plan, by including provisions that will provide generously for your spouse in the event of divorce.

Your prenuptial agreement will clarify what property, which of your assets, and which of your spouse's assets continue to be separate property after you marry, including your interest in a family business. Your prenuptial agreement can waive the rights that you and your spouse have to take an elective share of each other's estates. It will also provide for how property will be divided if you divorce and may limit spousal support.

Even without a prenuptial agreement, if you're careful with your assets, you should be able to keep many of your premarital assets out of your marital estate. This separation is more difficult in community property estates, or if you use marital assets to make loan payments or to maintain or improve the premarital asset. Also, simply keeping your assets separate will not be sufficient to protect those assets from being included in your spouse's "elective share" of your estate. Still, if you leave your spouse a greater inheritance than state law requires, it's very unlikely that your spouse will instead choose to receive the elective share.

If you decide to use a prenuptial agreement, make sure that you introduce the idea well in advance of your marriage ceremony — at least several weeks in advance and preferably several months. You and your spouse should both have independent legal representation to help you understand the agreement. If you have significantly more money than your prospective spouse, you can pay his lawyer fee, but he should pick his own lawyer.

More tools to consider

Some states permit *contract wills,* which can't be changed after the death of the first spouse. However, this type of will can be unduly limiting, particularly if the surviving spouse remarries or has more children, and may complicate probate. Before considering a contract will, be sure you fully understand how the joint estate plan would affect you as the surviving spouse.

A more complicated estate planning tool that may be useful in second marriages is the *Family Limited Partnership* (FLP). You control the assets in your FLP, while your children are limited partners who have an ownership share but no control over the assets. The FLP is often costly to create and comparatively burdensome to maintain. Chapter 6 discusses FLPs in more detail.

Don't forget to update the beneficiary designation for your insurance policies and retirement accounts. If you don't, you may find that you leave a windfall to your ex-spouse instead of your current spouse and children.

Estate Planning for Your Business

If you own your own business or a share of a family business, your estate plan should include a business succession plan. A will isn't enough, and your living trust is probably inadequate. Business succession is a complicated process and is usually best implemented over a course of years. If you're a business owner:

- ✔ If you're active in your business, your succession plan should provide for the continued operation of the business in case of your incapacity or death.

- ✔ Your succession plan should describe who will own your interest after your death, and who will take over your management role.

- ✔ You may also carry life insurance to help fund the continued operation of the business; to hire additional staff to perform the tasks you previously performed; or to provide a cushion for liability the business may incur as a result of interruptions in its services.

- ✔ Your succession plan should be flexible enough that it can be adapted to the changing needs of your business, as well as changes in your wishes and those of your heirs.

You need to be aware of possible estate tax consequences of business ownership. Your estate plan should anticipate the possibility that your business could fail upon your death, but that when calculating your estate taxes the IRS may try to value your business as if it continues to operate. As part of your estate plan, you should document the factors that may limit the value of your business to a buyer or that may make it difficult to sell. That documentation will make it easier for your family to argue that, upon your death, the business had little or no value.

Many small businesses falter or fail when their founder leaves the business or dies. Sometimes this failure is unavoidable, particularly if the business is entirely dependent upon the owner. The nature of the business may make its value largely dependent upon the continued involvement of the owner, as with a law practice or dentist's office, or the owner may operate the business in a manner that leaves it with little value to a buyer, such as by choosing to maximize short-term income and not investing profits back into the business. A good succession plan can help ensure that your business continues to function after your death.

Sometimes you will want to transfer business ownership or management to another family member, perhaps a child. Other times, you will want to sell the business to somebody outside of your family. Remember that it can take a long time to find a buyer for your business, and the buyer may expect training and support. If you intend for your business to be sold after your death, you should still implement a plan for its operation and management pending sale and for support of the new owner.

Inheritance of your sole proprietorship

When you're the sole owner of your business and you want to leave it to your heirs, you need to consider many factors:

- **Who will manage your business**? If one of your children is already managing your business, it's easy enough to have your child continue in that role. But if not, are any of your heirs both willing and able to take over the business? If it's necessary to hire a manager, who will make the hiring decision and how will the position be funded? How quickly can the new manager take over, so as to minimize or eliminate any interruption in operations.

- **Will your death cause an interruption in the cash flow of your business?** If so, you may want to purchase insurance to help your business maintain its liquidity.

- **Who will inherit ownership?** Will you give the business to one of your children, balanced against bequests of other assets or life insurance proceeds to your other children? If you give equal ownership interests to your children, will you also give them equal say in the operation of the business? If so, by what mechanism will disputes between them be resolved?

Discussing your succession plan

You may have a very clear idea of who will take over your business when you die, and how your heirs will share ownership or management responsibility. But you need to talk to your heirs about your plans and make sure that you're on the same page. A poor choice of manager, or conflicts between comanagers, create a substantial possibility that your business to fail.

You may discover that the child who manages your business is losing interest in the business and intends to sell the business upon your death. If your child manager has grown your business, your child may resent the idea that ownership will be shared equally with her other siblings upon your death. Some children will threaten to quit if they feel that their hard work will end up creating a windfall for siblings who have their own lives and careers apart from the business.

You may be inclined to leave your children equal ownership and management roles in your business. Conflicts often arise between co-owners. For example, your children have different visions of how the business should operate, or one wants to invest profits in the business while the other wants to withdraw the maximum salary and dividends. Your conversation with your heirs will help you anticipate and plan for this type of conflict.

The FLP (see Chapter 6) may be a useful tool in leaving your business to your heirs, while also possibly reducing its value for the calculation of estate tax. In an FLP, you retain control of your business as the managing partner, while transferring ownership of shares to your children. Your children are limited partners and thus do not have any say in your management decisions. You can use the annual gift tax exemption, presently $12,000, to gradually transfer ownership to your children while reducing your taxable estate.

Even if you choose not to implement a FLP, perhaps due to its cost or complexity, you may nonetheless use an annual gifting strategy to transfer shares of your business to your children. Annual gifts have an additional benefit, in that as your business grows in value so do the shares you have already transferred. If you wait until you die, today's $12,000 gift may represent a six-figure increase in your taxable estate. Although your children will face increased capital gains tax if they sell the gifted shares, as opposed to getting a step up in basis when inheriting them at your death, the potential tax savings remain substantial. For more on estate taxes, and my skepticism that that repeal will become permanent, see Chapter 6.

You can also sell shares to your children during your lifetime, financing the sale with a low-interest promissory note. Similar to a gift, your children receive the shares at a much lower value than they're likely to be worth at the time of your death. You may still implement a gifting strategy, using your annual gift tax exclusion to forgive part of the debt owed on the note.

Inheritance of your share of a business

Every small business with more than one owner should have a buy-sell agreement addressing the right to purchase shares from a partner who wants to leave the business, or from a partner who becomes incapacitated or dies. You probably don't want a stranger buying or inheriting your partner's interest, or exercising the proxy rights of an incapacitated partner and then trying to assert a say in how your business is operated. Without a buy-sell agreement, you may get exactly that or may give that "gift" to your partners.

If you own a share of a business, whether it's a family business or a business you run with partners or investors, you face many of the same issues as with a sole proprietorship (see preceding section). If you manage the business or have a significant management role, you and your partners need to plan for a successor manager.

A key difference is that your partners have an interest in how your shares are distributed. Some businesses have buy-sell agreements, detailing how shares are to be valued and when your shares may be purchased by the other partners. Depending upon what you and your partners decide,

- ✔ The business may buy life insurance to help fund the purchase of a deceased partner's shares.

- ✔ The buy-sell agreement may provide for your partners to pay for your shares in installments.

- ✔ Your partners can purchase your shares for cash, obtaining financing, if necessary.

The buy-sell agreement may be triggered upon a partner's death or incapacity, giving your partners the opportunity to purchase your shares from your estate rather than having them inherited by somebody they would prefer not be involved in the business. You, of course, get the same benefit should misfortune fall upon one of your partners.

Appointing the People Who Will Carry Out Your Estate Plans

You may be used to taking charge of every detail of your life. But no matter how independent you are, you can't administer your own estate. You have to get help from somebody else. So what do you do?

You seek out helpers who are trustworthy, responsible, and financially stable, and who are young and healthy enough that they're likely to remain both willing and able to manage your affairs after your death or incapacity. Your choice will usually be a person, but at times you may choose an institutional trustee or lawyer to administer your trust or will. The following sections help you make the right choices and choose helpers who will protect your estate and respect your wishes.

Choosing your personal representative or trustee

Your *personal representative,* also called an *executor,* is the person who manages your estate during the probate process. Your trustee manages the assets held by your trust. During the administration of your trust or estate, your trustee and personal representatives will be the primary target of anybody who is unhappy with your estate plan or the way it is being administered.

Whenever you choose somebody to assist with your estate plan, you should talk to them before adding them to your will or trust. This discussion isn't a sales pitch where you're trying to convince somebody to become your trustee. It's more like a job interview, where you try to be absolutely certain that your candidate is trustworthy, reliable, and willing to perform a difficult job. Find out the answers to the following questions:

✔ Do they want the job?

✔ Do they truly understand how difficult it may be?

✔ Do they have the necessary knowledge and skills to fulfill their role?

✔ Do they have the time to perform their role?

✔ Do they live near you? If not, how much travel will be involved if they accept the job?

✔ Are they comfortable interpreting your will or trust?

✔ Are they financially stable? Will they have any temptation to "borrow" money they're supposed to safeguard?

✔ Do they expect to be compensated? If so, and you wish them to agree to a particular rate or amount of compensation, is the compensation you're offering acceptable?

✔ Do they understand your goals and wishes?

✔ Will they stand up for your wishes, even if friends and relatives are pressing them to make a different decision?

Estate administration involves number crunching. Accountings must be prepared for a probate court, and possibly for trust beneficiaries. There may be a lot of bills to pay and savings, retirement, and investment accounts to close out. Tax returns must be filed on behalf of your trust and estate. Your trustee may also be responsible for managing or leasing property and making investment decisions. Either your trustee or personal representative may have to liquidate estate assets — for example, to pay taxes owed by your estate.

While it's reasonable for your trustee or personal representative to hire professionals to assist with these tasks, you need to choose somebody who is comfortable working with numbers. Their math skills increase the quality of oversight of your assets and reduce the chance that your estate will unnecessarily incur expenses for professional services.

If your personal representative or trustee will take control of your business, be sure that she's competent to manage your business affairs. Remember the recommendations for business succession planning, discussed earlier in this chapter in the section on "Estate Planning for Your Business." Don't let your business falter or fail due to a lack of preparation for your death or incapacity.

Chapter 11 details other tips for choosing a trustee, including an institutional trustee.

Should you choose copersonal representatives or cotrustees?

Sometimes you may have more than one person in mind to help with the administration of your estate. For example, one person may be very good with numbers, but not have much time to devote to estate administration, while another may have ample time but be terrified of preparing accountings or tax returns. Perhaps you have two children and fear that one will resent the other if you designate one but not the other. A possible resolution is to appoint them as joint administrators of your estate.

There's no limit on how many people can jointly administer your estate, although at a certain point, a saying comes to mind: "Too many cooks spoil the broth." Don't unnecessarily complicate the administration of your will or trust by appointing a panel of administrators. Also, as hard as it is to find a trustee or personal representative who is both qualified and willing, the more people you add, the more likely it is that you will end up including somebody who is not an appropriate choice.

The biggest concern in appointing more than one person as trustee or personal representative is that conflict will occur. Even if you're sure that your choices will get along, include a mechanism for dispute resolution. Your dispute resolution mechanism may involve assigning tie-breaking authority to one person, providing for mediation or arbitration, or even tossing a coin or drawing the high card from a deck of cards.

One factor you may have in mind when choosing a trustee or personal representative is whether she'll work for free. That expectation may be reasonable if your trustee or personal representative is a primary beneficiary of your estate or if your estate is simple. But working for free is otherwise a lot to ask of somebody. For a larger or more complicated estate, either task can become a part-time job, and in some cases, a full-time job. Compensation makes it much less likely that your trustee or personal representative will resent the job or will resign when they realize just how much work is involved.

Choosing a successor

It takes two, baby. Or more. Your first choice as personal representative or trustee may not be able to fulfill that role for many reasons:

- ✔ Your first choice may become ill or die.
- ✔ Completing the tasks involved may take more time and effort than your first choice is willing or able to give.

✔ Despite your prior discussions, your first choice may simply change his mind and decline the appointment.

✔ Your first choice may not be sufficiently competent or capable and may have to be replaced by a court.

By designating a successor (or more than one successor), your trust or estate will continue to be managed by somebody you choose.

If the person you chose as trustee or personal representative becomes unwilling or unable to serve, unless you have designated a successor, the probate court will choose somebody to take over the job. The person appointed may be a complete stranger who has no familiarity with your goals and wishes and will charge fees that may significantly exceed what a friend or relative would agree to accept.

Discussing your estate plan with your helpers

After you have chosen your trustee, personal representative, and successors, you need to make sure that she understands your wishes. You should sit down with her, whether alone or together, and have a conversation about your estate plan and goals.

Go over your will or trust and explain what each provision means. Encourage your helper to ask questions.

Finding Professionals to Assist You

The more complicated your estate plan, the more likely it is that you will require assistance when preparing and implementing your plan. Common situations in which professional assistance is recommended include

✔ You're planning for business succession.

✔ You're using estate tax avoidance strategies.

✔ You're doing estate planning for second marriages

✔ You're leaving assets to a disabled heir who receives public assistance

✔ You're disinheriting an heir.

If you're doing anything unconventional with your assets within the state of Louisiana, you can easily run afoul of that state's *forced heirship laws.* You should consult a lawyer to make sure that your estate plan is properly formulated and that it will be upheld by a court.

Getting help from a lawyer

Your first task in getting help from a lawyer is finding a responsible estate planning lawyer. Your ideal lawyer will be experienced not only with planning estates, but with planning estates that are similar to yours. Similarity goes beyond size and extends to similarity of assets. If you have a small business, you need a lawyer familiar with business succession issues. If you're on your second marriage, need to create a special needs trust for a disabled child, or want to disinherit an heir, seek a lawyer who is experienced with those issues. You may want a lawyer who has probate experience and whose estate planning documents have stood up in probate court.

Easier said than done? Certainly. You won't find that type of detail from a Yellow Pages ad, and if you call a law office and ask, you're almost certain to hear that the lawyer you have contacted has qualifications that far exceed your needs (whether or not that is true). So what do you do? Try to get referrals from people you know who have hired estate planning lawyers. If you have an accountant you trust, request a referral. You can also interview members of the American College of Trust and Estate Counsel (ACTEC), using its online directory (available at `www.actec.org`).

Hiring an accountant

Just as when you hire a lawyer, referrals are very useful when you need to hire an accountant. Your friends, family, business associates, and your lawyer may have suggestions. You can also consult your state's CPA Association. You can find a directory of CPA Associations on The American Institute of Certified Public Accountants Web site at `www.aicpa.org/states/stmap.htm`.

When you have selected some possible CPAs, you should interview them. Questions to ask include

- How long have you been in practice?
- What are your qualifications and credentials?
- What is your experience with situations like mine?
- Do you specialize in servicing people with situations like mine?
- Will you personally handle my needs, or will the work be performed by somebody else within your office?

    ✔ How much do you charge, and does that price include all costs and fees?

    ✔ What services will I receive for that payment?

When you choose an accountant, consider the condition of the accountant's offices. Are they neat and organized? That's what you should expect. You can also rely upon your instincts. Do you trust the accountant and feel comfortable with the idea of working with the accountant? If not, it's a big world. You have a lot of other accountants to choose from.

Using professional trust services (institutional trustees)

Your first thought upon hearing the words *institutional trustee* is probably, "that sounds expensive." The most common institutional trustees are banks, brokerages, lawyers, and trust companies. They typically charge annual fees between 1 and 3 percent of the value of the trust.

An institutional trustee is thus likely to charge more than a friend or relative who serves as trustee, and you can't expect that an institutional trustee will waive its fees. Unless your trust is valued at $400,000 or more, using an institutional trustee is probably not financially prudent. In fact, many institutional trustees will decline to service smaller estates.

Using an institutional trustee provides the benefit that your trustee is likely to be in operation for the entire life of the trust. At the same time, responsibility for your trust may be handed off from employee to employee, due to staffing changes or employee turnover. You should inquire about continuity issues when you interview potential trustees.

You should consider having the trust periodically reviewed by a third party, to make sure that assets are being properly invested and maintained. This review adds an additional cost to your trust, but helps protect your heirs from mistakes or misconduct. Your institutional trustee should carry insurance to protect you from losses resulting from any such problems.

An institutional trustee is likely to be objective when managing your estate. Except as clearly authorized by the trust, pleas from your children for the extra disbursement of funds will probably fall on deaf ears. An individual may be swayed by a family relationship or feelings of friendship. Similarly, while your children may decide that it makes no difference if they spend the money that they're supposed to hold in trust for your grandchildren, your institutional trustee will do exactly what you instructed and make sure that your grandchildren receive your gift. Your institutional trustee will also not go through a period of grieving after your death or shy away from recovering trust assets from your friends or relatives.

Loss of the personal touch

Historically, your institutional trustee may have been your small town bank manager who had worked in the same bank for many years and had a long-term personal relationship with you. The banking industry has evolved. Today, it's exceptional to have that type of personal relationship with your banker.

Although a lack of relationship can help the trustee remain objective, the loss of a personal relationship may also affect your estate. While each of a succession of professional managers may do a perfectly competent job, they may miss a pattern that might be obvious to a trustee who has managed your trust from its inception.

A story that may not be true, but is illustrative of the problem, involves a wealthy woman who created a pet trust for the benefit of her dog.

The trust provided for the woman's housekeeper to remain in her home and to draw a considerable salary to care for the home and dog for the duration of the dog's life. She hired an institutional trustee to manage the trust.

A succession of employees of the trust company made dutiful inspections of the house at least once each year and confirmed that the dog was still alive. More than a decade later, when the dog would have been more than 20 years old, a newly assigned employee recognized that something was amiss. An investigation revealed that the dog had died. The housekeeper had purchased look-alike dogs and was on her third dog when her trickery was detected.

Institutional trustees are readily able to consult other professionals. While your individual trustee may struggle to find a lawyer or accountant who can give them advice on a minor problem, your institutional trustee can easily obtain advise from lawyers, accountants, investment professionals, and other experts. Also, even with staff turnover, the institutional trustee's experience with trusts avoids the learning curve of an individual trustee who has little or no prior experience managing a trust.

Issues of self-dealing may arise with institutional trustees. The trustee may be inclined to invest the trust's assets through the institution. You may want to mandate that part or all of the trust's assets be invested through other institutions so that the trustee will make the most suitable investments instead of favoring his employer's investment vehicles. For smaller trusts, some institutions will restrict investment options. Be aware of your institutional trustee's practices before you choose it.

Chapter 5

Providing for Your Children and Dependents

• •

In This Chapter

▶ Choosing somebody to care for your minor children

▶ Safeguarding your child's inheritance

▶ Providing for your child's continuing financial needs

• •

*P*roviding for children is often the first concern of somebody creating an estate plan. Young children will need somebody to care for them and to manage their assets. An estate plan can also help adult children by providing for college or for supporting children with disabilities.

Choosing a Guardian

As the parent of a minor child, you are undoubtedly concerned about who will take care of your children in the event of your death. In most cases, a surviving parent can provide care, but these issues can be particularly pressing for single parents.

Although in most cases your children will be cared for by their surviving parent, when that's not possible, a court will appoint somebody to care for them. Although your choice of *custodian,* or personal guardian, for your minor children is subject to court approval, in most cases, a court will defer to your wishes. To best protect your children, you should select a primary custodian and an alternate custodian, somebody who will care for your children if the primary custodian becomes unable or unwilling to serve.

In some cases, you and your spouse may disagree as to who should be the children's custodian. You should strive to reach agreement, even if your choice is less than perfect, as otherwise the decision will be made for you by a court.

Making the decision

Most of the time, parents want to keep their children together and will choose a custodian who is willing to care for all their children. In some situations, such as where your children have a large difference in age, you may want to designate more than one custodian based upon the individual needs of your children. For example, you may provide for a teenager to remain with a nearby family through the end of high school, while a grandparent cares for your younger children.

Questions to consider in choosing a custodian include

- **How old is the custodian?** Your designated custodian should be a legal adult under the laws of your state. In most cases, that's the age of 18, but in a few states, the age of majority is 21.

- **How qualified is your custodian?** Does your choice have good parenting skills and an appropriate personality and temperament? Can they provide a stable household environment?

- **Does your custodian have any physical limitations?** Caring for children, and particularly for young children, can be physically taxing.

- **Does your custodian have other priorities?** Will your choice have the time to care for your children, even if doing so affects their work life, social life, or lifestyle?

- **Does your custodian have other children?** If so, how old are they, and how well would your children blend into the household?

- **Does your custodian share your moral and religious beliefs?** Will they continue to raise your child in your faith, or in a manner consistent with your morals?

- **Can your custodian afford to take care of your children?** If your estate is not sufficient to provide for the financial needs of your children, will your choice be able to make up the difference?

You should discuss these issues with possible custodians prior to making your choice. While I'm not suggesting that you interview possible custodians as if they're applying for a job, this is a major decision, and it should thus be an informed decision.

You may choose to draft a letter to the custodian, to be kept with your will, which will remind them of your wishes for your children's care. While the letter will not likely have any legal effect, it will remind the custodian of your wishes and may help ensure that they're followed.

What if you can't agree on a guardian?

You and your spouse have given a lot of thought to the question of who should care for your children if you die, but you just can't agree. Please don't give up yet. The consequences of not choosing a guardian are potentially far more serious than the consequences of picking somebody you believe is second best.

Start by interviewing your candidates. You may find that one of the preferred choices is unwilling to take on the responsibility of your children, or that a candidate looks less appealing once you've thoroughly examined their qualifications.

If, after your interviews, you're both convinced that your preferred guardian is the best choice, take a look at the big picture. Are you arguing over the lesser of two evils? Or are you choosing between two qualified, appropriate candidates? If your disagreement is over two suitable, willing guardians, consider a compromise, or even choosing by coin toss. Pick one candidate as guardian and the other as successor.

Choosing a guardian other than the noncustodial parent

In the case of divorce, if the noncustodial parent still has custody rights the law will presume that custody should go to that parent upon your death. You may be concerned that the noncustodial parent is not a suitable custodian. Although you may not be able to prevent that from happening, you can take steps to help protect your child:

- ✔ Designate a preferred custodian in your will. The other parent may die first or may opt not to take custody.

- ✔ Discuss your concerns with your designated custodian.

- ✔ Document the factual basis for your concerns and keep the documentation with your will.

- ✔ Consult a family lawyer in your state to formulate a plan to help keep the child out of the other parent's custody.

- ✔ If necessary, provide for your estate to retain the services of a family lawyer who handles custody and guardianship proceedings.

If the noncustodial parent has abandoned the child or has a history of mental illness, abusive conduct toward the child, or substance abuse, you may be able to initiate guardianship proceedings shortly before or after your death, in which a court can consider appointing your preferred custodian as the child's guardian. Please remember that custody and guardianship laws are different in each state, and this will not always be possible.

Managing Your Child's Assets

If you're married, you may choose to leave your estate to your spouse and trust that your spouse will take care of your children's needs. If you're separated or divorced, or simply wish to do so, you can make bequests to your minor children. However, from both practical and legal standpoints, children have very limited authority to manage their own assets.

When a child has assets beyond a few thousand dollars, an adult must help manage those assets. If you don't designate a custodian for your child's estate and the other parent is not available to care for your child, the funds will fall under court supervision and may be managed by a stranger, who will charge fees for services provided. Even if the court appoints a relative who does not charge fees, legal and accounting expenses may be incurred when they prepare annual reports for the court.

You will probably choose the same person to be your child's custodian and to manage their assets. Most of the time, that person will be a surviving parent. Yet some people are wonderful with children, but terrible with money. If the person you select as caregiver for your children has poor financial skills, you can choose a different person to be custodian of their estate. Similarly, if you're divorced and prefer that your ex-spouse not control your children's inheritance, you may designate a different person or financial institution to serve as custodian.

The same considerations apply when choosing a custodian to care for your child or your child's estate (see preceding section), but the emphasis shifts to the financial. Your choice should be a legal adult who is responsible with money, trustworthy, and has the time to handle your child's assets. You will want to designate the primary custodian and also identify an alternate.

Conflict may arise between the person who oversees your child's assets and the child's custodian. You can minimize conflicts by:

- ✔ Trying to select people who will work in a cooperative, collaborative manner.
- ✔ Discussing in advance your wishes for how your children will be supported and how you want the children's assets to be used for their support.

Depending upon your wishes and the size of your estate, you may create a trust to hold some or all of your children's assets. The trust can include detailed provisions as to when money should and should not be paid out and can even provide a mechanism for resolving conflicts between the caregiver and the trustee. For more on trusts, see Part III.

Providing for Your Child's Needs

You've taken care of your child's physical care and financial well-being through adulthood. (See the section "Planning for the Care of Your Minor Children," earlier in this chapter.) But what about providing for your child's higher education? What if your child has special needs, and an inheritance may jeopardize needed government benefits? What if you want to be sure that your child doesn't fritter away the inheritance you worked so hard to provide?

The principal tool for managing your child's inheritance is the *trust fund*, through which you designate a responsible person to hold and manage your children's inheritance. A trust also gives you greater control over when your children will receive an inheritance, even after adulthood. While a few states let you postpone a child's inheritance by a few years if you express that intent in your will, a trust is a much more powerful tool for controlling when and how your child will receive an inheritance. (For more on trusts, see Part III.)

Your child's education

You may already have a savings account for your children's future education. However, more formal savings tools, such as qualified tuition plans, Coverdell Accounts, and accounts under the Uniform Transfers to Minors Act, may provide tax advantages as you save toward your child's college. Even diligent savings will not be sufficient to cover college expenses, and you may also want to provide for college through an inheritance, insurance, or trust.

You can use any form of trust to help fund your child's college education, but using a trust for college savings does have some drawbacks. The trust will have to file an annual tax return and is taxed on its income, and the balance of the fund may affect your child's eligibility for financial aid.

529 plan

A qualified tuition plan, commonly called a *529 plan,* comes in two forms:

- A **savings plan,** into which you deposit funds to later be used for college expenses. Be aware that management fees for this type of account can be high, and investment choices are limited, so despite the tax advantages, earnings may be low.

- In most states, a **prepaid college tuition plan,** where you can pay toward tuition at in-state colleges, with the savings guaranteed to increase in value at the same rate as college tuition. These plans are usually limited to state residents. You can apply the savings to private and out-of-state colleges, but even a fully funded plan may not fully cover those costs.

Anybody can contribute to a 529 plan, so they provide an easy way for members of your extended family to help contribute to your child's future education costs. Most states offer full or partial tax deductions for contributions to the plan. The assets are exempt from federal income taxes and are often also exempt from state and local taxes, and earnings accumulate on a tax-deferred basis. If your child dies or decides to not go to college, you can transfer the plan to another member of your family. For financial aid purposes, the plan is valued at an amount equal to the refund value of the plan.

Coverdell Account

A *Coverdell Account* (previously known as an education IRA) is funded with post-tax dollars and is maintained for the benefit of one beneficiary. You can contribute to a Coverdell Account for any child below the age of 18. As long as the money is used for education-related expenses, no tax is incurred on either the principal or interest earned when you make a withdrawal. Unlike other savings options, you can use the fund for K–12 education costs as well as for college costs. You have much greater flexibility with the investment of the funds than with a 529 savings plan. As the funds are considered to be an asset of the parents, there is no financial aid consequence to Coverdell Account savings.

Despite their advantages, Coverdell Accounts also have serious disadvantages. Total annual contributions are limited to $2,000 per year, and high-income parents may be subject to even lower limits. Also, your child must use the money from the account by the age of 30, or the account balance will be disbursed to your child subject to a 10 percent penalty and will be subject to taxes on its earnings. It may be possible at that time to change the beneficiary or roll over the account to another beneficiary, so another child or qualifying relative can benefit from the money without incurring those penalties, but the rollover process is very complex. You can find information on transfers and rollovers on the IRS Web site (presently at www.irs.gov/publications/p970/ch07.html). Due to the low limits on contribution, the account's management costs can consume or exceed its earnings.

UTMA trust

You can also use trusts and similar vehicles to save toward your children's college expenses during your lifetime. One popular option is an account created under the Uniform Transfers to Minors Act (UTMA). Unlike other trusts, the terms of an UTMA trust are defined by statute. Gifts made into an UTMA account are irrevocable. The money you place into the minor's UTMA account will fall under their control when they reach the age of majority, which in most states is the age of 18. Most states permit you to set a turnover age of 21.

If you're concerned that your child is more likely to buy a car than budget for college, then the UTMA trust is unlikely to be your tool of choice.

Section 2503(c) trust

An option very similar to an UTMA is the Section 2503(c) trust, which is also created for the benefit of a person under the age of 21. You can make annual contributions to the trust up to the amount of the annual gift tax exclusion, presently $12,000. You can apply the principal and interest earned to college expenses. You can provide the child with the option to continue the trust past the age of 21, if he chooses not to withdraw their money at that time.

Crummey trust

A popular form of trust that also takes advantage of the annual gift tax exclusion is called a *Crummey trust*. That name is not a judgment on its merits — it was named after its creator.

A Crummey trust can continue past the age of majority, but there is still a catch. The beneficiary is allowed to withdraw the gift only during a window of 30 to 60 days after each contribution. While most children understand that such a choice will probably result in that gift being the last you make, the money can still present a temptation.

Few choose this type of trust for college savings, as administrative costs of Crummey trusts tend to be high, and their entire balance will be treated as an asset when your child seeks financial aid.

Life insurance policy

One approach is to purchase a life insurance policy to pay college expenses. The best approach is to create a life insurance trust, to be funded by the policy upon your death. As your estate is not the beneficiary of the life insurance benefit, the money is not subject to estate taxes. The trust can provide for the payment of tuition and living expenses during college and for how any balance is to be distributed to your child after graduation.

Your child's special needs

If your child has a physical or mental disability that may require a lifetime of care, you may be torn between how to provide for your child and concern about how an inheritance would affect your child's government benefits. Parents sometimes feel that their choices are limited to the following:

- Disinheriting the child.
- Directing a bequest to another child, with the understanding that the sibling will use the bequest to benefit their disabled child.
- Ignoring possible financial consequences, and making a bequest to the disabled child.

These approaches are all far from perfect, and each can frustrate your goal of providing for your child. Fortunately, you have another option — the special needs trust. This type of trust can hold your child's inheritance without putting government benefits at risk or causing them to be discontinued.

Creating a special needs trust is complex, as is the interplay of Medicaid, SSI and other government benefits. For special needs planning and the creation of a special needs trust, you should get help from a qualified lawyer.

Your child's financial stability

While your child is not likely to object to inheriting a large sum of money as a young adult, you may be frightened by the idea. No matter how mature and responsible your child may be, she may not be wise with her inheritance.

While a few states provide you with a limited ability to delay inheritance, if you state that wish in your will, most will allow your child to take control of an inheritance at the age of 18. None will delay inheritance past the age of 25.

If you do not want your child to inherit as a young adult or want to provide for inheritance of only a portion of your bequest at that time, your best solution is to create a trust. A trust will not only give you that flexibility, but will also allow you to provide for special disbursements in the event of special events, achievements, or emergencies.

If your child has a history of substance abuse, irresponsible gambling, or wild spending, you can utilize a form of asset protection trust called a *spendthrift trust* to help ensure that your child can't squander his inheritance. The trust disburses money on a schedule or under circumstances you define. Your child can't borrow against the balance of the trust fund, nor can creditors attach it as security for loans. A valid spendthrift trust will even survive your child's bankruptcy.

An *asset protection trust* can also help protect your child's inheritance in the event of divorce. While most states will compel the trust to pay child support or spousal support from the trust, the funds within the trust will not be considered part of the marital estate and thus will not be subject to division in divorce.

Chapter 6

Dipping into Your Pocket: The Tax Man (and Others)

In This Chapter

▶ Planning for tax liabilities

▶ Avoiding gift and estate tax

▶ Paying your estate's outstanding bills

▶ Minimizing the cost of administering your trusts and will

*I*t's an unfortunate truth that if you owe money during your life, your estate will owe money when you die. And the saying, "Nothing is certain but death and taxes?" There is probably no context where that statement is more true than with estate taxes.

When you plan your estate, you should consider the probable liabilities of your estate, including outstanding bills, mortgages and other loans, income taxes, estate and gift taxes, and the cost of probate proceedings. With a good estate plan, you can reduce the cost of probate and trust administration, provide for the payment of your bills and debts, and do a lot to avoid estate taxes.

In this chapter, I provide an overview of estate taxes, common tools used in tax planning and tax avoidance, and the costs and benefits of those tools.

Tallying Up Your Estate's Tax Liabilities

Your estate has two primary sources of tax liability:

✔ Income taxes from your last year of life

✔ Estate and gift taxes

Your estate consists of the value of all property in which you had an interest at the time of your death. Your personal representative will prepare an inventory of your estate's assets and their worth, including assets held by your living trust. Based upon the value of your estate, you may owe both state and federal estate taxes.

You can take one of three general approaches to estate taxes:

- ✔ **Acquiescence:** Even though you know that the IRS will take a significant percentage of your estate, you do nothing to prevent that event from happening.

- ✔ **Acceptance:** You enter into a basic estate plan, perhaps using a bypass trust so that your estate benefits from the exemptions of both you and your spouse, but otherwise accept that part of your estate will go to the IRS.

- ✔ **Resistance:** You engage in more aggressive tax avoidance strategies to minimize your estate's tax exposure.

I recommend engaging in some amount of resistance. If your estate is taxable, you will almost always be able to find ways to significantly reduce its tax burden.

Federal estate taxes — a moving target

With current estate tax exemptions, most estates don't have to pay estate taxes. As of the time of writing, the estate tax exemption is $2 million. The exemption rises to $3.5 million in 2009, and the estate tax is eliminated in 2010. Yet the repeal is temporary. Unless new legislation is passed, the estate tax exemption will revert to $1 million. At present, the nonexempt balance of your estate is taxed at the rate of 45 percent.

Few expect that the estate tax repeal will be made permanent. The greatest uncertainty is for estates valued between $1.5 million to $4 million, as after the next round of legislation, the estate tax exemption is expected to fall somewhere within that range.

When owed, estate taxes take a significant bite out of your estate. The current estate tax rate is 45 percent. If you don't plan and implement an effective tax avoidance strategy, once you have taken advantage of your estate tax exemption, the IRS will take almost half of your assets.

The generation-skipping transfer tax

A close cousin of the federal estate tax is the *generation-skipping transfer tax* (GST). The idea of generation skipping is simple: If you have a large estate and leave it to your children, they'll also pay estate taxes when they in turn leave their estates to their grandchildren. By placing part of your estate in a generation-skipping trust for the benefit of your grandchildren, you avoid the second round of estate taxation. Also, the money directed to your grandchildren is largely protected from your children's creditors or from being claimed by an ex-spouse if one of your children divorces.

The generation-skipping transfer tax has a lifetime exemption in the same amount as the estate tax exemption, currently $2 million. You can allocate your exemption among your generation-skipping gifts. Above the exemption, the double hit of estate tax and generation-skipping taxes is almost confiscatory, and the combined tax can easily consume 80 percent of your bequest.

Consider the following examples:

- ✔ During your lifetime, you make a $1 million gift to your grandchild. You don't allocate either GST or gift tax exemptions to the gift. Applying current tax rates and assuming that you live at least three years after making the gift, your total cost for that $1 million gift is more than $2 million ($1 million, plus $450,000 in gift taxes, plus $450,000 in GST taxes, plus $202,500 in gift tax on the GST tax).

- ✔ If you want to leave $1 million to your grandchild through your estate, again without allocating either gift tax exemptions or GST exemptions to the gift, estate and GST taxes will be approximately $1.6 million, meaning that for $1 million to reach your grandchild, it will cost your estate $2.6 million.

Although the generation-skipping transfer tax is slated to expire along with the estate tax, you can realistically expect that both will return with the next round of estate tax legislation.

The rules governing the generation-skipping tax are complicated, and you can accidentally make a gift that implicates this tax.

State estate taxes

Most states impose estate taxes or inheritance taxes. Your estate pays estate taxes. The recipient of an inheritance pays inheritance taxes.

Prior to estate tax reform, many states imposed *pick-up taxes,* which are taxes in the amount of the federal State Death Tax Credit (SDTC). State estate taxes that fall within the SDTC don't raise the total tax burden on your estate. Due to the phase-out of the federal estate tax, many states have amended their estate tax laws to ensure continued revenue. That is to say, even if the federal estate tax repeal is made permanent, in most states, you'll continue to pay state estate taxes.

Gift taxes

If you make a lot of gifts during your lifetime, you may have to pay gift taxes. Gift tax exemptions fall into three categories under federal tax law:

- **Your annual exemption, presently $12,000 per person, per year**. (If you're married, you and your spouse can each make gifts up to the amount of the annual exemption, such that you could give each of your children up to $24,000 per year without incurring gift taxes.)

- **Your lifetime exemption, presently $1 million.** Gifts falling within the annual gift tax exemption don't count toward your lifetime exemption.

- **Gifts to your U.S. citizen spouse of any amount.** These gifts are exempt from gift taxes and aren't counted toward your lifetime exemption. If your spouse isn't a citizen, the gift tax exemption is substantial, in the amount of $128,000 in 2008 and indexed to inflation.

In addition, some gifts aren't subject to the gift tax:

- **Gifts of tuition made directly to the educational institution (not to the student).** Gifts directed into a 529 College Savings Plan also have a five-year gift exclusion so that you can gift up to $60,000 into a plan in a single year instead of spreading the gift over five consecutive years — but you have to wait five years before making another gift to the recipient.

- **Gifts of medical expenses or health insurance made directly to the medical facility or insurer (not to the patient).** Gifts made directly to the patient in excess of the standard annual gift tax exclusion are *not* exempt, even if the patient uses your gifts to pay medical bills and insurance costs.

- **Gifts to tax-exempt charities.** Your gift to a tax-exempt charity is exempt from gift taxes and may also provide an income tax deduction.

- **Gifts to a political organization.** A gift made to a qualifying political organization for its own use is exempt from gift tax, but does not give you an income tax deduction.

Also, if you add a joint account holder to your savings or investment accounts, no gift occurs until they withdraw money.

How gift taxes affect you

You're probably looking at these exemptions and exceptions and wondering, "How many people actually have to pay gift taxes?" The answer: Not many. But without a gift tax, it would become easy for large estates to partially or completely avoid estate taxes, through the creative use of gifts and trusts.

The lifetime exemption is not as glorious as it may sound. The amount of gifts falling within that exemption is counted toward your taxable estate. Also, for gifts that exceed the annual gift tax exemption, estate taxes are normally imposed on gifts made within three years of death as if they remain part of the estate. If you take advantage of your *annual* exemption during your last month of life, giving each of your children $12,000, those gifts will reduce your taxable estate. But if you make a gift of $500,000, your gift in excess of the $12,000 annual exemption is still treated as part of your estate for the calculation of estate taxes.

Filing gift tax returns

If you make gifts, you may be required to file a Form 709 Gift Tax Return for that tax year. Whether or not tax is due, you must file a gift tax return if you meet any of the following criteria:

✔ You make gifts valued at more than your annual exemption to any individual other than your spouse, unless they fall under one of the exceptions. (See the "Gifts" section, earlier in this chapter.)

✔ You make a gift of a future interest, even if the value of the future interest is less than your annual exemption. A *future interest* is an ownership interest in property that doesn't include the right to present possession or use of the property. For example, if you transfer real estate so that you retain a life estate, but somebody else (your *remainderman*) gains possession after you die, the remainderman has a future interest in the real estate.

✔ You and your spouse split a gift. In that case, you must both file gift tax returns. For example, if you and your spouse give your child $24,000 and want to take advantage of both of your annual gift tax exemptions, you will split the gift and will each file a gift tax return reporting a $12,000 gift.

✔ If you make a gift of community property, property you hold with your spouse as joint tenants, or property you hold as tenants by the entirety, the IRS considers half of the gift to be made by your spouse, and both you and your spouse must file a gift tax return.

You don't need to file a gift tax return for a year in which you make no gifts to your spouse, don't make any gifts in excess of your annual exemption to any individual, and all the gifts you made were of present interests.

There is no such thing as a joint gift tax return. You and your spouse are each responsible to file your own Form 709.

Gift taxes are payable by you, as the donor. However, if you fail to pay gift taxes owed, the IRS may seek to collect the taxes from the recipient of your gift.

If you die before filing your gift tax return, your personal representative must file the return on behalf of your estate.

Minimizing Tax Costs and Liabilities

You can take comfort in your ability to avoid estate taxes through the use of trusts and gifting strategies. Please be aware that tax avoidance strategies can be much more complicated than they may appear.

Although this chapter discusses many techniques that you can use to reduce your estate tax exposure, many of them are difficult to implement. If your estate is large enough to incur estate taxes, you should consider seeking professional estate planning services.

The uncertain future of the estate tax, with unpredictable future gift and estate tax exemptions, make creating a solid tax strategy difficult. Whatever your strategy, you should update your estate plan after the next round of estate tax legislation.

Although the future of the estate tax isn't certain, the most likely outcome of estate tax reform is an increased exemption and not total repeal.

Beware the following estate planning myths:

- ✔ **Myth: Your revocable living trust is a shield from estate taxes.**

  Fact: You may believe that your revocable living trust protects your assets from the tax man, but that isn't correct. While a basic revocable living trust helps you prepare for incapacity, avoid probate, and manage the distribution of your assets, it does nothing to avoid estate taxes. Everything you put into your revocable living trust is included in the value of your estate when you die. You can incorporate tax-saving tools into your revocable living trust, but there is no automatic tax benefit.

- ✔ **Myth: Adding your heirs to the title of your real estate and financial accounts automatically shields those assets from estate taxes.**

  Fact: Adding a joint owner to real estate or a bank account normally allows that asset to pass to the joint owner outside of probate, but does not reduce the value of the asset to your taxable estate. Chapter 17 discusses additional reasons not to use joint ownership as an estate planning tool.

Leaving your estate to your spouse

One of the easiest ways to avoid estate taxes is to give your assets to your surviving spouse. Your spouse enjoys an unlimited marital deduction, and thus your gift is free of estate taxes. But, as you probably expected, this strategy isn't perfect.

From a practical standpoint, you may not want to leave your spouse in full control of your estate — for example, in a second marriage, where your spouse remarries after your death or may not be inclined to follow your instruction to leave money to children from your first marriage.

In addition, by leaving your entire estate to your spouse, you also may be missing an opportunity to avoid a lot of taxes:

✔ You and your spouse each enjoy an estate tax exemption, currently valued at $2 million.

✔ If you give your entire estate to your spouse, although your gift to your spouse isn't taxed, your spouse's bequests aren't taking advantage of your $2 million exemption.

✔ If you leave $2 million (or the amount of the exemption at the time of your death) to your other heirs, that money doesn't become part of your spouse's estate. When your spouse dies, their estate also benefits from the $2 million exemption, effectively doubling the amount you can leave to your heirs tax-free.

 If you leave part of your estate to your other heirs, will your spouse have enough money? You can create a *bypass trust* (also known as a *credit shelter trust*) and leave the money to your other heirs through that trust. Although you must limit your spouse's access to the trust, you can provide for the trust's income to go to your spouse, permit your spouse to withdraw up to 5 percent of the value of the trust annually, and even allow your spouse to use the trust's assets as necessary for support or medical expenses. You can also appoint your spouse as trustee. Yet as the trust assets aren't part of your spouse's estate, it's not subject to estate tax when your spouse dies.

Making gifts

Another significant tax avoidance technique is gifting. You can reduce your taxable estate by making gifts to tax-exempt charities and political organizations. You can also plan a gifting strategy for your lifetime so that you can pass assets to your heirs tax-free:

✔ You can take advantage of your annual gift tax exclusion by making annual gifts of up to $12,000. If you and your spouse both make gifts, you can give a single recipient up to $24,000 per year without incurring gift taxes.

✔ You can make unlimited gifts of tuition, the cost of medical care, or the cost of health insurance, making the payment directly to the institution or insurer. Don't make these payments to the beneficiary of your gift, or you'll lose the benefit of this exemption.

> ✔ You can reduce the value of your estate by making gifts to tax-exempt charities and political organizations. Note that if your primary goal with your charitable giving is to limit estate taxes, you need to update your plan any time the exemption increases.

You can also take full advantage of your $1 million lifetime gift tax exemption while you're alive. For you and your spouse, that's a combined total of $2 million.

Capital gains taxes

For tax purposes, *basis* is the value used to calculate taxable gains and losses when property is sold. Generally, your basis in your home is its value at the time you bought it plus the value of certain improvements (for example, a new roof or replacement of a furnace).

When your heirs inherit your property, under current law, they receive stepped up basis. The value of the property is determined as of the date of your death, and the basis is stepped up to that amount. If your heirs sell the inherited property, they pay only capital gains taxes on the increase in its value during the time they owned it.

When you give somebody a gift, the recipient gets carryover basis, meaning that the basis they receive is the same as yours. When you add somebody as a joint titleholder during your lifetime, you open up the possibility of gift tax exposure.

Imagine that you purchased a vacation home for $60,000 in 1980, and it has a present value of $300,000. If you give the home to your child, you use $300,000 of your lifetime gift tax exemption. For capital gains taxes, your children receive carryover basis of $60,000, the amount you paid for the property. If, on the other hand, you continue to hold the home in your estate, and it's worth $350,000 when you die, the additional $50,000 in appreciation will be part of your estate and subject to estate taxes. However, your heirs will inherit your home with a stepped up basis of $350,000. You must weigh potential estate tax benefits against capital gains consequences for your heirs.

Charitable remainder trusts

In addition to outright gifts to charities, you can enter into more complicated arrangements. The most popular is the *charitable remainder trust.*

In a traditional charitable remainder trust, you make a gift to charity and receive an annual income in return. For example, you place $1 million into your charitable remainder trust, with the trust providing for an income to you of 10 percent, or $100,000 per year. The charity (or trustee you appoint to manage the trust on behalf of the charity) invests the money and receives the balance of the trust upon your death.

Not all charities are created equal

If you give money to an established charity or educational institution, you have a pretty good idea of how your money will be used. But what if you want to support a small charity or offbeat cause? You have to be careful to avoid charities that aren't competently managed or that are run by people who are more interested in lining their own pockets than contributing to the charity's cause.

My advice is to thoroughly investigate the charity before giving it any money. Ask for its annual report and financial statement. If it refuses to provide those documents, I suggest finding a different charity for your donation. With those documents in hand, evaluate how much of the charity's spending goes to its charitable causes, versus paying for salaries, overhead, and fundraising.

You can find out about charitable giving and investigate many charities through the Better Business Bureau's Wise Giving Alliance Web site at www.give.org.

In a *reverse charitable remainder trust,* the charity receives the income stream from the trust during your lifetime, and the balance of the trust passes to your heirs upon your death.

As the trust has a charitable nature, assets you transfer into the trust may be sold without payment of capital gains tax. You can thus use a charitable remainder trust to avoid capital gain taxes on assets that have significantly appreciated since you acquired them. Your $50,000 investment in Google is now worth $250,000? If you sell your Google shares, you will pay capital gains tax on the $200,000 gain, but if those shares are held by your charitable remainder trust, no taxes are paid and the full $250,000 can be reinvested by your trustee.

 When creating your gifting strategy, don't forget your own future needs. I'm not suggesting that you avoid estate taxes by making so many gifts that you're unable to support yourself. Remember, you can also reduce your taxable estate simply by spending your money.

Using trusts to avoid estate taxes

You can use many other trusts to avoid estate taxes. Commonly used trusts include

- ✔ **The qualified personal residence trust (QPRT), also known as a house trust:** You place your house into a trust, naming your children as beneficiaries. This action effectively freezes the value of your home for estate tax purposes. Once the trust owns the home, the appreciation is attributed to your trust and not your estate. When the trust ends, your children become the owners of your home and your landlords. In order for this trust to succeed, you must continue to occupy your home as your residence and you must survive the term of the trust. Although your QPRT can last for as long or as short a time as you want, if you die before the trust ends the IRS will treat the home as part of your estate.

✔ **The grantor retained interest trust (GRIT):** You place an asset into the trust, retain the right to receive income from the asset, but otherwise place it outside of your estate. At the end of the trust, the trust's assets are transferred to the beneficiary. Neither you nor your spouse may serve as trustee. The tax code also limits the effectiveness of these trusts in transferring assets to your spouse, siblings, and children. As with the house trust you can make the term of the trust as long or as short as you want, if you die before the trust ends the IRS will treat the trust's assets as part of your estate. Closely related to this trust are the grantor retained unitrusts (GRUTs) and grantor retained annuity trusts (GRATs).

✔ **The generation-skipping trust, sometimes called a dynasty trust:** You place money in trust for the benefit of your grandchildren. You may allow your children to receive the income generated by the trust. Because your children never own the trust assets, those assets never become a taxable part of their estates. (For more on this topic, see the section "The generation-skipping transfer tax," earlier in this chapter.) Gifts above your generation skipping tax exemption are taxed at an extremely high rate.

✔ **The irrevocable life insurance trust (ILIT):** The trust purchases a life insurance policy and is named as the beneficiary of that policy, keeping the insurance proceeds out of your estate. The insurance policy must be acquired by the trust at least three years before you die, or the proceeds will be included in your taxable estate.

Please note that all these trusts are irrevocable. Once you create them, you can't change your mind and pull your assets back out. Also, they're complicated to create and are best drafted by an estate planning professional.

Chapter 12 discusses these trusts in more detail.

Creating a Family Limited Partnership

The *Family Limited Partnership* is another popular estate planning tool for larger estates. When used properly, the Family Limited Partnership can reduce estate and gift tax exposure, protect assets from creditors, and facilitate business succession. In a typical Family Limited Partnership:

✔ You and your spouse create a formal limited partnership, a separate legal entity with its own taxpayer identification number, and transfer assets into the partnership. You and your spouse each hold 50 percent ownership of the limited partnership.

✔ You and your spouse retain all management authority, but make gifts of your limited partner interest to your children.

✔ Due to the lack of input into management of the business and lack of marketability, your children's limited partnership shares are discounted in value. For example, if you hold $1 million of assets in the limited partnership and make a gift of 2 percent of the partnership to your child, before the discount, the gift would be worth $20,000 and would exceed your annual gift tax exclusion. With a 40 percent discount due to restrictions on the shares, the value of your gift would be only $12,000 and would fall within the annual gift tax exclusion.

You can create a Family Limited Partnership where your children (or other beneficiaries of your gifts) manage the partnership and you hold the limited interest. The discount is applied to the share held by your estate, such that if your partnership shares are worth $2 million, a 40-percent discount would reduce its taxable value to your estate to $1.2 million.

As you can see, this tool can accelerate the transfer of assets to your heirs and significantly reduce your taxable estate. The Family Limited Partnership may also help protect your assets from your creditors.

By the same token, the IRS is very aware of Family Limited Partnerships and is hostile to them, particularly where it deems the discount claimed by your estate to be excessive. Many mistakes are common in creating and administering a Family Limited Partnership, and these errors can reduce or eliminate its value as a tax avoidance tool. I recommend that you hire an estate planning professional to create your Family Limited Partnership.

Please recall that this list of estate tax avoidance techniques isn't exhaustive. Your estate planner may recommend additional tools based upon your goals and the size of your estate.

Seeing the Big Picture: Tax Avoidance Should Not Dictate Your Estate Plan

Even if you detest the idea of giving the IRS a penny of your estate, you need to step back and consider how tax avoidance strategies affect your estate plan. Tax planning can be complicated and expensive for you:

✔ Creating an effective estate tax avoidance plan is complicated. If you try to do it yourself, you may make a mistake such that your estate pays taxes despite your efforts.

✔ Professional tax planning services can be expensive, and the more complicated your plan, the more expensive those services will be.

✔ With the estate tax in a state of uncertainty, your estate tax avoidance plan may soon require significant revision.

✔ While you can avoid estate tax through gifts and certain irrevocable trusts, you limit or eliminate your own ability to use those assets.

Your estate plan can also complicate the administration of your trusts and estate, resulting in increased fees and costs. It can complicate when and how your heirs receive their inheritances.

When you create your estate plan, consider how you can avoid estate taxes. But don't lose track of the primary purpose of an estate plan: leaving your assets to your heirs in the manner of your choosing.

Paying Your Estate's Debts

Although your heirs can't inherit your debts, your estate remains on the hook. Your creditors may make claims with your estate for money you owe, and your bills are paid prior to the distribution of your bequests to your heirs.

Often, your heirs can take advantage of exemptions that partially shield your estate from your creditors. When an exemption applies, your heirs can retain ownership or use of certain property, even if it means that creditors go unpaid. The availability and amount of these exceptions are different in each state.

✔ Under the homestead exemption, your primary residence may be fully or partially protected from your creditors, and certain family members may be granted a right to occupy your homestead despite the claims of creditors. In some states the homestead exemption is very small, only a few thousand dollars, while other states shield the entire value of your home.

✔ The personal property exemption allows your spouse and minor children to retain certain items of personal property. The amount of this exemption is usually between $10,000 and $50,000.

✔ Some states permit a court to grant *family allowance,* payments of money to help support your surviving spouse and minor children. The payment is usually based upon the amount of money your family needs to support itself in the same manner as when you were alive, and payments usually last one year. Some states will continue family allowance payments until the estate is closed, even if that takes more than a year.

Your administrator must remember to follow proper procedure and not simply pay off your bills as they come in. If your estate has limited assets, that approach may leave your estate without sufficient assets to pay your higher priority bills.

Although state laws vary on the procedure, the following steps outline the general process of how your estate pays your bills:

1. **Your personal representative gathers information about your debts.**

2. **Your creditors are notified that you have died and that they must make a claim against your estate within a specified period of time, usually one to four months.**

   Notice is normally given by publication or by mail.

3. **Creditors submit their claims.**

   If a creditor receives proper notice and doesn't submit a timely claim, the claim is likely to be barred (that is, the creditor forever loses any right to payment).

4. **Your personal representative accepts or rejects creditors' claims.**

5. **If a claim is rejected, the creditor must promptly file a claim with the probate court.**

6. **The list of approved claims to the probate court for approval.**

7. **If the list is approved, the listed debts are paid from your estate's assets.**

If your estate lacks sufficient funds to pay all your debts, the debts are prioritized according to state law, and creditors with higher priority are paid first. Each state has its own law defining which debts have priority. The following list is typical, although the details may be different in your state:

- Expenses of estate administration, including court costs, attorney fees, and the fees of your personal representative.

- Secured debts, such as mortgages, deeds of trust, and liens

- Funeral expenses

- Expenses of your last illness

- Spousal and family allowance

- Wage claims made by your employees

- Debts and taxes with priority under federal law

- Debts and taxes with priority under state law

- All other debts

Medical costs and Medicaid reimbursements

Your final medical bills, to the extent that they're not covered by insurance, have high priority for payment. Another liability arises if you received Medicaid benefits. State Medicaid recovery laws permit state governments to pursue the assets of your estate as reimbursement for Medicaid benefits you received during your lifetime.

Typically, the state files a claim against your estate, specifying the amount to be reimbursed. The claim applies to all the property you own at the time of your death. Reimbursement claims typically includes the cost to Medicaid of

- ✔ The cost of nursing home care, or of home or community-based care
- ✔ Hospital services
- ✔ Prescription medications

Your heirs do have some degree of protection through hardship exemptions and, more typically, through deferrals. A hardship exemption requires a demonstration of undue hardship, a standard that is both subjective and difficult to meet. Medicaid recovery will typically be deferred in situations where:

- ✔ You have a surviving spouse.
- ✔ Your household includes minor children, or adult children who are blind or permanently disabled.

Once your surviving spouse dies or your minor child reaches adulthood, the state will again pursue your assets.

The federal government encourages states to seek reimbursement from Medicaid recipients, and states are becoming more aggressive in pursuing reimbursement. You can't simply transfer assets out of your name to avoid reimbursing the state. The law provides for *look-back periods* during which transfers into trusts and transfers for less than market value can result in Medicaid ineligibility. Also, the net result of your gift may be that the government can immediately reach assets to pay for your care that would otherwise have been subject to an exemption or deferral.

Please remember that despite Medicaid reimbursement, your estate may save money by taking advantage of Medicaid benefits. A nursing home that may charge $65,000 per year for private pay clients may charge only $45,000 per year for Medicaid clients. Even if your estate ultimately pays the $45,000 annual cost, you still save $20,000 per year over private payment.

If you expect to receive Medicaid benefits, you should consult a qualified professional to assist you with Medicaid planning. While Medicaid planning probably will not shield your estate from the government or increase the amount you can leave to your heirs, it can make your life a lot more comfortable. For example, you may be able to preserve your savings to cover items not paid for by Medicaid, including:

- ✔ A private room
- ✔ Supplemental care, such as a geriatric care manager or companion caregiver

- ✔ Eyeglasses, hearing aids, and dentures
- ✔ Beauty shop visits

This type of Medicaid planning is legal and ethical. You don't need to feel guilty about preserving your assets.

Payment of bills, loans, and mortgages

Most of your bills aren't paid until the probate court approves the list of approved claims submitted by your personal representative.

Some of the obligations of your estate require payments to be made before the estate closes. Your personal representative will pay your mortgage payments, utility bills, and homeowner's insurance premiums while your estate remains open. Your personal representative may also have to make car payments and maintain auto insurance, if you own a car at the time of your death.

If your estate includes real property that is subject to a mortgage, your mortgage lender will require repayment. If your estate can't afford the mortgage, your heir may take the property subject to the debt and attempt to assume the mortgage or refinance, or the real estate may be sold to pay the mortgage debt.

You can obtain insurance to protect your heirs from mortgages. You can purchase mortgage life insurance, which pays off the mortgage balance when you die. You can also consider simply purchasing a term life policy sufficient to pay off your mortgage. Term life insurance is usually cheaper than mortgage life insurance.

Payment of funeral expenses

Your personal representative is responsible for arranging your funeral, and paying the costs of your funeral and burial. Funeral expenses may include

- ✔ The funeral home bill
- ✔ The cost of the reception after your funeral
- ✔ Stipends for clergy
- ✔ Your gravestone

Most states give funeral expenses very high priority, such that if your estate has limited assets, the funeral costs are paid before most other bills. A state may prioritize payment of funeral expenses ahead of federal taxes, although a tax return must still be filed.

Covering Administration Costs

No matter how you leave your estate to your heirs, there will be costs. Some of the costs are unavoidable, while others may be reduced with the estate planning tools discussed in this book. The most significant costs your estate will incur are usually legal fees, as well as the fees and expenses of your trustee or personal administrator. Those costs are described in the following sections.

Don't forget that the costs of administering your estate include the costs of caring for your property and of distributing your bequests. For example:

- ✔ If you have real estate, it must be maintained and insured.
- ✔ Somebody will have to clean your belongings out of your house or apartment.
- ✔ If the real estate is sold, your estate may pay commissions to a real estate agent.
- ✔ If you make bequests of property that must be stored or shipped to your heirs, unless you provide otherwise, your estate will bear the cost of storage, shipping, and insurance.

Court costs

The actual cost of opening an estate in probate court is modest. Filing fees are usually no more than a few hundred dollars. Litigation can increase court costs if, for example, the estate

- ✔ Files a lawsuit, such as a wrongful death claim, and incurs the costs associated with the lawsuit
- ✔ Defends itself against litigation, such as a will contest

This amount doesn't mean that probate is a bargain. Remember that court costs don't include either lawyer fees or fees paid to the administrator of your estate.

Legal fees

Although a personal representative can probate your estate without the help of a lawyer, anticipate that your estate will pay legal fees.

The amount of legal fees permitted varies by state, with some states authorizing the attorney to charge a "reasonable fee," others awarding a fee to be set by the court, and some setting the fee as a percentage of the value of your estate. Where an attorney handles the probate process, expect the total fee to be between 2 to 5 percent of your estate.

Administrator's fees

The personal representative of your estate is entitled to compensation for services performed in the administration of your estate. The amount an executor may charge depends upon state law and typically is 2 to 5 percent of the value of your estate. The fee may be higher depending upon the complexity of your estate. If state law provides for hourly fees, or fees based upon the reasonable value of services performed, your personal representative's fee will be subject to court approval.

Your personal representative may require professional assistance with your estate, and your estate pays for those services as well. In addition to legal fees, for example, your personal representative may require help from an accountant or appraiser. You can help minimize these expenses by

- Discussing your estate with your personal representative
- Making sure that your taxes are paid and that your finances are in order
- Ensuring that your personal representative knows where your property is located
- Making sure that your personal representative knows what types of services are likely to be required by your estate, and what they can reasonably be expected to cost

Often a relative or close friend will agree to serve as personal representative without a fee, or for an agreed-upon fee. Discuss this fee with your personal representative and successor and describe the agreed compensation in your will. Serving as personal representative is hard work and can be emotionally difficult. Unless the personal representative is your sole or primary heir, I suggest providing compensation.

Absent an agreement, expect that your personal representative will charge and collect a fee. Be careful about setting too low a fee, as the role of personal representative is often difficult and time-consuming, and an undercompensated personal representative may resign.

If your personal representative has to post a bond, your estate will pay the cost of the bond. The bond is similar to insurance for your estate, in the event that the personal representative mishandles or misappropriates assets. If you want, some states permit you to waive the bond requirement in your will, or you can specifically require that the executor post a bond.

Trustee's fees

You can avoid much of the expense of probate by passing your assets through a trust. Yet a trust carries expenses of its own.

Like your personal representative in probate court, your trustee can charge fees. Your trustee may also require professional services, including legal and accounting services.

You may define within your trust the compensation your trustee is to receive. If you don't, your trustee will be permitted to charge a reasonable fee for services rendered. That fee may be hourly, or it may be a percentage (often about 1 percent per year) of the value of the trust's assets. Professional trust services often charge annual fees in the range of 0.75 to 1.25 percent of the trust's assets.

Be careful to understand what services your trustee will provide, and what services are offered at an additional fee. If you're using an institutional trustee, you should have a clear understanding of their fees and the services your trust will receive for those fees, including:

- ✔ One time fees, such as fees for setting up the trust accounts, or trust termination fees

- ✔ Annual fees, and the services included in the annual fee

- ✔ Service fees not included in the annual fee, such as fees for preparing tax returns or annual trust reports

- ✔ Extraordinary fees (fees for services outside of the normal scope of trust administration), and how those fees are assessed

Don't rule out institutional trustees based upon cost alone. Sometimes an institutional trustee will be the best choice for your trust (see Chapter 4).

Part II
Everything You Need to Know about Wills

"I just think we need to make provisions in our Will for disposition of our property. Who'll get Park Place? Who'll get Boardwalk? Who'll get the thimble and all the tiny green houses?"

In this part . . .

This part guides you through the process of creating your will. You figure out what a will can and can't do and why your will is a key part of your estate plan. You find out about pitfalls you may encounter when writing your will, and how to properly execute your will when it's complete. You understand why you must regularly review and update your will, and how to make changes. You also find out about the probate process and how to avoid will contests.

Chapter 7

Writing and Signing a Will

. . . .

In This Chapter

▶ Deciding what type of will you need

▶ Reviewing your assets

▶ Choosing your heirs and making bequests

▶ Executing a valid will

. . . .

*Y*our will is an essential part of your estate plan. No matter what else you do to plan your estate, your will serves purposes that no other estate planning document can fill. Through your will, you can

✔ Designate who will care for your minor children and their money

✔ Detail your preferences for your funeral and the disposition of your body

✔ Plan how your estate will pay your bills

✔ Provide a backup plan in case something is accidentally left out of your estate plan or a bequest fails

Most people are able to compose a simple will, which is all some people need. This chapter outlines what goes into a will, and how to properly execute your will.

More complex estate plans utilize both a will and trusts. If your estate is large, you need to engage in tax planning, or you want to do things that may be legally tricky (such as disinheriting an heir), you'll probably benefit from having a lawyer draft your will.

Deciding Whether a Will Serves Your Needs

In one sense, asking yourself whether a will serves your needs is an easy question. Everybody has needs that can be served by a will, so everybody should have a will.

But what I'm really asking is whether your estate plan can be managed with just a will. If you don't have estate tax concerns, aren't concerned about probate or having your will made part of a public court record, and simply want your estate to be distributed to your heirs when you die, a simple will may be all you need.

Until you're near retirement age, a living trust probably won't help you, but it will cost you time and money to create and update, and it will be more cumbersome for you to work with assets that you transfer into the trust. Sure, even younger people can suffer a sudden illness or die unexpectedly, but if you're in pretty good health, you can cover your bases pretty well with a will, durable power of attorney, and healthcare proxy.

Trusts are most useful in your estate plan when

- ✔ Your estate may be subject to estate taxes. Presently your estate must be worth $2 million or more to pay federal estate taxes.
- ✔ You want to avoid probate court.

Most states have significantly improved the probate process, and smaller estates often qualify for simplified probate. It may be cheaper to probate your estate instead of creating and funding a trust.

Simplicity often leads you to a will

The fewer assets you have, and the less complicated your plans for the distribution of your estate, the more likely it is that a will is all you need.

Similarly, if you're married and want to leave most or all of your estate to your spouse, you probably don't need a complicated estate plan. Your spouse should automatically inherit your share of jointly owned property, and you may not have much left to go through probate.

Do you own real estate in more than one state? The probate court in the state where you die doesn't have authority over real estate located in another state or country. To probate out-of-state real property, the administrator of your estate will have to start a separate probate action in the state where the property is located. You can easily avoid this complication with a living trust. (See Chapter 12 for more on this process.)

Do you own your own business? If so, even during your prime working years, you should start thinking about business succession. If your business may falter or fail without you, you also need to create a plan for your incapacity. During the time it takes for a probate court to appoint somebody to take over your business, it may suffer significant losses or become broken beyond repair. (Chapter 4 discusses business succession planning.)

You can create and fund trusts with your will. You can get the estate tax benefits of a bypass trust or restrict when and how your heirs receive their inheritances, by including pour-over provisions in your will to fund an existing trust or providing for the creation and funding of an entirely new testamentary trust.

If you live in Louisiana, whatever your circumstances, your estate may be too complicated to plan by yourself. Your state has *forced heirship* laws that require you to leave bequests to certain heirs and has strict requirements for the execution of a valid will. If you reside in Louisiana, I suggest that you hire a lawyer to draft your will.

For people in other states, the larger and more complex your estate, the more likely it is that you'll benefit from having a professionally drafted will. If you require tax-planning services, want to disinherit an heir, or have children from a prior relationship, a lawyer can help you figure out exactly what you need to do to plan your estate and help you avoid traps that can seriously disrupt your plan for your assets.

For more information on estate planning traps, see Chapter 8. For tips on how to find an estate planning lawyer, see Chapter 4.

Assets not covered by a will

As you review your assets, consider whether they're jointly owned or already have a designated beneficiary. If you're married, many of your assets are probably jointly owned with your spouse. Your insurance policies and retirement accounts name a beneficiary.

When joint ownership or a beneficiary designation define who will receive property upon your death, it doesn't matter what you put in your will. Whatever your will says, the assets pass according to the title or beneficiary designation and never become part of your probate estate. These transfers are thus said to occur *outside of probate.*

The following sections address the different types of assets not covered by a will.

Insurance, annuities, and retirement accounts with designated beneficiaries

When you designate a beneficiary for an insurance policy, annuity, or retirement account, the asset is transferred to your beneficiary upon proof of your death. These assets are generally still included in your estate for the calculation of estate tax, but the probate court isn't involved in the transfer of the asset to your beneficiary.

Your heir may receive significant benefits from receiving a retirement account outside of probate. (See Chapter 15 for additional information on retirement accounts.)

Insurance can be a very important part of your estate plan, and it may be possible for you to keep insurance proceeds out of your taxable estate. If the insurance payout will cause your estate to become taxable, see Chapter 16.

Property with a right of survivorship

If you're married, you and your spouse probably jointly own your home. If your deed says that ownership is *by the entireties* or refers to a right of survivorship, your co-owners should receive your interest in the property without going through probate.

The various ways that property may be titled, and how that affects the transfer or inheritance of property, are detailed in Chapter 17.

Joint bank accounts

The money in your joint bank accounts is available for either account holder to withdraw, at any time. Unless you set up the account to require the consent of all account holders, your joint account holder doesn't need your permission to withdraw funds. When you die, your interest in the account passes to your joint account holders.

You need to be careful with joint bank accounts for several reasons:

✔ The IRS will try to count the entire balance of your joint account in your taxable estate and will require the joint account holders to prove that they contributed money to the account balance.

✔ Your joint account holder can empty your account. There are many sad stories where an elderly person added a younger sibling or child to the account to "help" pay their bills and manage their assets, only to have the "helper" pocket the money.

If you intend to maintain total control over the account until your death, you may be better served by adding a transfer-on-death provision to your account rather than joint ownership (see the next section).

Transfer-on-death accounts and titles

As an alternative to joint ownership, you can give somebody an interest in property or financial accounts that doesn't take effect until you die. Although the asset is included in your estate for gift tax purposes, the *transfer-on-death provision* transfers ownership to your beneficiary upon your death without the necessity of probate. You keep total ownership and control of the asset during your lifetime.

You need to be careful using this technique. If your family circumstances change, your transfer-on-death provision may become outdated, as in the following cases:

✔ If you set up a deed to transfer ownership to your three children upon your death and a child dies before you, the property will go to your surviving children unless you included your grandchildren as contingent beneficiaries.

✔ If you later have or adopt another child, unless you update the provision, that child won't inherit.

✔ If you set up an asset to transfer on death to your spouse, you must remember to update that provision after divorce, or your ex-spouse will receive the asset.

Exploring the Types of Wills

Wills come in many different types. For the most part, the difference is one of complexity. The basic elements of a simple will are also present in a highly complex will, but additional provisions have been added.

The statutory will

Most states offer a *statutory will,* a very simple will that, if properly executed, will be accepted by a probate court. Statutory wills are often made available as fill-in-the-blanks forms, so they're pretty easy to complete. You may be able to get a form by asking your state representative's office to provide one, and in many states, they're available for download from the state legislature or state courts Web sites.

At the same time, statutory wills are very simple. They can help you implement a basic estate plan, but aren't meant to help with tax planning or more complicated estates. While unquestionably "better than nothing," a statutory will is most useful if you have a very small estate and desire a very simple estate plan.

The handwritten (holographic) will

A *holographic will* (or in Louisiana, an olographic will) is written entirely in your own handwriting and is signed by you, but isn't witnessed. Most states disfavor holographic wills and recognize them only under narrow circumstances, such as when they're prepared by a soldier who is engaged in combat.

A cousin of the holographic will is the *oral will,* sometimes called a *nuncupative will,* where there is no written document at all. A court will entertain an oral will in a few circumstances — typically only where the person making the will faces imminent death, where disinterested witnesses produce a written record of the will shortly after the person's death, and where only small amounts of money are involved.

Sometimes you can go through the trouble of writing or articulating a will, but you can't produce a written will that is properly witnessed. Make sure that your wishes will be respected by following your state's formalities for the execution of your will. (See Appendix A for state-by-state guidance on executing a formal will.)

A will of your own

Your will is more powerful than you may realize. In addition to parceling out your estate to your heirs, you can create and fund trusts, implement parts of your estate tax avoidance strategy, designate caregivers for your minor children, and outline your preferences for your funeral and memorial service.

As a general rule, when you create a will, it's sensible to

- ✔ **Follow state law formalities for the execution of your will.** Otherwise your will may be rejected by a probate court.

- ✔ **Whenever possible, keep your estate plan simple.** Don't complicate your will unless you're truly convinced that the added complexity is necessary to your estate plan.

You can find will forms that you can customize to your circumstances on the CD accompanying this book.

Other wills

When I discuss a simple will, I'm usually talking about a will that appoints an administrator, perhaps designates people to care for your minor children, and allocates your estate between your heirs. But you can do a lot more with your will.

- ✔ **Testamentary and pour-over wills:** You can create a trust with your will or direct your estate to put assets into a trust. (For more on trusts, see Part III.)

- ✔ **Joint wills:** You can create a joint estate plan with your spouse and may also be able to make your joint estate plan legally binding even after your death.

- ✔ **Self-proving wills:** You can add an affidavit to your will to simplify the process of submitting it to probate.

Testamentary and pour-over wills

When you create a living trust, you traditionally transfer assets into your trust during your lifetime. That transfer of assets simplifies probate and helps with disability planning.

But what if you never get around to transferring your assets into your trust or want to keep ownership in your own name during your lifetime? You can use your will to create or fund a trust. How is this done?

- ✔ **A pour-over will funds an existing trust.** A pour-over clause may add additional funds or assets to your living trust. But you can also execute a trust that you have no intention of funding during your lifetime and direct assets into the trust from your estate.

- ✔ **A testamentary trust will includes language that creates a trust that becomes operative upon your death.** You can even make the creation of the trust conditional — for example directing inheritances for your minor children into a trust, but allowing them to directly receive their inheritances if they reach adulthood before you die.

Testamentary trusts can be useful as part of a tax-avoidance strategy. For example, if you're married, you can create a testamentary bypass trust to maximize estate tax exemptions for your combined marital estate. Chapter 12 describes the many trust options.

Joint wills

In simple terms, a *joint will* is executed by both you and your spouse. When the first spouse dies, the surviving spouse inherits the entire estate. When the surviving spouse dies, the estate is distributed according to the terms of the will.

A joint will is a simple way to provide for your spouse and heirs, but it's not much more complicated for you and your spouse to both execute your own separate wills.

If your joint will doesn't prevent the surviving spouse from changing the will after you die, your spouse may change your common estate plan. If you're trying to provide for friends or relatives that your spouse doesn't care for, or for children from a prior marriage, that may be a risk you don't want to take.

If you want to be sure that if you die first, your spouse can't change your joint estate plan, many states permit you to enter into a contract will. You and your spouse enter into a joint estate plan.

- ✔ As long as you remain alive, you and your spouse may change the plan or even scrap it.

- ✔ Upon the death of you or your spouse, the estate plan becomes binding and irrevocable.

For a smaller estate, a contract will may be a sufficient means of ensuring that your heirs receive their inheritances, even if your spouse might prefer to disinherit them after your death. But a contract will does have disadvantages:

- ✔ Your spouse may not be able to sell or dispose of assets that are identified in the joint estate plan. For example, will your spouse be able to sell the marital home and move into a condo or apartment? What if your spouse can barely afford the house payments, let alone the cost of maintenance?

- ✔ Your other heirs' inheritances may be tied up for the life of your spouse, which could be 20 or 30 years. Do you want your children to receive their inheritances when they're getting established in their lives, or when they're approaching retirement age?

If you're considering a binding, joint estate plan, you should consider using a trust. The bypass trust is powerful estate planning tool that lets you direct assets to your heirs while providing lifetimes support for your spouse. You can also use trusts to allow your younger spouse to remain in the marital home for a period of years following your death, with the home then being inherited by your children from a prior marriage. For more discussion of estate planning for second marriages, see Chapter 4.

Self-proving wills

It's unlikely that somebody is going to challenge the validity of your will. Most of the time, everybody agrees that the will submitted to the probate court is genuine. But if a disagreement occurs, tracking down witnesses to your will can be difficult. Your witnesses may have moved, and some may even be dead.

A *self-proving will* includes an affidavit, executed and signed by your witnesses in front of a notary public. When the affidavit is properly executed, your will may be submitted to probate without any statements from your witnesses.

Elements of a Will

In order to be effective, your will must describe who you are, what assets you have, who you want to receive your assets, and how your assets are to be divided. Beyond the basic elements, your will appoints a personal representative to administer your estate and can also appoint caregivers for your minor children. It can create or fund trusts to hold and manage your assets after your death. Your will can also describe your funeral and burial preferences.

Appendix C provides a form to help you assemble the information necessary to complete your will. This form is also available on the CD accompanying this book.

Who you are

The popular conception is that a will commences with the declaration, "I, John Smith, being of sound mind and body. . . ." However, it's not necessary to describe your health. And if you're not mentally competent, it doesn't make any difference to say you are.

All you really need to do is identify yourself sufficiently so that people will know that it's your will.

What are your assets

Part of the estate planning process is figuring out what you own. Your possessions will typically include

- Personal assets:
  - Cash, savings, and checking accounts
  - Investments
  - Home furnishings
  - Jewelry
  - Art and antiques
  - Collectibles
  - Your wardrobe
- Real estate, including your primary residence and any vacation property
- Insurance policies and annuities
- Retirement plans

If you're a business owner or are a partner in a small business, your estate also includes your interest in the business.

Not all your assets will go through probate. Insurance policies and retirement plans probably have a designated beneficiary. Your home may automatically go to your spouse as the joint title holder. But you should still consider those assets when planning your estate, as they can affect how you distribute your other assets. For example, if one of your children is the beneficiary of a life insurance policy, you can leave a larger bequest to your other child to balance out the inheritances.

You should also take inventory of your debts, including mortgages and bank loans, credit cards, and car loans.

Your estate will pay off your debts before your heirs receive their inheritances. If some of your property has to be sold to pay your debts, a specific bequest of that property will fail, or your estate may not have enough money left over to fill all your bequests. For guidance on inventorying your assets and debts, see Chapter 3.

Who are your beneficiaries

After you know what you own, you need to figure out who you want to give it to. Put together a list of your possible heirs. Be overinclusive. You don't have to leave something to every person on your list.

Here are a few ideas to get you started:

- ✔ Your family, including
  - Your spouse
  - Your children and stepchildren
  - Your grandchildren and great-grandchildren
  - Your parents
  - Your sisters and brothers
  - Aunts, uncles, and cousins
  - Nieces and nephews
- ✔ Your friends
- ✔ Educational institutions
- ✔ Charities

You need to also consider the circumstances of your heirs. Young children may benefit from having their inheritances left to them in a trust, providing for their support and payment of educational expenses over a period of years. An heir who doesn't manage money well may benefit from a spendthrift trust. An heir who receives public assistance due to a disability may benefit from a special needs trust. You can find more discussion on estate planning for these special circumstances in Chapters 4 and 5.

What are your bequests

You know what you own. You know who your heirs are. You now need to figure out who gets what (and who gets left out).

The law limits your ability to disinherit your spouse and sometimes your minor children. Chapter 8 discusses the limits on disinheritance.

When you're drafting a will in Louisiana, you operate subject to your state's *forced heirship laws.* These laws compel you to leave minimum bequests to certain heirs, principally your spouse and children, and define very narrow grounds under which you may disinherit an heir or provide a lesser bequest than the law specifies. These laws make it very difficult for people to plan their estates without the assistance of a lawyer.

Avoiding failed bequests

Your bequests may fail in one of two ways:

- ✔ Your heir may die before you or may decline an inheritance.
- ✔ You may leave a bequest of property that is no longer part of your estate when you die.

The first problem is pretty easy to address. If you have a specific item of property that you want to remain in the family, designate an alternate beneficiary. For example, if you leave your grandmother's engagement ring to your eldest daughter, name her younger sister as the alternate beneficiary.

Naming an alternate beneficiary is also important as your bequest to an heir who dies before you may pass to that heir's descendents, rather than staying in your estate. If you don't designate an alternate beneficiary for Grandma's engagement ring, it may end up going to your son-in-law.

If you leave a bequest of a specific asset that is no longer in the estate, your bequest failed. This problem can arise with anything that is sold, lost, spent, or destroyed, including cars, collections, investments, and cash. For example:

- ✔ Your will bequeaths "My house at 1212 Cherry Tree Lane" to your son. You subsequently sell the house, move, and don't update your will to leave your new home to your son. His gift fails. Your first house is no longer in your estate, and your new home doesn't automatically get substituted for the old. Although a more generic description, such as simply saying "my home," may prevent the failure of your bequest if you own a different home at the time of your death, it won't help if you no longer own a home.

- ✔ You have an investment account worth $500,000. You leave $100,000 to your brother, with the balance to be split between your children. Before you die, you suffer an illness that runs up large medical bills. After your medical bills and the other debts of your estate are paid, only $80,000 remains in the account. Part of your brother's gift fails, as he receives only $80,000 of the $100,000 you intended him to receive. But although you intended them to each inherit $200,000, your children receive *nothing* from the account.

Sometimes a gift will fail by accident or oversight. Say that you have two children, Jack and Peter. Your will leaves bequests to "My children, Jack and Peter." You later have a third child, Sue, but forget to update your will. Even though she's one of your children, you've excluded her from that bequest. Note that this omission may not leave her empty-handed and may in fact cause her to inherit *more* than her siblings. (See the discussion of estate planning for unknown heirs in Chapter 8.)

With a bit of extra thought, you can help make sure that your bequests succeed.

- ✔ You can use generic descriptions, such as "my personal residence" or "my car" so that changes in your assets are less likely to cause a gift to fail.
- ✔ You can gift in percentages ("20 percent of my stock account to my brother, and the rest divided equally among my children") rather than in specific dollar figures.
- ✔ You can give class gifts, "to my children" or "to my grandchildren," rather than naming specific individuals.

Additional suggestions for making sure that your intentions are honored, and to minimize the chances that your estate plan will go horribly wrong, are found in Chapter 8.

Creating a moral obligation or a binding inheritance

Sometimes you have reasons why you don't want to leave property directly to the intended recipient. Here's a common example: Perhaps you have a child who is disabled and receives public assistance. Rather than creating a special needs trust, you may choose to leave that child's share of your estate to another sibling, trusting that your children will take care of each other.

Most of the time, things work out the way you want. Probably 95 percent of the time, the heir who holds an inheritance for the benefit of somebody else will do exactly what you wanted. The rest of the time, perhaps out of personal financial hardship or perhaps out of greed, the person holding the money will spend it, and the person they were supposed to look after has no legal remedy.

Even when things work out, this arrangement can burden a family relationship. The child trusted with the money may come under constant demands for more money, perhaps amounts w–ell in excess of what you left, from their sibling.

If you want to create a moral obligation on your heirs, you can take some comfort in the odds. But be sure that you also consider the burdens and risks you may create.

Reference to a tangible personal property memorandum

Some states allow you to make reference in your will to an external document that lists items of personal property and who inherits them. This memorandum allows you to leave your household furnishings and personal possessions to specific people, change the list to add new items, remove things you no longer possess, or change who gets what, without changing your will.

The formal requirements for the memorandum can be very different, depending upon the laws of your state. Some states are content with a list you sign and date, while others require formal witnessing and execution. Not all states permit this type of memorandum.

If your state permits and you create a memorandum, make sure that you keep it in a secure place known to your personal representative. If it gets lost or misplaced, it can't be followed.

What happens with the residue (if any) of the estate

After all your bequests are made, odds are that something will be left over. Items of personal property that weren't specifically described in your will, some of the money that was set aside to pay the expenses of your estate — your clothes, a bequest that failed Whatever it is, the leftover items are the *residue* of your estate.

A *residuary clause* describes how those leftovers are to be distributed to your heirs. For example, "The residue of my estate is to be divided equally between my children."

If you don't include a residuary clause, anything left in your estate will be distributed according to your state's laws of intestate succession. Truly, including a residuary clause is so easy that you have no excuse not to have one.

Payment of debts by the estate

Your estate is obligated by law to pay your debts. Your personal representative provides notice to your creditors, consistent with the laws of your estate, those creditors submit claims for payment, and your estate pays those debts found to be valid.

Help your personal representative by leaving, along with your will, a list of your debts. That list will make notifying your creditors of your death and their obligation to submit claims to your estate so much easier for your personal representative.

Most wills include a clause directing your personal representative to pay your bills. Some are more demanding, suggesting that your personal representative should affirmatively seek out and pay your creditors.

A clause relating to your debts can't reduce your estate's obligations to pay its debts under state law. It can only enlarge the responsibilities of your personal administrator. I thus consider this clause to be optional and in most cases suggest leaving it out of your will.

Describing your funeral and burial wishes

If you have specific wishes for your funeral and burial, you can describe them in your will. Topics you may want to address include

- ✔ Whether you want to be cremated or buried or have other wishes for the disposition of your body.
- ✔ Where you want to be buried
- ✔ What type of funeral and memorial service you desire and any specific people you want to have invited to your service
- ✔ Any poems, scripture, songs, quotations, or readings you'd like shared at your service

Your estate plan should anticipate the payment of funeral expenses. Funeral costs, along with your other bills, are paid before any distributions are made to your heirs.

Designating a personal representative

Your personal representative, also called an executor, manages your estate in the probate court. This role is important and sometimes difficult, so you need to choose somebody who has the necessary interest and qualifications to administer your estate. You want somebody who is mature, financially responsible, and trustworthy.

You can describe in your will how your personal representative is to be compensated. Unless your personal representative is your primary heir, I suggest providing for payment.

You should also designate an alternate personal representative, in case your first choice is unable or unwilling to serve. If you don't choose a personal representative or don't have an available alternate when your first choice is unavailable, the probate court will appoint somebody to administer your estate.

For more information on selecting a personal representative, see Chapter 4.

Designating a guardian for any minor children

If you're providing for your minor children, you should designate a person you want to care for your children if you die. You can separate physical care from finances, designating one person to take physical care of your children and another person to handle their money.

You'll also want to designate successor caregivers, just in case your first choice is unable to fulfill their duties. Chapter 5 offers a lot of suggestions on how to select caregivers for your children and provide for their care and support.

Your signature

After you finish drafting your will, you must sign and date it. Some states require that you sign your will in front of your witnesses. Others allow you to sign it at an earlier time, as long as you inform your witnesses that it's your signature and acknowledge that the document is your last will and testament.

Executing a Valid Will

The specific requirements for executing a will are different in each state. Appendix A summarizes state laws.

Every state requires your will to be witnessed by two legally competent individuals. Many states limit the inheritance that may be received by a witness to your will, so use witnesses who aren't also your heirs. See Appendix A for more information on state laws governing who may, and who may not, witness your will.

Choosing the right witnesses

If someone challenges your will, your witnesses may be crucial to establishing the authenticity of your will and signature. What does that mean? It means that you want your witnesses to be

- ✔ Credible
- ✔ Available
- ✔ Disinterested

Disinterested doesn't mean uninterested. It means that they don't stand to profit from their actions. If one of your heirs contests your will and it was witnessed by another heir, a court may be skeptical of your witness's testimony. Also, as a check on self-interested testimony, most states limit the amount you can leave to an heir who serves as a witness. In short, pick witnesses who are not heirs.

You may also want to pick witnesses who are younger than you are, and who have relatively stable addresses. Although some states allow you to use minors as witnesses as long as they're competent to testify in court, most states don't. You're best served by choosing witnesses who are legal adults.

Signing and executing your will

Although the specific requirements for execution are different from state to state, I suggest taking a conservative approach to executing your will. If you want to know the minimum requirements for your state, consult Appendix A. If you want to go a bit overboard:

- ✔ Consider using three witnesses instead of two and make sure that they're all legal adults.
- ✔ Don't use your heirs as witnesses.
- ✔ Have a signing ceremony where all your witnesses see you sign your will and sign on as witnesses in front of you and each other and your notary.
- ✔ At your signing ceremony, complete a self-proving affidavit before a notary.

If you go the extra mile, even if you significantly exceed what your state demands of you, you reduce the chances that a challenge will be made to the validity of your will.

Chapter 8

Navigating the Land Mines

*T*his chapter covers some of the trickier aspects of estate planning, including disinheriting an heir, addressing possible unknown heirs, what a will should never say, the potential disaster in not keeping a will current, the potential impact of state laws about inheritances and wills, and what to do if you lose your will.

Identifying Common Land Mines

As you prepare your estate plan, you should be aware of the following pitfalls:

✔ Disinheriting an heir is more difficult than you think.

✔ Your bequests may conflict with state law (and state law usually wins).

✔ You should resist the temptation to share harsh words and feelings.

✔ Odd things may happen if you die at the same time as your spouse and haven't provided for that possibility.

One of the biggest errors you can make is assuming that once you have written your will, your job is done. You must periodically review and update your will. If you don't, the distribution of your estate may be very different from what you expect.

Disinheriting heirs, known and unknown

As a general rule, you can decide how your estate will be distributed. You can disinherit whomever you choose. You can leave your other heirs as much or as little as you want.

Yet the process of disinheriting an heir can be trickier than you may think. State law may prevent you from fully disinheriting a spouse or child. Mistakes in your will may permit your disinherited child to inherit despite your clear wishes.

When you disinherit an heir, be clear in your language. You don't need to explain your decision. Examples of clear statements disinheriting an heir include

- ✔ "For reasons known to him, I leave nothing to my son, George."
- ✔ "I disinherit my daughter, Rebecca."

You may have heard that you should leave a nominal bequest, such as $1, to your disinherited heir. You don't have to follow that advice, and doing so creates unnecessary work for your personal representative who has to track down and provide the $1 check to your disinherited heir.

What if the heir you disinherit is inclined to contest your estate? Even if your disinheritance is upheld by a court, your estate will be tied up in litigation and incur legal fees. You may want to leave a more substantial bequest, coupled with a *no-contest clause* (a clause disinheriting anybody who contests your will). An heir given the choice of a $20,000 inheritance or initiating a will contest and possibly walking away with nothing may choose to take the check.

A disinheritance clause governs only your heir's right to inherit under the terms of your will itself, and not any legal right of inheritance under state law. Whatever you provide in your will, your heir will be eligible to inherit any portion of your estate that is distributed under intestate succession laws. To fully disinherit an heir, you must include a residuary clause in your will, directing the distribution of the balance of your estate after all specific bequests have been made.

Limitations on disinheritance

In community property states, your spouse is entitled to half the marital estate under community property laws. You're free to leave your half of the estate to whomever you choose. However, common law states allow your spouse to *opt against the will, choosing* a statutorily defined inheritance. If you disinherit your spouse, expect that your spouse will choose that option.

Is disinheritance the right choice?

Your children don't talk to you. Your son can't hold a job. Your daughter is a drug addict. You don't want them to get any of your money. So you should disinherit them, right?

Perhaps not.

Money is a powerful motivator. If you discuss your estate plan with your children and warn them that you intend to disinherit them, you may inspire significant improvement in their conduct. You can argue that you don't want to coerce your children, but is the alternative truly better? And what starts out as coercion can grow in to something else.

Your son may not like to hear you say that unless he gets a steady job and settles down, he won't get a penny of your estate. But five years later, he may be married and employed. The children who never call you may suddenly be making regular visits and phone calls.

I'm not suggesting that you be a sucker. You can wait to see whether their efforts are sincere. But you may find that after your children know your grievances and have an opportunity to change, your reasons for disinheritance evaporate.

You may be able to limit your spouse's statutory inheritance rights through a prenuptial agreement. For more on prenuptial agreements, see the section "Handling spousal rights and community property," later in this chapter.

Many states also limit your ability to disinherit your dependent children. Their principal goal is to prevent your children from becoming dependent upon public assistance.

Louisiana has a unique set of laws known as forced heirship laws, which restrict your ability to disinherit your children and descendents. If you intend to disinherit a legal heir in Louisiana, in order to be sure that your disinheritance is legal and effective, you should get help from an estate planning lawyer.

Disinheriting or providing for unknown heirs

If you're concerned that an heir may appear and make a claim for your estate, be sure to address that in your will. Imagine, for example, that you were a bit wild in your younger days and are concerned that a child you don't even know about might appear to make a claim against your estate. What can you include in your will to protect your intended heirs? An extremely broad clause can read

> *I intentionally and with full knowledge of the consequences do not provide in my will or living trust for any of my children not identified within my will and trust, including children conceived, born, or adopted by me after the execution of my will, and intend that this disinheritance specifically defeat the application of any statutory heirship interest.*

Be clear when providing for or disinheriting illegitimate children

Jim was a wealthy widower who had been married for more than 50 years. But during the early years of his marriage, he had an affair. His lover had a child, Elizabeth, whom "everybody" believed to be Jim's daughter. Jim treated Elizabeth very well during his lifetime, but never formally acknowledged her as his daughter. Elizabeth experienced some financial problems shortly before Jim's death, and he let her stay rent-free in an apartment building he owned. In his will, he left her a life estate in the apartment, giving her a permanent, rent-free place to live.

After Jim died, Elizabeth challenged his will claiming that she was an "omitted child." She sought DNA testing to prove paternity. Even though she inherited under the will, she claimed that the inheritance was insubstantial in value and wasn't in the nature of a parent-child bequest. She argued that Jim's other children received much larger gifts.

The probate court allowed DNA testing, and Elizabeth was found to be Jim's biological daughter. After a hearing, the probate court held that the life estate was a substantial gift, and that Elizabeth hadn't been omitted from Jim's will. But then the court reversed its ruling and allowed Elizabeth to seek a larger share of Jim's estate. Faced with an uncertain outcome and the possibility of an expensive, drawn-out lawsuit and appeal, Jim's other heirs agreed to settle Elizabeth's claim. Elizabeth not only inherited her apartment, but also received a six-figure check.

I suspect that if the case were litigated, the courts would have concluded that the probate court was right the first time: Jim's bequest to Elizabeth was substantial, and she wasn't an omitted child. I also understand why Jim's other children chose to settle her claim so that they could avoid legal fees, receive their inheritances, and move on with their lives.

Jim could have avoided this problem either by expressly disinheriting any illegitimate children or by stating that his bequest was made with the knowledge that Elizabeth might be his biological daughter.

With a clause like this one, you may provide specific bequests to your known children, but shut the door to claims by others. Here's a simpler clause:

> *Except as otherwise provided herein and in my living trust, I have intentionally omitted to provide for any of my heirs, children, or persons claiming to be my heirs, whether or not known to me.*

These clauses are broad enough to disinherit children known to you, including children born or adopted after your will is executed, so be extremely careful in using this type of clause.

You can soften the effect for after-born or adopted children:

> *Except as otherwise provided herein and in my living trust, I have intentionally omitted to provide for any persons born and living as of the date of this will who claim to be my heirs, including my children and legal heirs, or whether or not known to me.*

If you provide your children with a class gift ("I leave my children the residue of my estate" or "I leave my children 60 percent of my estate"), while an unknown child's claim will reduce the amount inherited by your known children, all your children will inherit equally. You can also provide a gift for your known children and a different, conditional bequest or class gift for children who are born, adopted, or discovered after you execute your will.

You probably heard about the battle over the estate of Anna Nicole Smith, with numerous men claiming to be the father of her young daughter, her sole heir. But did you know that her will disinherited her daughter? Ms. Smith left her entire estate to her son, with a broad disinheritance clause that excluded after-born children from inheriting. She never updated her will. Tragically, three days after her daughter was born, Ms. Smith's son died. He had no wife or children, so Ms. Smith's bequest to him lapsed. Ms. Smith hadn't named a contingent beneficiary, so when her gift lapsed, the bequest went to her legal heir, her daughter. Ms. Smith almost certainly would have wanted this result, but she was saved her from her serious estate planning mistakes by nothing more than dumb luck.

Your best option is to provide as you see fit for any possible illegitimate children or unknown heirs and update your will if your family situation changes.

Don't accidentally disinherit your children and create a context where they may be able to make claims against your estate. Make sure that your will provides for your children, even if in the alternative. ("I leave my estate to my spouse or, if she dies before me, to my children.")

Avoiding invalidating part or all of your will

State laws are likely to affect your will in two contexts. First, they may require that you leave a substantial share of your estate to your spouse and possibly also provide for the support of your minor children. Second, conditions you impose on your heirs may conflict with public policy and be ignored by a court.

If you're careful, you can keep your estate plan within the confines of state law.

Handling spousal rights and community property

States take two general approaches to marital property:

- ✔ In a community property state, although you continue to own the property you bring into your marriage, most assets acquired during the marriage belong equally to you and your spouse. Gifts and inheritances you receive during marriage are your separate property, but if you put that money into a joint bank account, you risk that it will be treated as community property.

✔ In a common law state, you continue to own and accumulate separate property during your marriage, but if you divorce, your spouse can make an equitable claim for a share of your property.

In a community property state, your spouse already owns half of the marital estate. You can't use your will to reduce that share or take it away, but you're free to distribute your separate property and your own half of the marital estate as you want.

In a common law state, the law prevents you from disinheriting your spouse. In practical terms, if you leave your spouse less than approximately half of your estate, your spouse can make a claim for a larger share.

In many states, you and your spouse can avoid the effects of state law by entering into a contract redefining how your assets will be distributed:

✔ A *prenuptial agreement,* also known as a premarital agreement or prenup, defines how you and your spouse own assets you bring into your marriage or acquire during your marriage and how your estate will be divided if you divorce.

✔ A *postnuptial agreement* has the same effect as a prenuptial agreement, but is executed after you're married.

✔ You can enter into joint wills or trusts to create a contractually binding estate plan. For more on contract wills, see Chapter 7.

Be careful about entering into a marital agreement, before or after marriage. Not all states permit them, and some may permit one but not the other or impose different criteria for when they're enforceable. If your prenuptial agreement is deemed unfair or incomplete or that your spouse didn't understand its terms, a court may refuse to enforce it. If you intend to use a marital agreement as part of your estate plan, you and your spouse should each consult separate, independent lawyers in association with the drafting and execution of the agreement.

Your real estate remains subject to the laws of the state where it's located. A move to a different state is most likely to affect you if you and your spouse own real estate in a community property state and then move to a common law state. For a list of community property states and more information on how community property laws may affect you, see Chapter 3.

If you move to another state, you should review your will under the laws of your new state, particularly if you're moving to

✔ A common law state from a community property state

✔ A community property state from a common law state

✔ Or from Louisiana

Providing for your dependents

Some states prohibit you from disinheriting your dependent children if your estate has sufficient assets to provide for their support. Massachusetts law, for example, provides that death doesn't extinguish a parent's duty to support a minor child. Florida's state constitution protects your spouse's right to inherit your house if you have a minor child.

These restrictions aren't universal, and some states do permit disinheritance of minor children. You probably intend to provide for your children, but if you don't, you should verify your state's laws.

Controlling your heirs from beyond the grave

You may want to use your will to force self-improvement upon your slothful child or finally get your daughter to divorce your annoying son-in-law. What if you make their inheritance conditional upon their taking specific actions? Your son inherits only if he is up by 7 a.m. every morning and works a full-time job. Your daughter inherits only if she gets a divorce.

As you probably suspected, it's not that easy. Courts won't enforce conditions on bequests that are considered to be against public policy or that are too onerous to monitor. A condition that requires your beneficiaries to endanger themselves or others, or commit a crime also won't be enforced.

If your conditions are reasonable but your heir doesn't want to fulfill the condition, your heir may decline your gift. You should designate an alternate beneficiary to receive your bequest in the event that the condition isn't met or your gift is declined. If you don't, your condition may be disregarded such that your heir inherits even if the condition is not met.

The following sections cover some restraints that don't fly with courts.

Marriage

Total restraints on marriage won't be upheld. ("I leave $100,000 to Becky if she never marries.") However, a provision of support ending upon marriage is permitted. ("I leave Becky an income of $10,000 per year so long as she remains unmarried.")

Some states forbid total restraints on second marriage, while others allow such restraints. ("I leave my widow an income of $20,000 per year, so long as she doesn't remarry.")

A partial restraint on marriage may be upheld if it's deemed *reasonable*. Reasonableness is a subjective standard, so the outcome can be unpredictable. As a general rule, a condition is likely to be held unreasonable if it prevents marriage under most or all foreseeable circumstances. Here are some examples of what will and won't fly:

✔ A condition requiring that your niece not marry before the age of 24 may be deemed reasonable, while a condition that she wait until the age of 55 will likely be deemed unreasonable.

✔ A court will probably reject a condition that your nephew not marry a woman who is more than four feet tall.

✔ Most courts will uphold a condition requiring that your beneficiary marry within your religious faith.

Religion

A restraint on religion may be permissible. Religion-based restraints on marriage are often upheld. Other religious conditions are also permitted. ("I leave $100,000 to Joe if he attends morning Mass every Sunday, unless prevented by illness or while on vacation in foreign lands, for the next five years.")

However, a restraint that creates a religious conflict between parent and child won't be upheld. A clause providing "I leave my daughter, Jillian, $100,000, provided she raises her child in the Methodist Church" would likely be upheld if Jillian is a Methodist, but not if she is Jewish.

Conduct

Conditions meant to improve behavior, such as requiring abstention from unlawful drugs or alcohol or that your heir stop gambling, will generally be upheld. But you must be clear in your meaning, or the condition may fail. (How would a court understand the meaning of your provision, "I leave $50,000 to Alex, provided he lives a clean and virtuous life.")

Also, you should describe how performance will be monitored, keeping in mind the cost and burden to your estate. If you don't designate a person to monitor compliance of your otherwise reasonable condition, the probate court will appoint somebody to monitor compliance, and your estate will pay the bill. And the longer your condition remains in effect, the more costly it is to monitor compliance.

Keeping a problem with one clause from affecting the rest of your will

You can include within your will a *severability clause* that provides, in the event that any portion of your will is found to be unenforceable, the remainder of your will remains in full force and effect.

Without a severability clause, a mistake in your will may cause your entire will to be disregarded by the probate court. If you include a severability clause, the probate court should ignore the invalid provision but uphold the rest of your will.

Lashing out from beyond

Most wills are diligent and methodical in their language. They're not very interesting to read, but they get the job done. But that's not always the case. Some wills include a parting shot at somebody the testator doesn't like. This approach is risky for various reasons:

- ✔ You may trigger a defamation (*testamentary libel*) lawsuit against your estate.

- ✔ You give ammunition to anybody who contests your will, as they may characterize your angry words as evidence of mental instability.

- ✔ You may harm your legacy. Your parting shot may overshadow the memories you want people to hold.

- ✔ Your target may never hear your words. Also, although the formal reading of the will is a hallmark of Hollywood movies, it's not required and is rarely done.

- ✔ Your comments may backfire and result in inheritance by the subject of your attack.

How could defamatory statements lead to *inheritance*? By indicating that you omitted the target of your statements from your will by *mistake*. Consider the following examples:

- ✔ "I was going to give my best friend, Jake, $1 million, but he's a shameless gigolo who slept with my wife."

- ✔ "I give each of my grandchildren $50,000, except for Sally who is a criminal and a drug addict."

In either case, you risk that Jake or Sally will argue to the probate court that you had testamentary intent and disinherited them by mistake. Jake will argue that he's not a gigolo, and your wife may testify that no affair occurred. Sally may establish that she has no criminal record and testify that she isn't addicted to drugs. Even though you never actually intended to give Jake a penny and would have disinherited Sally anyway, a court may grant them an inheritance.

If you want to disinherit an heir, keep your language short and to the point. You don't need to offer lengthy explanations or apologies.

Handling simultaneous death of spouses

Although it's unlikely to happen, you and your spouse may suffer a common catastrophe. A serious car accident can result in both of you dying at the same time, or within days of each other.

In the event of simultaneous death, unless you provide otherwise in your will, most states have laws that will distribute your estates as if each of you survived the other.

These laws often treat deaths as simultaneous based upon the common cause, even when one spouse survives the other by days or, in some cases, months.

You can define in your will what constitutes *simultaneous death.* For example, you can provide that deaths are simultaneous if your spouse died within 30 days of you. The period of time you define should be less than six months, as beyond that timeframe your gift to your spouse may lose its tax-exempt status.

You and your spouse almost certainly own joint property. When you die, your joint property goes to your spouse. But if you're both treated as a surviving spouse, automatic inheritance of joint property can't occur, and probate litigation becomes necessary.

For larger estates, simultaneous death may significantly increase estate tax. When you die, your bequest to your spouse passes free of estate tax. As a presumed surviving spouse, you can't take advantage of that exemption. The easiest solution is to include within your will a provision that, in the event of simultaneous death, the wealthier spouse is assumed to have died first.

But what about your children from your first marriage? If your estate plan presumes that your spouse survives you, your assets go into your spouse's estate and may go only to your spouse's children. As the wealthier spouse, you can

 ✔ Accept the increase in estate taxes and designate your children as the alternate beneficiaries of part or all of your estate.

 ✔ Create an estate plan that uses a bypass trust to maximize estate tax benefits for your estate, while protecting your children's inheritance. (See the discussion of estate planning for second families in Chapter 4.)

You've probably designated your spouse as the beneficiary of your life insurance and retirement and financial accounts. If you and your spouse die at the same time, unless you have named an alternate beneficiary, the proceeds of your insurance and accounts will go into your probate estate. To prevent that event, be sure to designate alternate beneficiaries for those policies and accounts.

Realizing Why You Must Update Your Will

Your will is a snapshot of your estate and your plan for its distribution, at a particular point in time. The most obvious reasons to update your will involve changes to your family, particularly marriage, divorce, birth or adoption of a child, or the death of an heir. Yet you have much more to consider.

Your goals and wishes may change over time

As time passes, you may be surprised at the twists life throws at you:

- ✔ You disinherited your ungrateful daughter or your drug-addicted son. You have renewed your relationship with your daughter, and your son just celebrated ten years of sobriety. Do you still want to leave them out of your will?

- ✔ Your will provides for your estate to be divided equally among your children, but your wealth grows considerably. Do you want to give part of your estate to charity? Do you need a better tax-avoidance strategy?

- ✔ After you write your will, you adopt a young child. Your older children have graduated from college and have established careers. Do you want to make a special provision for your youngest child's education?

- ✔ You leave money to your grandchildren to provide for their college education. After the youngest graduates from college, do you still want to provide that money?

- ✔ Your son is caught embezzling from his employer and is sent to prison. Will your bequest end up reimbursing the state for the cost of his incarceration?

- ✔ Your daughter's business has failed, and she is deep in debt. Will your bequest go to her, or will her creditors end up with the money?

Your periodic review of your will allows you to identify aspects of your estate plan that are no longer consistent with your wishes or your original goals.

Your assets may change over time

Over the course of time, your estate will change:

✔ You will acquire new assets.

✔ Your assets will change in value.

✔ You may sell an asset or give it away, or it may be lost or destroyed.

If you don't update your estate plan, the distribution of your assets may turn out very differently than you intend. For example:

✔ You own two office buildings, each worth $250,000, and leave one to each of your children. One building shoots up in value while the other, located in a less desirable area, doesn't.

✔ You leave your $50,000 stamp collection to your son and your $50,000 Hummel figurine collection to your daughter. Your stamp collection is destroyed in a fire.

✔ When you write your will, you have $100,000 of eBay stock and $100,000 of Pets.com stock. You give the eBay stock to your daughter and the Pets.com stock to your son. The eBay stock is worth millions, while Pets.com stock is worthless.

Assume that the value of your estate is $600,000. Your home is worth $300,000, and you have $300,000 in other assets. You provide in your will, "I leave my home to my daughter, Jane, and the remainder of my estate to my son, Louis." Now consider these scenarios:

✔ Your salary is raised, and you're fortunate in your investments. When you die, your home has appreciated to $600,000 in value, but your other assets are worth $2 million.

✔ You sell your home and move into a much more expensive home, applying much of your savings to the down payment. When you die, your home is worth $800,000 and your savings are $50,000.

✔ You sell your home and rent an apartment in an assisted-living community. When you die you have no home, but have $1,000,000 in other assets.

Although you intend equal inheritances, your children's actual inheritances are highly unequal.

You may want to provide for your brother as well as your children. Based upon the $600,000 value of your estate, you provide, "I leave my brother, Hamilton, $100,000, with the residue of my estate to be divided equally between my children." Unfortunately, you die after a long illness, and your assets are used to pay for your medical and nursing home care. Your remaining estate is $150,000. The first $100,000 goes to your brother, and each of your children receives $25,000, a *tenth* of what you intended.

You can *partially* avoid this problem by using percentages instead of dollar figures. If you write, "I leave my brother, Hamilton, 16 percent of my estate, with the residue of my estate to be divided equally among my children," your brother will inherit $24,000 of your reduced estate, and your children will each receive $63,000.

At the risk of sounding like a broken record, you can only prevent this type of inequity by periodically reviewing and updating your estate plan.

Family changes may invalidate your will

If you've left your entire estate to your spouse, your divorce will invalidate your will. This is good news, right? It is in part. You probably don't want your ex-spouse to inherit your estate. But don't forget: If you don't execute a new will, the probate court will distribute your estate according to your state's intestate succession laws as if you have no will.

What if you haven't left your entire estate to your spouse? Divorce still invalidates your bequests to your ex-spouse. As for the rest of your will:

✔ Your other bequests aren't affected. Provisions you made for your ex-spouse's children remain valid.

✔ The portions of your estate that you left to your spouse will be distributed under your state's laws of intestate succession.

The only way to be sure that your wishes are followed is to execute a new will.

Family changes may dramatically alter who inherits under your will

Beyond divorce, other changes to your family unit can significantly affect inheritance under your will. Your bequests are most likely to be affected if, after executing your will:

✔ You marry or remarry.

✔ You have a child or adopt a child.

✔ One of your heirs dies.

If you marry after you execute your will, when you die, your spouse will inherit an amount determined by state law, most likely *at least* half of your estate, and perhaps your entire estate.

If you add a child to your family but don't update your will to provide for the child, your child can ask that the probate court declare that the omission was accidental. If the court agrees that your child was accidentally omitted from your will, the court will grant your child and inheritance under your state's intestate succession laws.

For a dramatic example of what this ruling can mean, consider the estate of Barron Hilton. Pretend for this example that his estate plan is embodied in a will. With $2.3 billion in assets, Mr. Hilton has announced his intention to leave 97 percent of his estate to charity, dividing approximately $69 million among his other heirs. If he wrote his will before the birth of his last child, a typical intestate succession law would give half of his estate to his spouse, dividing the balance between his surviving children. With eight children, the omitted child's intestate share is roughly $140 million. That's more than twice the combined inheritance of all other family members.

Now imagine a more typical scenario. George Smith has a $1.5 million estate. He leaves his wife half of his estate, leaves each of his four children $100,000, and divides the rest of his estate among other relatives and charities. Prior to his unexpected death, he and his wife have a fifth child. Under a typical intestate succession law, George's wife receives half of his estate, and each child is entitled to an equal share of the remainder. The omitted child could thus inherit $150,000, substantially more than any other sibling. But worse, George's estate didn't get any larger. That $150,000 has to come out of the money he had intended to leave to other heirs.

You can partially prevent these outcomes by making class gifts rather than specific bequests. State laws normally only regard your child as having been omitted if the child is "not named or provided for" in your will. By naming your children as a class, you provide for all of your children.

Thus, if George leaves $400,000 "to be divided equally among my children," each child inherits an equal $80,000. Yet this division may not be George's intention. He may prefer that all his children inherit $100,000, and that the money come out of his other bequests. Unless he updates his will, he won't get to make that choice.

The death of an heir may also disrupt your estate plan. If the beneficiary you name in your will dies before receiving your bequest, the bequest is deemed a *lapsed gift* and is disregarded in the distribution of your estate. In simple terms:

- ✔ If your will provides for an alternate heir, a lapse simply shifts the bequest to the alternate heir. ("I leave my car to my brother, Joe, but if he predeceases me to my cousin, Emily.")

> ✔ If your will doesn't provide for an alternate heir, but has a residuary clause, the lapsed gift is distributed pursuant to the residuary clause.

> ✔ If your will has neither an alternate heir nor a residuary clause, or the residuary gift lapses, your lapsed gift is distributed under the laws of intestate succession as if you had no will.

But that's the beginning of the story, not the end. Most states have *anti-lapse statutes* that attempt to designate a substitute heir. For example, if you name your brother as your heir and he dies before you, a typical anti-lapse statute makes his children the beneficiaries of your bequest. Most anti-lapse statutes also apply to class gifts, such that if you name "my brothers" as your heirs, the children of a brother who dies before you will take his share.

But anti-lapse statutes won't fix every lapse:

> ✔ Anti-lapse statutes apply only to pass lapsed gifts to your legal heirs (those who would inherit if you died without a will).

> ✔ Anti-lapse statutes may distribute your estate in a manner you would consider unfair.

If you don't want anti-lapse statutes to apply to your bequests, when drafting your will, you should make your intentions explicit. In some states "*mere words of survival*" (such as, "if they survive me" or "my surviving children") do not prevent the application of an anti-lapse statute unless your will further demonstrates your intention to override the anti-lapse statute.

By way of example, imagine that you have three siblings, a brother and two sisters. You have no children. Your brother, Horton, dies before you write your will. You provide, "I leave $200,000 to be divided equally between my surviving siblings, Sarah and Jessica." Both Sarah and Jessica die before you do.

> ✔ Horton's child argues that your use of the word "surviving" creates a condition, and that the entire gift has lapsed as you have no surviving siblings.

> ✔ Sarah's four children argue that your bequest was a class gift to your surviving siblings and, as Jessica died first, Sarah would have inherited the entire bequest as the last surviving member of the class. They thus argue that the $200,000 should be divided between them.

> ✔ Jessica's child argues that the bequest wasn't conditional upon your sisters surviving you, but merely described that you had two surviving siblings at the time you wrote your will. She argues that the anti-lapse statute should result in her receiving $100,000, with the remaining $100,000 divided between Sarah's children.

The odds are pretty good that a court will side with Jessica. Your state's anti-lapse statute probably applies to class gifts and may compel the court to disregard the word "surviving." Even if not compelled to do so, the court may agree with Jessica's child that the language was not intended as a condition. Thus, of your six nieces and nephews, the likely outcome is that one inherits $100,000, four inherit $25,000, and one gets nothing.

The best way to prevent this event is to update your will. If you want, you can also provide in your will that you don't want anti-lapse laws to be applied to your bequests. If you do, you should be explicit that you don't want anti-lapse statutes to apply to lapsed or failed gifts. Without your clear expression, the probate court will apply those laws.

Knowing What to Do If You Lose Your Will

If you store your will in a suitable location, you shouldn't lose it. (See Chapter 2 for more information on storing your will.) But, as they say, to err is human. If you've lost your will, take these steps:

1. **Draft a new will.** If you can track down a copy of your will, you can use it as a basis to redraft and update your will. For the sake of clarity, include a clause in your new will that explicitly revokes any prior wills.

2. **Notify your executor and your heirs of the new will.** If two valid wills are submitted to a probate court, the court will normally follow the more recent will. But if your heirs don't know about the new will, they may find and submit only the earlier will.

3. **If you've distributed any copies of your old will to other people, collect those copies and, if you choose, distribute copies of the new will.**

If you later find the will you lost, make sure that you revoke it, whether by physically destroying it or by marking each page of the will as void. Chapter 9 discusses revocation of a will in more detail.

Chapter 9

When You Already Have a Will

*Y*ou completed your will, executed it, and breathed a sigh of relief. You have every right to congratulate yourself and to take a break from thinking about your estate plan. But keep it in the back of your mind that your work isn't over. You must periodically review your will and update it to reflect changes in your life and your wishes.

Under some circumstances, if you fail to do so, changes in your life may invalidate part or all of your will. In most circumstances, the more time that passes from the execution of your will, the less likely it is that the distribution of your estate will be consistent with your intentions when you drafted it.

So when should you review your will? How do you make changes? What if you want to revoke your will? This chapter contains those answers.

Reviewing and Updating Your Will

In life, change is inevitable. After you execute your will:

✔ Your family will change, whether by death, marriage, divorce, separation, childbirth, or adoption.

✔ You will acquire new assets and get rid of some old ones.

✔ You may want to increase, decrease, or eliminate bequests to friends, former friends, and charities.

✔ You may reconsider your choice of personal administrator or guardian for your minor children.

✔ Changes in inheritance laws or estate taxes may affect your will, frustrating your intentions or invalidating some of your bequests.

Any of these changes may significantly alter your estate plan. Not only may your wishes change, the law may create rights for a new spouse or child that will alter the distribution of your estate. To be sure that your wishes are followed, you must update your will.

You've probably heard that you should review your will every three or four years. I suggest an annual review on a specific date, perhaps the day you change the batteries in your smoke detectors. You do that every year, right? (See how easy it is to have something you know you should do for the good of yourself and your family, but let it slide?)

Changes in your family circumstances

Any major change in your family, including marriage, divorce, childbirth, adoption, and death, can disrupt the most careful estate plan.

If you move to another state, review your estate plan to make sure that it's consistent with the laws of your new home state. This advice is particularly true if you're married and are moving between a common law state and a community property state. (For more discussion of community property laws, see Chapter 17.)

Divorce or separation

If you divorce, in most states, the portions of your will providing for your spouse become invalid. If you're in one of those states, that law saves you the worry that your spouse will inherit from your estate, but it's not the end of the story:

✔ Although the bequests you made to your spouse will lapse, they'll be distributed under the *residuary clause* of your will (the clause distributing anything left over after your specific bequests are made) or your state's laws of *intestate succession* (the laws governing how your estate is distributed if you don't have a will).

✔ If you remarry your ex-spouse and haven't revoked your will, the provisions for your spouse will usually again become valid.

Some states will invalidate your entire will if you divorce. So update your will and write your ex-spouse out of the picture in the manner you choose.

Separation has no effect on your bequests, nor does it diminish your spouse's ability to choose a greater inheritance as allowed by state law.

Although some states offer legal protections for registered domestic partners, if you're in a domestic partnership, don't assume that separation or ending your relationship will affect your will. That is, if you leave assets to your domestic partner, unless you amend or revoke your will, expect your domestic partner to inherit it.

Remarriage

When you get married for a second time (or third, or fourth . . .), you have to consider not only how you will provide for your spouse, but also how your new estate plan will affect your intentions for your children from a prior marriage.

Further, your spouse's *statutory inheritance* (the percentage of your estate the state requires you to leave to your spouse) is very likely to reduce every significant inheritance included in your existing will. Some bequests are likely to be eliminated. It's very unlikely that your estate plan as administered will resemble what you intended when you executed your will.

Estate planning for second marriages, and dealing with mixed families, is a complicated subject. I discuss this topic in more detail in Chapter 4.

New children (born or adopted)

When a child joins your family, it's a joyous occasion. But as any parent knows, with that joy comes an awful lot of responsibility. One such responsibility? You guessed it: updating your estate plan.

Updating your estate plan is important not only because you want to provide for your new child. If you don't update it, your current estate plan may be seriously disrupted. Your new child may even inherit a far greater portion of your estate than any other heir.

How so? States have laws protecting the rights of *pretermitted* (accidentally omitted) heirs. Most often, the omitted heir is a child born after the execution of your will. These laws are different in each state, but one possible result is that the omitted child receives an intestate share of your estate — the percentage the child would have received had you died without a will.

Imagine that your will gives your other children less than their intestate share, perhaps because you're also leaving bequests to other relatives and to charity. If your omitted child gets a full intestate share, your other bequests are reduced to provide for that share. Some items of property that you had intended to go to your heirs are sold. Perhaps some of your bequests go unfilled. Your other children may inherit far less than your omitted child.

The outcome is similar if you have no other children. Your child's share of the estate still comes out of your other bequests, and your intended bequests may not be fulfilled.

In some states, the bequests you make for your other children may be reduced proportionately so that your omitted child receives an equal share. But what if you left real estate or items of personal property to your children, and not cash? To give your omitted child an equal share, those assets will likely have to be liquidated.

You can minimize the need to update your will by providing class gifts, such as "I leave 50 percent of my estate to my children." Although the pool gets divided into smaller shares with each new child, you don't need to change your will to provide for subsequent children. My advice, whether or not you use class gifts, is to make childbirth or adoption an occasion to update your will.

See Chapter 8 for tips on providing for or disinheriting children unknown to you or not born at the date you execute your will.

Deaths of intended heirs

When one of your beneficiaries dies, the distribution of your bequest may change based upon the laws of your state, the terms of your will, and whether or not the beneficiary has heirs:

- ✔ Your bequest will lapse and become part of the residuary of your estate.
- ✔ The bequest will be distributed to the heirs of your intended beneficiary.

The impact of a major beneficiary's death on your estate plan can be profound. Consider, for example, what might happen if your spouse dies before you do. Did you draft your will with that possibility in mind? If not, your estate plan will probably be left in shambles.

Also, you may not want your bequest to go to the heirs of your designated beneficiary. In many cases, the only way to prevent that occurrence is by amending your will.

You may designate alternate beneficiaries in your will. Consider this example: You leave your wedding ring to your eldest daughter, Joan, and she tragically dies before you. Her surviving heir, your son-in-law, is a nice enough guy, but why should he inherit a family heirloom? If you designate your younger daughter, Katie, as the alternate heir, even with Joan's death your ring stays within the family. If Joan has children, you also have the option of designating a grandchild as the alternate heir.

Changes in your wishes

If you wrote a will a few years ago and haven't reviewed it, take a look at it now. Unless you did little more than leave everything to your spouse and children, you'll probably be a bit surprised by some of the bequests you made.

Say that you were going to give your best friend Harry $500,000 until your wife . . . well, you know the cliché. But the fact remains, your wishes will probably change over time. Not only because you're angry with somebody, but also because the life circumstances of your beneficiaries will change.

Although lives can change in countless ways, here are some common examples:

- ✔ Your will provides for bequests intended to make sure that your grandchildren can afford college educations. Since you wrote your will, they've all graduated from college.

- ✔ Your son has fallen deeply into debt and is hounded by creditors. If you leave him a cash bequest, his creditors will snatch it up to service his debts.

- ✔ Your cousin has had a financial windfall since you wrote your will and simply doesn't need your money.

The primary purpose of your will is to distribute your estate in the manner you want, so make sure that your will reflects your wishes.

Changes in your financial situation

As you get older, your estate is likely to grow. It also may decline in value, whether due to the cost of medical care, a drop in the stock market, or some other unforeseen financial setback. Even when the changes are good, they can disrupt your plan for your estate.

 Review your estate plan upon your retirement. You should also create or update your plan for incapacity, as described in Chapter 14.

Do you still have the described assets?

You probably have treasured items or family heirlooms that you want to leave to specific people. But what happens if these items are no longer part of your estate when you die? Lawyers call it *ademption*. Your heir will call it "Getting a whole lot of nothing."

Here are a few examples:

- ✔ You collect vintage cars and have a 1931 Bugatti Royale Kellner Coupe. You draft your will, leaving it to your brother. The next year, a car collector sees it and persuades you to put it up for auction. It fetches the highest price ever received for a car at auction, $8.7 million. You die three years later. You still have much of that cash in your estate, but the car is gone, and your brother gets nothing.

- ✔ You leave an heir a cash gift and don't have enough cash in your estate to cover the gift. Assets from the residuary of your estate will be sold to cover the bequest.

- ✔ You leave your son, Augustus, "My vacation home in Traverse City, Michigan." But during your retirement, you decide that you want to vacation in a warmer place. You sell your Traverse City cottage and buy a condo in Florida. If you don't update your will, your bequest to your son will adeem, and the condo will be distributed as part of the residuary of your estate.

- ✔ You have a $600,000 estate comprised of a $200,000 house, $200,000 in savings, and $200,000 in personal property. You decide to leave your house to your eldest daughter, Joan, the cash to your son, Sean, and the residue of your estate (everything else) to your youngest child, Ellen. Medical expenses from your last illness and the cost of probating your estate consume most of your savings. Joan still gets the house, the residue of the estate is sold until Sean gets his $200,000 in cash, and Ellen may get little or nothing from your estate.

During your periodic review of your will, verify that the assets you describe remain in your estate. Consider whether you're likely to have enough cash in your estate to cover any monetary bequests. If you don't, update your will.

Have you acquired additional assets?

As your estate grows, will your new assets be distributed as you intend under your old will? For example:

- ✔ You purchase a vacation home.
- ✔ You inherited a house full of antiques from your parents.
- ✔ You're an avid stamp collector, and you add many valuable stamps to your collection, doubling its value.

Right away, you need to consider two things:

- ✔ **Do your new assets affect your specific bequests?** For example, if you leave your car to one child and your stamp collection to the other, do you need to balance the bequests due to the increased value of the stamp collection?

- ✔ **Will your new assets end up in the residuary of your estate?** If so, is that consistent with your goals? For example, if you intended the residuary to be a few thousand dollars and left it to charity, will your new vacation home also go to the charity?

If either of those conditions apply, most likely a will update is in order.

A fine legal mind, but not an estate planning lawyer

United States Supreme Court Chief Justice Warren Burger drafted his own will. He typed the document himself, dividing his estate between his two children. He made two costly errors.

First, he neglected to grant his executors the power to sell his property. They had to go to the probate court for that authority, resulting in unnecessary legal fees.

But the biggest cost came from his failure to plan for estate taxes. With some simple tax planning, he may have been able to completely avoid estate tax. But the thought apparently didn't even cross his mind, and about a quarter of his estate went to state and federal estate taxes.

What if your estate plan treats the bulk of your estate as joint or community property with your spouse? If you receive a gift or inheritance, it's your own separate property. Your will didn't even contemplate that you would have the new asset. Most likely, if you want it to go to somebody other than your spouse, you need to change your will.

You must also consider whether you'll owe estate taxes. If so, how will your estate pay them? With no plan in place, if you divide your estate between your heirs without considering taxes, the tax bite will affect the inheritance of some of your heirs and will likely cause some heirs to inherit unequally. For more information on tax planning, see Chapter 6.

Changing Your Will

As long as you remain legally competent, you may change your will at any time during your life. Your choices for amending your will are

- ✔ Amendment by *codicil,* a supplementary document that changes your will
- ✔ Executing a new will that revokes your prior will and reflects the changes you desire

If you attempt a different method of amendment, your change will probably be disregarded by the probate court. Worse, you may invalidate your entire will. Here are a few methods that don't work:

- ✔ Writing or typing a note in the margin of your existing will
- ✔ Writing or typing between the lines of text on your existing will (an *interlineation*)
- ✔ Erasing, crossing out, or scribbling over part of your will

Some states permit you to refer in your will to a *tangible personal property memorandum*. This document lists specific items of personal property, such as cars, boats, furniture, clothing, jewelry, decorative items, or a stamp collection, and states an heir for each listed item.

Although some states require your tangible personal property memorandum to be complete at the time your will is executed, other states permit you to amend the memorandum at any time. In those states, this memorandum can be a useful tool for changing your heirs for items of personal property without amending your will.

Adding to your will (amendment by codicil)

When you look at the U.S. Constitution, you can see that the original text is the same as it was when the Constitution was ratified. Not one word of the original text has been changed. The Constitution has been amended, many times. But each amendment is added to the end.

Amending a will by codicil works the same way. A codicil adds to your will, changes an existing provision, or invalidates part of your will, but the original text of your will doesn't change. You can execute as many codicils as you want. Your later codicils may amend or revoke earlier codicils.

Codicils are best used to make simple changes to your will. Where your changes are more complex, or where you have a series of codicils, you should execute a new will. Why?

- ✔ Figuring out exactly how your codicil interacts with the original text of your will can be difficult.
- ✔ If you have multiple codicils, you need to figure out both how the codicils interact with your original will and how they interact with each other.
- ✔ Your codicil may be lost or separated from your will, whether by accident or through the bad act of the person who first finds your will.

The more codicils you have or the more complicated your amendment, the more likely it is that your heirs will disagree over your intentions. Their disagreement or confusion can lead to unnecessary probate litigation.

Executing a valid codicil

A codicil is witnessed and executed in the same manner as your will. In essence, a codicil is a short will that supplements or revokes in part your earlier will. When you execute your codicil, remember the following:

- ✔ Your codicil must be dated.
- ✔ Your codicil should be witnessed and executed in the same manner as a new will.

Your codicil should be kept with your will.

Revoking Your Will

Your will doesn't become effective until you die. Thus, you may revoke your will at any time during your life. Be careful, as probate proceedings will become complicated if you don't revoke your will properly, or if your heirs find more than one will and disagree about which one is valid.

Once your old will is revoked, don't try to bring it back from the dead. As a general rule, you can't reinstate a revoked will. If you want to reinstate the terms of a revoked will, execute a new will that incorporates those terms.

A few states may permit you to execute a witnessed document stating that you want to revive your prior will, but even if you're in one of those states executing a new will is just as easy to do.

If you don't revoke your old will when you execute your new will, both remain in effect. Your new will is effectively a lengthy codicil to your old will.

Thus, if you do not revoke your prior will:

- ✔ If you make bequests of the same property in both wills, the new will governs.
- ✔ If you make a bequest of property in the old will but make no mention of that property in your new will, the old will governs.

For example, if your old will leaves your car to your nephew, and your new will leaves your car to your sister, your sister inherits the car. If your new will doesn't mention the car, your nephew inherits the car.

How to revoke a will

You can revoke your will in one of three ways (although your state may extend only the first two options):

- ✔ Execute a new will that explicitly revokes all prior wills and codicils.
- ✔ Physically destroy your will with the intention of revoking it. (You should collect and destroy all copies, as well.)

- ✔ In some states, execute a document that revokes your prior will. Typically, you must execute it in the presence of two witnesses.

The most common method of revocation is to execute a new will stating that all prior wills and codicils are revoked. I recommend this approach for several reasons:

- ✔ There won't be a gap in your estate plan, as you avoid creating a period of time when you don't have a will.

- ✔ If a prior will is found and submitted to the probate court, your intent to revoke that prior will is clear and in writing.

If you revoke a will by destroying it, remember that the probate court must find that you had the intent to revoke your will. If an heir argues that the will was lost or was destroyed by accident, the probate court may accept a copy for probate. Thus, if you choose to destroy a will by destroying it, destroy it in front of some witnesses who will be able to testify as to your intent.

What to do with a revoked will

You will usually get one of two answers if you ask what to do with your revoked will:

- ✔ You may destroy the original and all copies of your old will, preferably in front of witnesses who can affirm that you did so with the intent of revoking it.

- ✔ You may preserve the old will or preserve an unsigned copy while destroying the original, clearly marking on every page that it's revoked (by writing "Void" or "Revoked"). If you've executed a new will, also write on each page that it was superseded by your new will (for example, "Revoked By Will Dated April 17, 2008").

While you may believe that a provision in your new will declaring the prior will to be revoked is sufficient, you have to be careful. If you don't mark the old will as revoked, somebody may try to submit it to the probate court as your final will.

Why preserve an old will instead of destroying it? In case somebody challenges your testamentary capacity or claims you executed the will due to somebody's undue influence. If your prior will is largely the same as your current will, convincing a court that your final will doesn't reflect your actual wishes will be difficult.

Chapter 10

Estate Administration: What Happens in Probate Court

● ●

In This Chapter

▶ Probating an estate

▶ Paying your final debts

▶ Protecting your estate against will contests

● ●

*Y*our estate is the total amount of property you own at the time of your death. Probate is the process through which a court confirms the validity of your will, and supervises the settlement of your estate.

This chapter describes what happens when a will is submitted to a probate court, how the probate process works, and what happens if somebody contests your will.

Navigating Probate Court

Once a person dies, the estate is submitted to the probate court, and the process of confirming the validity of your will begins. A *probate court* is the court authorized to oversee the administration of your will and the settlement of your estate. If you have a will, the probate court determines whether the will is valid and then oversees the administration of the estate by the *executor* (the person appointed in the will by the decedent to oversee the estate). If you don't have a will or the will is determined to be invalid, the probate court appoints an administrator, and your property is distributed according to the state's laws of inheritance.

Probate proceedings begin when your personal representative or the custodian of your will files your will with the probate court, or when some other person files a petition seeking to administer your estate. The person who submitted the petition to the court is known as the *petitioner.*

The probate court's actions include

- ✔ Receiving your will and entertaining any challenges to its validity
- ✔ Appointing a personal representative (also known as an executor) for your estate
- ✔ Supervising the actions of your personal representative
- ✔ Requiring that legally interested parties (your legal heirs) are notified of the proceeding
- ✔ Settling disputes between people who claim to be entitled to your assets.
- ✔ Overseeing the payment of debts owed by your estate
- ✔ Approving the distribution of your estate's assets to your heirs

The probate court also oversees the final tax returns filed by your estate and the payment of any estate taxes.

Probate court proceedings are open to the public, and members of the public can examine the probate court file for your estate, which includes your will and bequests. Although some people are troubled by their estate being a matter of public record, except in cases involving celebrities, it's unusual for any aspect of an estate to be publicized.

Discovering How Estate Size Affects Probate Procedures

Probate has a reputation for being slow and costly, and that reputation isn't entirely undeserved. Fortunately, state legislatures have recognized that the type of probate procedures necessary to safeguard the assets of large estates are often unnecessary for smaller estates, and many smaller estates are resolved through a faster, less costly process.

For probate court, the size of your estate relates only to the assets that pass through the probate process. If you've used estate planning tools, such as a living trust to pass your assets to your heirs outside of probate, you can leave a substantial asset to your heirs while still taking advantage of simplified probate procedures.

Probate for small estates

Although probate laws are different in each state, most states offer two levels of simplified probate for small estates.

Some estates have very limited assets, perhaps just a few thousand dollars, so it may be possible to seek disposition of personal property without administration by a probate court. The person who pays the final expenses of the estate, such as medical bills or funeral costs, submits a simple petition to the court requesting reimbursement, along with

- ✔ The decedent's death certificate
- ✔ Paid bills claimed for reimbursement
- ✔ Documentation describing the asset to be released
- ✔ A copy of the decedent's will (if one exists)

If the court accepts that the petitioner is entitled to the decedent's assets, the court issues an authorization for the transfer or release of those assets to the petitioner.

For more substantial estates that don't exceed a certain limit (usually between $70,000 and $100,000) and where the estate's creditors are known, the estate will likely qualify for summary administration. *Summary administration* is a streamlined probate process that's designed to be faster and less expensive than the full probate process. This process has significantly less court oversight than with full probate proceedings.

In most states, absent any unexpected complications, simplified probate proceedings take two to four months. Being in probate for several months doesn't mean that your estate will be tied up in court proceedings throughout that time. Your administrator and the lawyer for your estate perform most of the work in probating your estate outside of court. If everything goes smoothly, the court hearing to settle your estate may take as little as an hour.

Probate for larger estates

Large estates continue to require *formal administration*, in which a personal representative is appointed to act on behalf of your estate. This process typically takes between six months and two years, depending upon the size and complexity of your estate.

Understanding the Role of the Personal Representative

The personal representative is typically required to be a legal resident of the state where your estate is probated or to be a close relative. The personal representative is often referred to as the *executor* or *executrix* of your estate.

Your personal representative is required to act in the best interest of your estate and can be held financially responsible for mismanaging the assets of your estate.

Upon your death, the personal representative you named in your will must decide whether or not to accept that role. If you discussed your estate plan with your personal representative and he agreed to serve, he'll likely accept the appointment. Upon your death, your personal representative should promptly locate and read your will.

Your personal representative arranges for your funeral and usually follows any funeral instructions you leave. If you don't leave instructions, your personal representative chooses how to conduct your funeral and burial.

Your personal representative also takes control of your property and financial accounts, obtains appraisals of your assets to determine their market value, and creates an inventory of your estate. Your personal representative also opens a checking account for your estate. All estate income is deposited into the account, and the estate's debts are paid from the account.

If necessary, your personal representative will start probate proceedings for your will. Your personal representative pays the debts of your estate, files all required tax returns, and distributes remaining assets to your heirs. Your personal representative's duties continue until all these tasks have been performed and the estate is completely settled.

Your personal representative has the right to be paid for his services. You can provide for compensation in your will, as agreed with your personal representative. If you don't provide for compensation or don't have a will, your personal representative may request compensation from the court. Depending upon the laws of your state, the compensation granted by a court will be an hourly fee or a percentage of the value of your estate. A member of your family often agrees to serve as your personal representative without charging a fee. Managing an estate is difficult work, and compensating your personal representative for his time and effort is perfectly appropriate.

The following sections describe some of the personal's representative's responsibilities in more detail.

Giving notice to legal heirs

In most states, your legal heirs (the people who inherit from your estate under state law if you don't have a will) are entitled to formal notice of probate proceedings. The purpose of notice is to give your heirs the opportunity to object to the validity of your will or to challenge the proposed distribution of your assets, before inheritances are distributed from your estate.

What if somebody makes a grab for your assets?

If you live alone, you may have a valid concern that the person who first learns of your death will loot your assets. Depending on the circumstances, your concern may relate to a nosy neighbor, a caregiver, a relative, or even an ambulance driver who responds to your home.

Although no plan can be perfect, you should consider finding asking someone you trust and who lives close enough to you to act quickly in an emergency to help you secure your assets in the event of your hospitalization or death. You may ask them to conspicuously watch your home as people come and go or to proactively secure certain property or possessions, as well as notify your personal representative or next of kin.

Some states permit probate without notice to your heirs, but the distribution of your estate may be left open to legal challenge for years. With formal notice, the opportunity to challenge the will or object to the distribution of assets normally ends when the estate is closed. For more information of how your will may be challenged, see the upcoming discussion on "Avoiding Will Contests."

Collecting property for distribution

Your personal representative must secure your personal property and real estate and take appropriate measures to safeguard your property. He needs to take control of

- Your home and its furnishings
- Other real estate holdings
- Your car and its keys
- Your safe deposit box and its contents
- Your savings and retirement accounts and any checkbooks
- Your interest in a business you own, or your share of a closely held business

Your personal representative must make sure that utility bills are paid for your real estate, and that your property is secured and properly maintained. Valuables should be protected from theft or loss. Although your existing insurance coverage may be adequate, your personal representative should contact your insurance companies to inform them of your death and to continue that coverage. Your personal representative may need to obtain additional insurance to fully protect your assets during the settlement of your estate.

If your estate doesn't have sufficient funds available to pay its debts, your personal representative may seek permission from the court to sell assets to pay those expenses.

Notifying and paying creditors

Your personal representative should cancel your credit cards and close any lines of credit.

As part of the probate process, your creditors can make claims against your estate for any money you owe at the time of your death. Which creditors are notified of the probate proceedings and how they present their claims to the probate court or to your personal representative vary from state to state. Creditors have a limited amount of time to submit their claims for payment, usually between three and six months from the date notice is given. In states where notice to creditors isn't required or is optional and isn't given, that period can be as long as 24 months.

If your estate doesn't have sufficient assets to pay all your bills, state law determines how creditors are paid, and the extent to which certain creditors go unpaid. Your heirs will not inherit your debts.

Your personal representative will pay all valid claims made by your creditors out of the assets of your estate. If your personal representative determines that a claim isn't valid, your creditor must file a motion with the probate court to obtain payment.

Distributing bequests

After any deadline for the submission of claims against your estate has expired and taxes are paid, your personal representative may submit to the probate court a proposed final distribution of your estate. In a typical estate, most creditors are paid out of the final distribution.

The final distribution describes the inheritances your heirs will receive from your estate. After the probate court approves the distribution, debts are paid, and inheritances distributed, your personal representative may seek an *Order of Discharge* from the probate court. That order ends the personal representative's duties to your estate.

Hiring a Lawyer

The personal representative of your estate isn't required to hire a lawyer. Your estate is less likely to need legal services if your personal representative is your sole heir, and no one is disputing your will or the distribution of your assets. However, you should anticipate that your personal representative will need to hire a lawyer to perform services for your estate, and your estate will pay the legal fees.

You can designate an attorney for your estate within your will. In many cases, the lawyer who drafted the will is designated as the attorney for the estate.

In many probate cases, the lawyer's role is largely advisory. In more complicated cases, the lawyer may have to help with court proceedings or defend against a will contest. Services the lawyer typically provides include

✔ Helping your personal representative understand her duties

✔ Helping your personal representative understand and interpret the provisions of your will

✔ Drafting deeds and conveyances required by the estate

The personal administrator can have the lawyer handle most of the probate responsibilities, but this approach can be expensive for your estate.

Most lawyers charge the estate an hourly fee for the services they perform. The lawyer may also agree to perform a specific set of services, or even all services required by your estate, for a fixed fee. In a minority of states, the lawyer can charge a percentage of the value of your estate as his fee.

Overseeing Probate: The Judge

The probate court judge appoints your personal representative, oversees the probate proceedings, and approves the distribution of assets from your estate. If any motions are brought before the court, such as a request for an interpretation of the language of your will, or if a will contest occurs, the probate court judge presides over the litigation. Will contests are discussed in the next section of this chapter, "Avoiding Will Contests."

Most of the time, the provisions of your will are easily understood. Yet sometimes a will includes an ambiguous or unclear provision. If the administrator or an interested party to your estate is uncertain what a provision means, he can ask the judge to review the language and issue a ruling as to its meaning.

The probate judge also supervises the actions of the personal representative. The judge may require the personal representative to post a bond to protect the estate's assets in the event of mismanagement or misconduct. The judge reviews inventories and accountings submitted by the personal administrator and approves the final distribution of your estate's assets.

If the judge believes that your personal representative is incapable of performing required tasks or is concerned that your personal representative has mismanaged the assets of your estate, the judge may dismiss your personal representative and appoint a successor.

The proposed final distribution of the estate must be submitted to the judge for approval. The judge listens to any objections to the final distribution and, depending upon evidence submitted, approves or rejects it.

If the proposed final distribution is approved, the debts of the estate are paid, and inheritances are distributed in accord with its provisions. If the proposed final distribution is rejected, the personal representative must prepare a new proposed final distribution, taking into consideration the reasons for the judge's ruling.

If somebody contests your will, the probate judge conducts a trial to determine the validity of your will. In some states, either the person bringing the contest or the estate may request a jury trial.

Avoiding Will Contests

A *will contest* is a formal challenge to the validity of part or all of your will. If you're worried about a will contest, relax. The vast majority of wills aren't contested, and most will contests are unsuccessful. Still, to make sure that yours is not the exception, you need to be aware of how and why will contests occur.

The person who contests a will must be an *interested person* in your estate. As a general rule, he is either named as a beneficiary in a prior will or entitled to a share of your estate under the laws of *intestate succession* (laws that identify heirs and distribute the assets of people who die without valid wills).

Claiming that an inheritance is unfair won't support a will contest. The contest must be premised upon a valid legal ground concerning the validity of the will, your capacity to make a will, or *undue influence* (somebody coerces you into making bequests against your better judgment), fraud against you, or mistake.

When a will contest succeeds, the most common outcomes are for the court to

✔ Disallow part of your will, but leave the remaining provisions in effect

✔ Disallow your will in favor of a prior will

✔ Disallow your will and treat you as having died intestate (with no will)

Some law firms specialize in will contests, typically charging the client a percentage of the money obtained from your estate. Your estate has to hire a lawyer to defend it against the challenge, and the distribution of your estate may be held up during months or even years of litigation. The cost of challenging your will can be free to the person making the challenge and potentially very costly to your estate and your intended heirs.

Although you can include a *noncontest provision* in your will, which disinherits anyone who contests your will, the provision may have limited effect. A non-contest provision prevents inheritance only if the heir bringing the challenge to your will is unsuccessful and doesn't save your estate the cost of defending against the challenge. Your noncontest provision must include a *gift over provision,* which describes how the forfeited share is to be distributed in the event of a will contest.

Even when a will contest is unsuccessful, some states won't apply noncontest clauses if your heir is found to have had good cause (see the next section) to contest your will. If the challenge is settled, as often occurs, the clause will have no effect. Further, if you disinherit an heir, that heir has nothing to lose in bringing a challenge.

You can minimize the chances of a challenge to your will based on fraud or undue influence by documenting your reasons for making bequests that may seem surprising or unfair. You can discuss your reasoning with your heirs so that they understand your intentions and won't be shocked when they see your will.

Validity

The first class of challenge to a will claims that your will isn't valid. The most common claims relate to the execution of the will:

✔ You did not sign the will.

✔ The will was improperly witnessed.

✔ The will was not properly notarized.

When you prepare your will with the help of a lawyer, it's unlikely that its execution will be successfully challenged. When you prepare your own will, you must take care to follow the instructions for proper execution of your will, as even a small mistake can result in its being declared invalid.

Another set of claims relate to the validity or authenticity of the will itself:

✔ The will is a forgery.

✔ The will submitted to the court isn't your most recent will. If proved valid, the newer will replaces the older will.

It may also be alleged that the will was procured by a fraud against you. Even though you were of sound mind and executed a will consistent with your testamentary goals, it's alleged that somebody intentionally deceived you into changing your bequests. For example, somebody may trick you into believing that she's a long-lost relative in order to be added to your will. Your child may try to get you to disinherit your new spouse by convincing you that your spouse is unfaithful. The facts rarely exist to support this type of fraud claim, but if it's proved that you relied upon fraudulent misrepresentations when making your will, and that the person making the misrepresentations intended to influence your will, the court may set aside part or all of the will.

In another form of fraud, somebody who is helping to prepare your will may misrepresent the content of the document in order to trick you into signing it. If it's proved that you did not know the content of the will you signed, the will isn't valid.

You can help ensure that your most recent will is submitted to the probate court by making sure that you void or destroy prior wills and keep your current will in a safe, secure place.

Mental incapacity

When you execute your will, you must have _testamentary capacity,_ meaning that you must be "of sound mind." In other words, you have the mental capacity to understand your assets, your relationship to your intended beneficiaries, and the effect of your will. If somebody challenging your will proves to a probate court that you lacked testamentary capacity, the probate court will declare your will to be invalid.

The most common allegations of incapacity are that

✔ **You weren't mentally competent when you signed your will.** This claim may be based upon advanced age or illness. Even where it's not disputed that you were competent at a later date, somebody contesting your will can allege that you were temporarily incompetent at the time you signed your will.

✔ **You were under the influence of alcohol or drugs when you signed your will.** Someone can make this claim even if you only take prescription medications.

Compensating your caregiver child without triggering an estate contest

If your adult child takes care of you during the later years of your life, you may decide that your child deserves an inheritance that rewards that hard work and sacrifice. But how will your other children react? Usually, the other children are grateful and understanding, but in some cases, they are resentful or suspicious of the unequal inheritance. You can, however, minimize the likelihood of a will contest or any hard feelings between your children after you die.

Talk to your children about your plans so that they're not surprised when they learn what is in your will and so that they know that your choice was freely made. Also, consider alternatives to unequal inheritance, such as paying your child a salary during your lifetime.

If your child lives with you and cares for you in your home, your instinct may be to leave your home to the caregiver child. Often, your home will be the most significant asset in your estate, and leaving your home to one child can result in very small inheritances to your other children. Consider instead allowing your child to remain in your home for a fixed number of years following your death, after which the home can be sold and the proceeds divided between your heirs.

The person making this challenge presents evidence to the court that you were of unsound mind when you created your will. Evidence may include medical records and testimony about unusual behaviors or irrational conduct around the time of the execution of your will.

The most common step taken by people who anticipate a challenge to their mental capacity is to have their doctors affirm that they were mentally competent when they executed their wills. For example, at the time you execute your will, you can visit your family doctor, describe that you're making a will, and have the doctor record in your medical chart that you displayed full testamentary capacity at the time of your visit. You can have your doctor write a letter, or more formally an *affidavit* (a written statement made under oath), reciting that you're mentally competent to execute a will and then keep that document with your will. You can do the same with an independent psychiatrist — somebody who has no treatment relationship with you and who performs an independent evaluation of your competence solely in relation to your will.

If you're very concerned about a will contest, you can also hire a *professional legal videographer* (a person experienced who makes legally admissible video recordings) to record a signing ceremony, where you discuss your will and your wishes for your estate, explain your reasoning for your choices, and then execute your will in front of your witnesses and notary. This video is simply a supplement to documentation you obtain from medical doctors.

The more documentation you create, the easier it will be for your estate to document your testamentary capacity. Statements from your doctors or a videotape demonstrating that you knew what you were doing can facilitate a quick resolution to a will contest premised upon your incompetence.

Undue influence

A claim of undue influence alleges that you weren't acting of your own free will when you made your will. Although your testamentary capacity isn't challenged, it's alleged that somebody interfered with your independent judgment when you executed your will. An appearance of undue influence may arise if you create a new will shortly before your death.

When evaluating allegations of undue influence, a court's considerations include

- ✔ Your relationship with the person alleged to have exerted undue influence.
- ✔ What motive may have existed to apply undue influence
- ✔ What opportunity the person had to exert undue influence
- ✔ Your ability to resist the alleged influence
- ✔ Whether the provisions of your will are consistent with the claim of undue influence
- ✔ Any connection between the alleged undue influence and the terms of your will

Merely pressuring somebody to create a will is not undue influence. The issue is whether the influence caused you to distribute your assets differently than you otherwise would have done.

Claims of undue influence are often directed at caregivers — whether they're family, friends, or hired help — who receive a larger share of your estate than your other heirs expect. Some caregivers do abuse their positions to try to get a larger inheritance, and this can happen even when family members provide your care. Even when it is your sincere wish to reward your caregiver, your other heirs may regard your bequest as unfair and may suspect undue influence. Similarly, your children of a prior marriage may accuse your new spouse of undue influence.

A claim of *duress* alleges that you executed your will in response to threats made against you. For example, someone may allege that you were held against your will or threatened with violence if you didn't sign a will.

If a court finds that you wouldn't have executed the will if not for the improper influence or duress, the court will invalidate your will.

Part III
Trust Me! How Trusts Work

The 5th Wave   By Rich Tennant

"Living trust? Avoid probate? I say we stick the money in the ground like always, and then feed this peddler to the sharks."

In this part . . .

This part explains what trusts are and whether you should use a trust in your estate plan. You find out how to separate hype from reality in understanding revocable living trust, and understand when you truly benefit from having a living trust. I introduce you to many other types of trusts and show you their roles in tax avoidance, business succession planning, and controlling how and when your assets are distributed to your heirs. You also find out how to fund your trust and the consequences of forgetting to do so.

Chapter 11

The Anatomy of a Trust

*B*eyond the living trust, you can choose from many other types of trusts as you plan your estate. This chapter outlines the reasons why you may want to use a trust and describes the parts of a trust, including who created it, why it was created, where the trust's assets are, who the trust is created for, who's in charge of it, and when it ends.

What's a Trust and Why You Need One

Like a will, a *trust* is a tool used in estate planning. Your trust is a legal entity you create to hold assets that, once transferred into the trust, are managed in accord with its written terms. Those terms of your trust describe how you want the trust's assets to be managed and distributed. You choose a person to manage the assets of your trust, the *trustee*, who agrees to accept that responsibility and to abide by the terms of your trust. You also choose the beneficiaries of your trust, and when they receive trust income or distribution of the trust's assets.

Any person who creates a trust is called the *grantor.* The grantor may also be referenced as the *settlor* or *donor* of the trust. For example, when you create a revocable living trust, you are the grantor. You then transfer assets into the trust, which is managed by the trustee for the benefit of your beneficiaries.

Some trusts are *revocable,* meaning that you can change your mind and take your assets out of the trust at any time you choose. Other trusts are *irrevocable* — once you create them and transfer assets in, you can't take those assets back out except as described in the trust document.

Some trusts are extremely complicated to create and fund and should be drafted by an estate planning professional. Chapter 12 describes the most common types of trusts used in estate planning.

Benefitting from Trusts

Planning your estate with trusts provides a variety of advantages over reliance upon a will alone. Your will remains an essential part of your estate plan, but you gain enormous flexibility by adding a trust to the mix. Trusts can help you provide for your spouse or child over an extended time, help provide supplemental income to people with disabilities, help protect people who aren't good at handling money, and help you avoid probate.

When a living trust may not be for you

There's a good chance that at some point in your life you'll benefit from a living trust, but perhaps not yet. Consider four leading factors when deciding whether you need a living trust: your age, your family circumstances, the size of your estate, and the location of your real estate holdings.

If you're below the age of 50, pay extra attention to the costs and burdens of a living trust. If you put your home into your trust, you create extra paperwork every time you move. You'll have many more years of transferring other assets into and out of your trust. You're likely to end up significantly revising your trust several times during the remainder of your life.

If you're in your 20s or 30s, these costs and burdens are even greater. However, if you're facing a disease that will leave you disabled and unable to manage your assets, a living trust may benefit you even at a young age.

If you have young children, your living trust can help you structure their inheritances and provide for the management of your estate by a trustee of your choice. However, you can accomplish the same thing by creating or funding a trust with your will. (Chapter 5 explains steps you can take to provide for your children.)

If you're moving on to your second marriage, particularly if you have children, your living trust can help you keep your assets separate from those of your spouse and can help preserve inheritances you intend for your children from ending up being inherited by your new spouse or stepchildren. (See Chapter 2 for information about estate planning for complex family situations.)

If you have a smaller estate, particularly if it's less than $100,000 in value, a living trust can actually make estate administration more costly and cumbersome for your heirs. In most states, you'll qualify for simplified probate, which should wrap up your estate quickly and with little expense. (See Chapter 10 to find out more about probate.)

If you own real estate in more than one state, putting your out-of-state holdings into a living trust simplifies the probate process and can save your estate quite a bit of money. Otherwise, to complete probate, your personal representative has to open a probate case in every state where you own real estate.

Not everybody needs a trust. Probate is often quite simple for smaller estates (see Chapter 10), and privacy concerns are often overblown. If you can achieve your estate planning goals with a simple will, you may want to stop there. As you review your estate plan, if your circumstances change, you're free to create and execute a trust.

They're flexible

Trusts offer you enormous flexibility to decide how your assets will be managed. You can place assets in trust during your lifetime, reserving control over them but providing for your trustee to take over if you become incapacitated.

You can create and fund your trust while you're still alive; while you're still alive and use your will to fund your trust (a *pour over trust*); or with your will (a *testamentary trust*).

If your trust is revocable, you can revoke your trust and transfer its assets back to yourself at any time.

You can provide for your incapacity

Your trustee's powers to manage trust assets are immediate. You can make those powers contingent upon a future event, such as your incapacity. But once you become incapacitated by whatever definition you choose to provide in your trust, your trustee can immediately take control of trust assets and start managing those assets for your benefit.

Having your trustee take over management of your estate is a lot easier than forcing your heirs to go to court to ask a judge to appoint a conservator to manage your estate. In relation to the trust's assets, banks and financial institutions are much more likely to defer to the instructions of a trustee, while they may be cautious about accepting the validity of a power of attorney. While a bank may require an original copy of your durable power of attorney before honoring the instructions of your attorney-in-fact, the same concerns aren't present with a trustee because the trust is the owner of its assets.

If your business assets are held in trust, your trustee can immediately step in to protect your business interests while your business succession plan is implemented.

Although a trust can provide significant benefit in the event of capacity, your trustee can manage only the trust's assets. The trustee has no authority over assets not owned by your trust. You should still execute a durable power of attorney and healthcare proxy, as described in Chapter 14.

You can avoid taxes

Trusts can be a powerful tool to avoid estate taxes. Common trusts include

- ✔ **The marital deduction trust (A/B trust):** This trust takes your marital exemption out of your spouse's taxable estate, while at the same time allowing your spouse to enjoy the income produced by the trust and, for purposes such as medical care or support, even access the trust's assets.

- ✔ **The Crummey trust:** This trust allows you to make tax-exempt gifts during your lifetime. These gifts accumulate in a trust to be distributed to your beneficiary at a later time.

- ✔ **Irrevocable life insurance trusts (ILITs):** An ILIT owns a life insurance policy in your name and is the beneficiary of the policy. When properly executed and funded at least three years before your death, the insurance proceeds aren't included in your estate.

Chapter 6 details tax avoidance strategies, and Chapter 12 describes specific types of trusts in more detail.

A revocable living trust, of itself, doesn't help you avoid estate taxes. The primary benefit of a revocable living trust is probate avoidance. You can include provisions in your revocable living trust that can help reduce estate taxes, but they're not inherent to that type of trust (see Chapter 12).

If you make mistakes with a trust designed to help you avoid estate taxes, the IRS may disregard the trust and treat its assets as part of your taxable estate. What sort of restrictions might you encounter?

- ✔ With some trusts used for estate tax planning, you may not serve as trustee, and you may not retain control over the trust's assets once the trust is created.

- ✔ With other trusts, the trust must be in effect for a minimum number of years before you die, or the assets are included in your estate.

- ✔ With still others, trust assets must vest with the beneficiaries within a specified timeframe.

If your estate is large enough to pay estate taxes, you should get professional assistance in drafting and funding your tax avoidance trusts. At present, the federal estate tax exemption is $2 million, meaning that estates valued below that amount aren't subject to federal estate taxes.

You can avoid probate

When you leave your estate to your heirs with a will or don't create an estate plan at all, a probate court distributes your estate. (For more on the probate process, see Chapter 10.) Using a trust provides some significant advantages:

- ✔ When you leave assets by will, your heirs have to wait months for the probate process to finish before your bequests are distributed to them. With a trust, your heirs may receive their bequests immediately.

- ✔ If you operate a business, your trust can become effective during your incapacity or immediately upon your death, and your trustee can be authorized to immediately start managing your business affairs. With probate, your business may languish for weeks or months while your heirs petition the court to appoint somebody to manage your interests.

- ✔ If you're in an estate where your personal representative and the attorney for the estate are paid a percentage of the value of your estate, having major assets held by your living trust may significantly reduce the cost of probate.

- ✔ You can usually avoid having a public probate record of assets that you distribute by trust (see the next section).

Although in this chapter I discuss some steps you can take to help ensure that your trust is upheld, trusts are very difficult to challenge in probate court. The more likely source of probate litigation is the alleged misuse of trust assets by your trustee, something you can minimize with a careful choice of trustee, careful definition of the trustee's powers, and a requirement that the trustee periodically provide an accounting of the trust's assets to your beneficiaries.

 Your estate will have assets that go through probate. If you have a small estate, you may have no need to avoid probate, and a living trust may be an unnecessary complication and expense in your estate administration. Also, if you don't have a trustworthy trustee, the judicial oversight from the probate process may better ensure that your bequests reach your intended heirs.

Probate avoidance may be a benefit of your estate plan, but your focus should be on creating the estate plan you want. Chapter 10 explains the probate process in detail.

A trust can help protect your privacy

If you leave your estate to your heirs with a will or choose not to plan your estate at all, your estate will have to be probated. The records of a probate court are public, meaning that anybody can go to the courthouse to seek your will, look at the inventory of your estate's assets, or find out who your heirs are and how much money they received.

A trust doesn't need to go through probate. Thus, in most cases, the terms of the trust are never made part of a public record. The size of your estate, the identity of your heirs, and the amount you leave to each remains private.

Selecting a Trustee

Depending upon the trust, the trustee may be you, a trusted friend or family member; a professional, such as a lawyer or accountant; or an institution, such as a bank

You may also designate cotrustees so that more than one person manages your trust. If you do choose cotrustees, you should also describe the powers they each may exercise individually and those that must be exercised jointly. For example, you might permit either trustee to pay your medical bills, but require both trustees to agree to the sale of a trust asset, such as real estate.

If you choose cotrustees, you should provide a mechanism for dispute resolution, be it a coin toss, drawing the high card from a deck of cards, or formal mediation or arbitration.

"I see things differently"

If a beneficiary challenges your trustee's actions, is your trustee the type of person who will scrupulously adhere to the terms of the trust? Or will she reply, "That may be what the trust says, but I see things differently"?

When you pick your trustee, anticipate the possibility that your trustee may have different goals and wishes than you do. It's great that your son is willing to serve as trustee without charging a fee and manage the money you're leaving to your minor grandchildren. But consider how your son's plans for your money may differ from your own.

It is not unheard of for a trustee to "borrow" money from a trust, perhaps with the full intention of paying it back. If your son encounters financial difficulties or simply chooses to augment his lifestyle with periodic "loans," what are the odds that the money will actually be repaid? I'll tell you: They're exceedingly small. Similarly, your son may feel that his children will inherit from him anyway, and thus that it's perfectly reasonable for him to spend the money rather than continuing to hold it in trust.

When your trustee is family and misappropriates funds meant for other family members, the odds are that your trust distribution will be redefined by your trustee's misconduct. In most cases, other relatives aren't willing to file a lawsuit to compel a family member to repay money taken from the trust. Would your grandchildren really sue their father? And even if they were willing to sue, the trustee typically doesn't have the money to repay the trust.

Anticipating conflicts

When you choose your trustee, be aware of how conflicts might arise between your trustee and your beneficiaries. Choose a trustee you trust to stand up for the outcome you want.

A common source of conflict arises when you have two classes of beneficiary, one who receives the benefit of your estate for life, and the rest who receive the benefit of your estate after the initial beneficiaries die. For example, you may give your spouse the benefit of your home and the income from your trust during her life, while your children from a prior marriage will receive the balance of your trust when your spouse dies.

Your children may pressure your trustee to invest trust assets in investments that have a high long-term rate of return, but which provide little or no present income or are high risk. Your spouse will likely prefer that investments produce a high income, even if those investments produce little or no long-term appreciation. Your trustee must be able to stand up to the competing demands and enforce your trust as it was written and as you intended.

Sometimes your beneficiaries will have different ideas than the trustee of when special distributions may be made or may harangue the trustee to try to obtain loans against a delayed gift. Your trustee should be able to withstand the pressure and make the choices you intended.

Making one of your children your trustee can be unwise if you expect that your other siblings will make such demands. Your trustee child is forced into a parental role, having to say "no" to your other children in circumstances where they believe they have every right to the money, or where they feel that they "deserve it" no matter what the trust says. This responsibility can create significant conflict and resentment between your children.

Questions to consider when selecting a trustee include

- Is the person responsible with money and capable of managing money and other assets?
- Is the person willing and able to carry out the terms of your trust?
- Is the person trustworthy and fully prepared to manage the assets of the trust solely for the benefit of the beneficiaries?
- Does the person have time to manage your trust?
- Is the person willing and able to provide regular accountings to the beneficiaries, consistent with state law and the terms of the trust?

Serving as trustee is difficult work, and not everybody is prepared to accept the task or perform it indefinitely. Your trustee will also grow older and may become ill or unable to serve. It is important to designate at least one successor trustee.

Your trust will continue even if you don't designate a successor. If your trustee dies or becomes unwilling to serve and you haven't designated a successor, your heirs will have to go to court to have a judge appoint a trustee. Expect that any person a court appoints will charge fees to the trust, and that those fees will not be limited by the terms of your trust.

Choosing Your Beneficiaries

Every trust must have at least one beneficiary. Common beneficiaries include your spouse and children; your friends; charities; and educational organizations.

You can designate individuals ("My daughter, Sarah") or classes ("My grand-children") as beneficiaries of your trust. Just make sure that your descriptions are sufficiently clear that your beneficiaries can be identified.

Transferring Assets into Your Trust

In order for your trust to be effective, you must transfer ownership of property into the trust. Although I prefer the term assets, you may sometimes hear the property held by a trust identified as the *res* or *corpus* of the trust.

A trust may be created to hold a specific asset, such as a house or life insurance policy. It may be more general, created to hold whatever assets you transfer over to the trust. But whatever the design and purpose of your trust, for any assets you intend to include in the trust, you should define the powers of the trustee and how you ultimately want those assets to be distributed to your beneficiaries.

When you create your trust, you can and should put the cart before the horse. Even though the trust won't become effective in relation to a particular asset until it's transferred into the trust, your trust should reflect your wishes and intentions.

Say, for example, that you own a primary home and a vacation home. You can describe in your revocable living trust how you want those properties used, managed, and maintained after your death. Then, after the trust is executed, you can deed the properties over to the trust. The same is true for investment accounts or other assets you intend to place in your trust.

Your trustee must know the location of your trusts in order to manage them. Make sure that your trust describes its assets clearly so that the trustee knows what and where they are.

Staying in control

With many trusts, you may retain significant control over trust assets even after they're transferred into your trust. If your trust is revocable, one obvious power you retain is the right to revoke the trust.

With a revocable living trust, you typically name yourself as the initial trustee and maintain full control of your assets. Even if your trustee takes control of your trust upon your incapacity, you can require your trustee to continue to defer to your wishes, to the extent that you remain able to make and communicate informed choices.

Other types of trusts, particularly those used for estate tax avoidance, require that you surrender most or all of your control of the asset to an independent trustee. Even then, you may be able to provide for your use and enjoyment of trust assets as long as the trust continues.

Giving (or limiting) your trustee powers

When you draft your trust, you may give the trustee very broad powers over the trust's assets, or you may grant narrow powers. Powers commonly granted within a revocable living trust include

- The power to manage and sell property, including real estate
- The power to rent or lease real property
- The power to borrow money for the benefit of the trust
- The power to invest the assets of the trust
- The power to litigate claims on behalf of the trust
- The power to compensate professionals, such as lawyers, accountants, and property managers who provide services to the trust
- The power to make special distributions of the trust's assets for the benefit of the beneficiaries (for example, to help with a medical emergency).
- The power to make certain gifts

You can provide the trustee with additional powers or restrict the trustee's powers. For example, you can authorize the trustee to sell the trust's assets in the event that the trust runs short of money, but require that assets be sold in a particular order or that certain assets (such as your home) be retained as long as the trust is able to avoid selling them. Ultimately, the trustee has as much or as little power as you choose to give.

Not all trusts permit significant restriction of the trustee's powers. You won't be surprised that you're most likely to be limited in your ability to restrict the trustee's powers with trusts created for estate tax avoidance.

Cancelling the trust

When you create a trust, you will create it either as a revocable trust or as an irrevocable trust. As you've already figured out, you can revoke a revocable trust at any time you choose. You cannot revoke an irrevocable trust, and once you transfer assets into the trust you cannot get them back out.

The trust you are most likely to use in your estate plan is the revocable living trust. You are most likely to use irrevocable trusts if you have a large estate, and you wish to avoid estate taxes.

Distributing trust assets

As with your will, when you draft your trust, you get to pick where your money goes. You may also impose limits on gifts, such as when trust income or assets will be distributed to your beneficiaries. For example:

- ✔ You can provide that your children will receive one quarter of their inheritance at the age of 18, one quarter of their inheritance upon graduation from college, and the balance upon reaching the age of 30.
- ✔ You can provide for your trust to pay for your grandchildren's educational expenses until they graduate from college and then provide for a lump sum payment of the balance.
- ✔ You can provide that your children will receive their inheritance upon marriage.

You can also create an asset protection or *spendthrift trust* to help protect your child's inheritance from being lost to creditors, divorce, or poor money management.

Be aware as you add contingencies that you may prevent your gift from ever reaching your beneficiary. If you want to be sure that your beneficiary will receive a gift even if the condition isn't met, make sure that you spell out that wish.

For example, if you want to encourage your son to go to college but recognize that he may never attend or may drop out, you can provide, "To my son, Ben, I give $100,000.00 to be distributed to him upon his graduation from college, or when he reaches the age of 35."

The process of adding conditions to a gift made through your trust is very similar to imposing restrictions on a bequest made through a will (see Chapter 8).

You can easily get carried away with contingencies, placing restrictions on when, how, or why a distribution is to be made. I suggest keeping your trust simple.

Be aware that some states will set aside your living trust, in whole or in part, in order to provide for your spouse's elective share. The elective share is the amount of your estate that your spouse is entitled to choose to receive under state law, in the event that you leave a smaller bequest in your will.

The rule against perpetuities

A *perpetuity* is a bequest that may never take effect, or may not take affect for a very long time. The rule against perpetuities is a very old estate planning rule, which is meant to prevent property from being indefinitely tied up in an estate. Typically, the rule provides that property must vest in an heir within "a life in being plus 21 years." This rule seems deceptively simple: You can leave money to your unborn grandchildren, as long as they get the money by the time they turn 21, right? While that's a reasonable application of the rule, it's much more complicated in operation.

For example, imagine that you create an irrevocable trust for the benefit of your grandchildren. Your spouse dies, and you remarry and have another child. Under the rule against perpetuities, your trust terminates when the youngest grandchild born *before* you created the trust turns 21. As your youngest child was not a "life in being" when you created your trust, under this rule your grandchildren born to that child could lose out on any benefit from your trust.

Also, the traditional rule will invalidate a gift even if it *might* vest outside of the maximum allowable period. Believe it or not, this was once applied to invalidate a conditional bequest that would have vested when the youngest heir turned 5, on the basis that the child might have children before reaching the age of 5.

Many states have modified this rule by statute, largely with the goal of preventing that type of unwanted outcome. For example, many states require gifts to vest within 90 years, with judicial reformation of your trust to provide for gifts that don't vest within that time. But you still have to be careful when you want to leave assets to people who have not yet been born, possibly including children or grandchildren you don't *expect* to be born.

Putting Your Trust into Effect

Once you have drafted your trust, you must execute it. That is to say, you need to sign and date it in front of witnesses in order to make it legal and effective. I suggest having a signing ceremony where the following people are present:

- ✔ You
- ✔ Your chosen trustee
- ✔ Three witnesses (in most states, two will suffice, but having an extra witness never hurts)
- ✔ A notary public

Most states require your trust to have at least two witness signatures. I suggest using three witnesses. Not only will that meet the requirements of all states, but you also have an extra witness available in the event that somebody tries to invalidate your trust.

Here's the basic process:

1. **When everybody is present and has established their identities to the satisfaction of the notary, the notary "swears everyone in, as if you all were going to testify in court.**

2. **In the presence of your witnesses and the notary, you will place your initials on every page of the trust and then sign your trust.**

   If you're also serving as trustee, you will sign both as grantor and then again as trustee in Step 3.

3. **Your trustee then signs to accept of the terms and conditions of the trust and to formally accept the duties of a trustee.**

   His signature helps ensure that your trustee will in fact serve and is okay with the amount of compensation you have authorized under the trust. This signature, as you would expect, is made in front of your witnesses and notary.

4. **Next, your witnesses initial every page of your trust and sign your trust, affirming that they saw you voluntarily sign your trust.**

5. **Finally, your notary will notarize the trust.**

   Although in most cases notarization is not required, it can help ensure that your trust is upheld in the event of a challenge.

Now your trust is signed and sealed, but you're not done yet. You must transfer assets into your trust (see Chapter 13).

When the Trust Ends

You define in your trust when the trust will end. That may be a relatively short period of time, for example, if your trust simply distributes your assets upon your death. But if you want to delay your gifts or make gifts in installments over a period of years, your trust may continue for a considerable amount of time.

You should provide for how the trustee will distribute any remaining assets of your trust after distributing all specific gifts. Even if you don't think your trust will have any remaining assets, the unexpected can happen. For example, a beneficiary may die or decline a gift, the trust may receive income from a source that you didn't anticipate, or you may forget to address an asset when you make your specific gifts.

Chapter 12

Dead or Alive: Picking Your Trust

. . . .

. . . .

*W*hatever your estate planning need, you can probably find a trust that will fill it. And the more complicated and specialized your estate planning needs, the more likely it is that you'll benefit from estate planning with trusts. In this chapter, I explore the types of trusts and help you determine which one best fits your needs.

Why So Many Choices?

The trust is an incredibly flexible estate planning tool, and it has been employed for generations. As tax laws proliferate, new techniques are developed to legally minimize tax exposure. Each new law or innovation can result in a new category of trust, designed to serve a specific need or purpose. When a trust succeeds in its goals, and those goals are shared by others, the trust is copied and refined.

You probably have a toolbox at home. It probably contains a dozen screwdrivers of various types and sizes, a hammer, some wrenches, a pair of pliers, and a range of other tools. When something needs to be fixed, you pick the tool you need to do the job. Estate planning with trusts is similar in concept. You identify the estate planning need and pick the trust that is best for the job.

Here's a sampling of what you can do with a successful trust:

✔ You can use trusts to minimize capital gains taxes, provide yourself with an income and charitable tax deductions, and avoid gift and estate taxes.

✔ You can provide for your minor children, children from a prior marriage, spouse, an heir with special needs, or even your pet.

✔ You can also protect your heirs from themselves and their creditors, meting out your gifts in installments or using special trusts for people who are bad with money.

✔ You can use trusts as part of the succession plan for your family business.

✔ You can provide for gifts to be distributed to multiple generations of your family, and at dates well into the future.

The Revocable Living Trust

You've heard of a revocable living trust. A lot of what you have heard is probably hype. Don't get me wrong — many people benefit from having a revocable living trust. But before you go through the trouble of setting one up, you need to be sure that you'll benefit from having one.

A *revocable living trust* is a document that outlines how your property, once transferred into your trust, will be managed and distributed to your heirs.

✔ It is *revocable* because as long as you remain alive and mentally competent, you may terminate the trust at any time and transfer its assets back to yourself.

✔ It is *living* because it is established during your lifetime and, in most cases, remains entirely under your control during your lifetime.

The benefits

When you create your living trust, you choose the person who takes over as trustee in the event of your death or incapacity. You define the terms of your trust and the powers available to your trustee.

You may also combine your revocable living trust with other types of trusts to get greater control over how your assets will be distributed to your heirs, or as part of a tax avoidance strategy. The following sections cover some additional benefits.

Providing for your care and support while you're alive

When you initially set up your revocable living trust, aside from the fact that your trust will own some of your assets, there's no significant change in the way you live your life. You continue to control your own assets.

But what if something happens to you, and you become incapacitated? With a properly prepared trust, your trustee can immediately start managing the assets in your trust pursuant to your instructions. Nobody needs to go to court to get that authority.

While you can get similar benefits from a durable power of attorney, financial institutions are often skeptical of your attorney-in-fact's claim to have authority over your estate. Often, they'll demand an original copy of your power of attorney, and sometimes they'll retain the original for a period of time. The goal is to prevent fraud, but this process can create a lot of hassle for your attorney-in-fact.

As your trust owns its assets, financial institutions don't have similar concerns about ownership or verification of the trust instrument. Your trustee will generally have a much easier time taking over the management of your assets than an attorney-in-fact.

Distribution of your assets after you pass away

Your revocable living trust can be very simple, instructing your assets to be immediately distributed to your heirs upon your death. Or it can be complicated, even creating and funding an additional trust or trusts.

You can delay distribution of your gifts for years, impose conditions that your beneficiaries must satisfy before they inherit, give out your gifts in installments, provide for the support of your spouse or minor children, or implement one of the more sophisticated trusts described in this chapter in the section "Choosing from Other Trusts."

In short, your estate is managed and distributed according to your wishes and instructions.

Additional benefits for married couples

The simplest living trust for a married couple is a joint trust. You and your spouse can create a joint living trust to hold your marital estate. If something happens to you, your spouse can continue to act as trustee without interruption. After your death, your spouse can amend the trust and add or change beneficiaries. When your spouse dies, the trust's remaining assets are distributed to the beneficiaries pursuant to the terms of the trust.

You can also incorporate a bypass trust, splitting your revocable living trust into two separate trusts upon the death of either you or your spouse. The bypass trust can help you avoid estate taxes and also allows you to provide for your spouse while ensuring that some of your assets go to other heirs, such as your children from a prior marriage. For more detail, see the section entitled "Trusts to protect your estate plan if you predecease your spouse: bypass trusts."

Possible drawbacks

Although the revocable living trust is sometimes pitched as cheap, easy, and something "everyone must have," reality is more complicated. Here's why:

✔ Your trust is a separate entity from yourself. Your property doesn't automatically become part of the trust; you must transfer property into your trust. After your death, your trust must file its own tax returns.

✔ Administration of your trust after your death may not be cheaper than probate and, particularly if your trust will continue for years after your death, may be significantly more costly.

✔ Probate proceedings occur under the supervision of a judge, but trusts are administered without judicial oversight. If your trustee is incompetent, irresponsible, or dishonest, your beneficiaries are vulnerable to mismanagement or misappropriation of funds.

Additional considerations relate to managing property in your trust and the time creditors have to make claims against your estate. You should not think of your revocable living trust as a tool to reduce or avoid taxes.

Managing your assets once they're in the trust

After you create a trust, you have to transfer ownership of assets into the trust. For the most part, this transfer is just a matter of paperwork. You don't lose your homestead exemption or trigger reassessment when you transfer your home into your living trust.

But after your property is in your trust, you may want to sell it. As your trust is now the owner of your property, you must either sell the property through the trust or transfer it back to yourself prior to the sale.

Don't transfer too much of your property into your trust. It's okay to have personal belongings and furniture as part of your estate, even if those items will go through probate. You'll be making frequent deposits and withdrawals from your checking account, so keep it in your own name. Putting your car into your trust can complicate car loans and may result in huge increases in the cost of insurance.

Battling creditors claims in the future

When your estate is probated, your creditors get a specific amount of time to make claims against your estate. When that time is up, as long as your administrator gave proper notice to creditors under your state's laws, your estate may be distributed to your heirs. If a creditor misses the deadline for making a claim, the creditor generally loses the opportunity to get paid.

As your trust may hold assets for many years after your death, your creditors don't operate under similar time constraints. Even if they miss the filing deadline for making a claim in probate court, they can try to collect your debts from your trust.

Facing more limited tax benefits than you may realize

You may have heard that if you create a revocable living trust, you won't pay estate taxes. The truth is, a revocable living trust of itself offers no protection

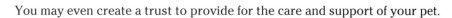

from estate taxes. None. Your taxable estate includes *both* the value of the property in your living trust and the value of your other assets.

To gain a tax advantage, you can combine your revocable living trust with another type of trust. If you're married, you can incorporate elements of an A/B trust (bypass trust) so that you can take full advantage of both your own estate tax exemption and that of your spouse. But you don't need a revocable living trust to take advantage of the other available trusts. You can create them even if you choose not to create a living trust.

The benefits of your revocable living trust are probate avoidance, disability planning, and, if you want, increased control over your estate and how it is administered and distributed after your death. Whether or not you choose to have one is peripheral to your tax avoidance strategy.

Choosing from Other Trusts

Many different types of trust are available to you. Some of the reasons you may choose a trust, beyond your living trust, include

- ✔ Avoiding estate taxes
- ✔ Implementing a gifting strategy during your lifetime, transferring some of your assets to your heirs or to charity while you're alive
- ✔ Planning for the succession of your business
- ✔ Avoiding capital gains taxes or income taxes
- ✔ Protecting heirs who have special financial needs or vulnerabilities

You may even create a trust to provide for the care and support of your pet.

When you read about these trusts, keep the following in mind: The government wants your money.

- ✔ Whenever your trust will keep tax money out of the pockets of Uncle Sam or will prevent the state from recouping money a beneficiary receives in the form of public assistance, the government has an incentive to try to invalidate your trust.
- ✔ Whenever your trust will keep money out of the hands of a beneficiary's creditors or prevent a spouse from grabbing a share upon divorce, the person who wants the money has an incentive to try to invalidate your trust.

The net result? Rules governing the creation and administration of many of these trusts are tricky, and small mistakes can erase the benefits of your trust. Given the amounts of money typically involved in these trusts and the consequences of getting it wrong, your investment in professional estate planning services will be well spent.

All those funny names

Did you hear that right? Your lawyer wants you to put your money into GRITs and QTIPs? Into a Crummey trust?

As you read this chapter, you'll find that many trusts have cumbersome names. But that's not confusing enough for lawyers who commonly refer to trusts by acronym. (Yes, I'm guilty, too.) A charitable remainder unitrust becomes a CRUT. A grantor retained income trust becomes a GRIT. A qualified personal residence trust becomes a QPRT (pronounced Kew-Pert). Or maybe your lawyer refers to a QPRT as a "house GRIT". And yes, a qualified terminable interest property trust is called a QTIP.

A Crummey trust isn't so crummy. It can be a very useful tool to avoid gift and estate taxes. Why the odd name? It's named after the tax-payer who first defended the trust in court, D. Clifford Crummey.

If you get a handle on the lingo, great. If not, don't worry. Your lawyer will know what you mean when you ask about an irrevocable life insurance trust. And if your lawyer starts talking about an ILIT (pronounced Eye-Lit), he won't think any less of you if you ask what he means. (Besides, he should know better than to use jargon with a client.)

Remember also that although these trusts are described separately, sometimes a single trust may fall into more than one category.

Trusts to avoid the tax man: Asset protection trusts

The term *asset protection trust* encompasses a wide range of trusts designed to shelter your money from taxes and creditors.

Many asset protection trusts are set up in foreign nations and are thus called *offshore trusts.* Sometimes the primary benefit of placing money in an offshore bank is to protect it from creditors, as the laws of some nations make it very difficult for anybody to successfully make a claim against your trust fund.

Some asset protection trusts are exceptionally complicated, and skirt as closely as they can to the limits of tax laws. If things go wrong, the government may invalidate the trust as a tax shelter and impose significant penalties on people who were relying upon the trust as a tax shelter.

Some asset protection trusts are scams, from start to finish. The people behind them will make any promise to get your money, and you'll pay substantial fees to participate. Yet if the IRS invalidates the tax shelter, you'll face thousands of dollars in fines and penalties.

If you want to try to shelter your assets, work with a domestic financial adviser who you trust and be sure to fully investigate the validity of any promised tax shelter. As with everything else in life, if it sounds too good to be true, it probably is.

Trusts for people who can't manage money: Spendthrift trusts

A spendthrift being somebody who is careless and wasteful with money, the *spendthrift trust* puts obstacles between the beneficiary and the trust assets. The beneficiary has no claim to assets in the trust until they're distributed and can't use the balance of the trust as collateral for a loan. Creditors can't garnish the trust's assets or distributions.

But that's just the beginning of the story. These obstacles also help protect trust assets from the beneficiary's creditors or the beneficiary's spouse in the event of divorce. Thus, even if the person is good with money, a spendthrift trust can be a useful tool to give money to somebody who may be facing divorce, substantial medical costs, or other financial hardships that may cause a windfall to be lost to creditors. You may also want to use a spendthrift trust when leaving money to children or young adults, rather than hoping that they'll manage money responsibly.

A spendthrift trust is irrevocable. To be effective, the trust instrument must contain language showing that the grantor intended it to be a spendthrift trust. The specific language is defined by statute and thus can be different depending upon the laws of the state in which you create the trust.

As the laws governing these trusts are different in each state, you have to watch for traps created by your state's laws. Some states limit the amount of money that you can place in a spendthrift trust. Some limit their effectiveness against creditors or permit child support to be garnished from distributions.

What if you want to shelter your own money in this way, creating a *self-settled spendthrift trust* for your own benefit? Most states will not allow you to be the beneficiary of a spendthrift trust that you create. The exceptions are limited and may not be enforceable across state lines.

With the state-specific elements of these trusts, you're wise to consult a lawyer when creating a spendthrift trust.

Trusts for doing good: Charitable trusts

The charitable remainder trust (CRT) is used to make a gift to charity, but you still reserve a benefit to yourself. This trust is particularly useful when you own property that has appreciated in value, such that its sale would trigger substantial capital gains taxes. By instead donating the property to charity, you not only avoid capital gains tax, you also get an income tax deduction for a portion of the money you transfer into the trust.

In its standard form, once you place property in your charitable remainder trust:

✔ You're the *income beneficiary* of the trust, meaning you receive income from the trust during your lifetime or over a fixed number of years.

✔ The charity receives any balance remaining in the trust after you die or after the term of the trust expires.

The most common variations of a charitable remainder trust are

✔ **The charitable remainder annuity trust (CRAT):** You receive a fixed percentage of your original investment. For example, you invest $100,000 in the trust and subsequently receive an annual distribution of $7,000, 7 percent of the trust, whatever the balance of the trust.

✔ **The charitable remainder unitrust (CRUT):** Each year you receive a distribution of a fixed percentage of the fair market value of the trust. Again assuming a $100,000 trust balance and a 7 percent payout, you'll receive a $7,000 distribution. But if the trust earns $12,000 in income, its value will increase to $105,000 after the distribution. The following year you'll receive $7,350 (7 percent of $105,000).

✔ **The charitable lead trust (CLT) or reverse charitable remainder trust:** Instead of receiving income during your lifetime, with the remainder of the trust eventually going to charity, you instead direct the trust's income to charity, and your heirs inherit the remainder upon your death. You avoid capital gains tax and enjoy income tax deductions for the continuing contributions during your lifetime.

Consider, for example, a stock investment that has appreciated substantially. Your $10,000 investment is now worth $200,000. You place the stock into a charitable remainder annuity trust, receiving an income of $15,000 per year from the trust. Or consider an apartment building you purchased for $100,000 that is now worth millions. If you transfer the apartment building into a charitable remainder trust, you can sell the building within the trust, the trust will invest the proceeds, and you receive an income from the trust. The trust pays no capital gains tax. When you die, the charity or charities you designate receive the balance of the trust.

Your charitable remainder trust must make distributions of at least 5 percent of its net value per year, although you can defer income as long as the net distributions meet the 5 percent minimum. One useful approach is to set up the trust before you retire, deferring income for several years, and then augmenting your income with larger distributions (and thus catching up with the 5 percent minimum) once you retire. You can incorporate a condition that, once payments are caught up, your trust becomes a standard CRUT. If you die before catching up, the trust's value at the time of your death is treated as part of your taxable estate, but your estate gets an offsetting charitable deduction from the donation of the trust's assets to charity.

Setting too high a payout will affect your charitable income tax deduction, and can potentially reduce the principal balance of the trust.

A charitable remainder trust is irrevocable. Once you make your gift, you can't take it back. However, you can give yourself the authority to change the charitable beneficiaries of the trust during your lifetime. In some circumstances, you can also serve as trustee.

Trusts to avoid gift taxes: Crummey trusts

If you want to make gifts to your heirs during your lifetime, you can take advantage of your $12,000 annual gift tax exclusion, giving gifts up to that amount to each of your heirs without worrying about gift tax exposure. If your spouse joins in the gifting plan, you can each make a gift, doubling the potential gift to $24,000 per year.

With a few years of giving, you can pass a great deal of money to your heirs, no strings attached. Once your gift is complete, the money is theirs to do with as they like. But what if you want to add some strings? Then you need to consider a Crummey trust, a form of irrevocable trust.

After creating the trust on behalf of your beneficiary:

- ✔ You make your annual gifts into the Crummey trust instead of making them directly to the beneficiary, informing your beneficiary of the gift.

- ✔ The beneficiary has a limited amount of time to withdraw the money from the trust. This right of withdrawal qualifies as a present interest in the gift, qualifying you for the gift tax exclusion.

- ✔ After the window for withdrawal expires, the beneficiary can no longer withdraw the gift, and it's managed and distributed pursuant to the terms of the trust.

But wait a second. If your beneficiary has the right to take out the money after you make your gift, how will you prevent them from simply taking the money out as soon as you make a deposit? Well, you can't. But what you *can* do is make it clear that the day your beneficiary withdraws the gift is the day you stop contributing to the trust. Even if you're not contributing a full $12,000 per year, most beneficiaries will leave the money alone when they realize how much money they stand to lose.

You can set up your Crummey trust to have multiple beneficiaries, which simplifies your annual gifting strategy by making all your gifts in a single transaction with the trust. You don't have to contribute cash. You can make gifts of stocks, bonds, other securities, or other types of property.

Trusts for people who receive government benefits: Special needs trusts

Recipients of public assistance typically have limits to the amount of income and assets they may have. If they have too much money, their benefits are reduced or terminated until their assets are depleted. A bequest to an heir who has a disability can be quickly depleted by the costs of residential care or medical bills.

At the same time, the cash benefits received through public assistance programs are quite low. Your heir may not have enough money for items that the government doesn't provide, but which can significantly improve quality of life, such as over-the-counter medications, books and magazines, certain dental care, soap, and shampoo.

The *special needs trust,* also known as a *supplemental needs trust,* is designed to help you improve your beneficiary's quality of life without jeopardizing their public assistance benefits. You place assets into the trust and appoint a trustee to manage the assets on behalf of the beneficiary. The trust isn't considered to be part of the beneficiary's estate and thus doesn't jeopardize their benefits.

Distributions from the trust are often modest, supplementing the beneficiary's care as opposed to providing for the support of the beneficiary. The trust language is customized to the circumstances of your beneficiary and provides specific examples of the types of supplemental care to be provided from the trust.

 The beneficiary of a special needs trust may not serve as trustee. The amount of distributions made from the trust needs to be carefully determined based upon the beneficiary's situation so as not to jeopardize or reduce their continuing benefits. When creating a special needs trust, it's advisable not just to get professional assistance, but to enlist the help of an estate planning professional who has special expertise in drafting these trusts.

Trusts to protect your estate plan if you predecease your spouse: Bypass trusts

If you have a large estate and expect to pay estate taxes, you can take some comfort in the unlimited exemption from estate taxes for gifts to your spouse.

But what happens when your spouse dies? Your spouse's estate takes advantage of the personal exemption from estate taxes, presently $2 million, and the balance of the estate is taxed.

A bypass trust is designed to allow both you and your spouse to take full advantage of the personal exemption. You create a bypass trust to hold up to $2 million of your separate assets and leave the balance of your estate to your spouse. When your spouse dies, the money in your bypass trust isn't counted toward your spouse's estate. Your spouse's estate takes its separate $2 million exemption, and you've doubled the amount of money that is exempt from taxes.

You may be thinking that this process is unnecessarily complicated. Why not just give away $2 million in assets from your estate instead of creating a bypass trust? Here are two leading reasons:

- ✔ You may not have such a large estate that your spouse will be financially secure after $2 million in assets are removed from the estate.

- ✔ Your spouse can draw an income from the bypass trust, and you can allow your spouse access to the principal of the trust as necessary to pay for her support and medical care.

Your spouse can serve as trustee and may even be granted authority to change the beneficiaries of the trust. You can set up the trust to maximize the amount of income and benefit to your spouse (a *maximum benefits bypass trust*), or you can limit the benefits to your spouse to maximize the eventual inheritance by the trust's beneficiaries.

The A/B trust

A bypass trust is commonly implemented through an *A/B trust,* jointly created by you and your spouse. That name refers to the fact that upon the death of you or your spouse, your marital estate is divided between two trusts:

- ✔ The *B trust* is the bypass trust. It contains the *lesser* of:

  - • The amount of the current estate tax exemption

  - • All your separate property, plus half of your community property

- ✔ The *A trust* (also called the *survivor's trust*) holds the rest of the marital estate

Your spouse's use of the A trust isn't restricted. Your spouse can benefit from the B trust as previously described, and the trust's assets eventually pass to your beneficiaries free of estate taxes.

The A/B/C trust

If you're extremely wealthy, you can create a third trust upon your death. The most common approach is for the third trust to be a qualified terminable interest property trust (QTIP), described later in this chapter. After fully funding the bypass trust, you place the rest of your separate assets in the QTIP trust instead of putting them into your spouse's survivor's trust. The QTIP trust doesn't provide further tax savings, but it allows you to continue to control and direct your assets rather than having them become part of your spouse's estate.

Trusts where you control the trust assets

Although most often when you create an irrevocable trust, you lose most or all control over the trust's assets, that's not always the case. Some trusts permit you to get significant benefits from the assets.

Grantor trusts (GRATs, GRITs, and GRUTs)

Here's a quick rundown of the acronyms:

- **GRIT:** Grantor retained income trust
- **GRAT:** Grantor retained annuity trust
- **GRUT:** Grantor retained unitrust

What does it mean to be *grantor retained?* It means that although you're creating an irrevocable trust, you retain the right to receive income from the trust for a period of years. At the end of the trust's life, the assets are distributed to your beneficiaries.

Until 1990, GRITs were a common tool for planning large estates. You'd transfer property into your trust. For gift tax purposes, the value of the property within the trust would be discounted from its fair market value due to your continued claim on the income generated by the trust. The assets might appreciate substantially over the life of the trust, but taxes would continue to be based upon that initial valuation.

Does that sound too good to be true? The government thought so as well and, in 1990, wiped out the GRIT except in the limited form of the qualified personal residence trust (QPRT).

But estate planning lawyers are clever and weren't about to let go of a good thing. So they figured out how to preserve some of these benefits:

- A GRAT allows you to transfer an asset into an irrevocable trust and receive an annual payment from the trust.
- A GRUT allows you to transfer an asset into an irrevocable trust and receive a distribution of a specified percentage of the trust's assets each year.

At the end of the trust term, the assets are distributed to your beneficiaries.

When would you use a GRAT or GRUT? If you have an asset that is appreciating at a rate higher than the annual rate of return expected by the IRS. For example, if you purchased Google stock in 2004 at $100 per share, that stock has more than quadrupled in value over four years. Had you put the stock into a GRAT or GRUT, the value of the gift would have been calculated based upon the IRS's presumed annual rate of return, which at the time was less than 5 percent. You pay gift tax based on that lower valuation, but your heirs receive the full benefit of your gift.

Qualified personal residence trusts (QPRTs)

A qualified personal residence trust (QPRT) allows you to give away your house at a substantially reduced value, even though you continue to live in it. This trust can provide substantial estate tax savings. But QPRTs are irrevocable trusts, and their use isn't risk-free.

Ideally, your home will not be mortgaged when you create your QPRT. Once your property is transferred into the QPRT, you can't refinance it.

If your home is mortgaged, normally the value of the gift will be treated as the net value of your home (market value less the balance of the mortgage). You continue to make the mortgage payments and may tax an income tax deduction for your interest payments. Your contributions to the principal balance of the mortgage are additional gifts to the grantees, so you must consider possible gift tax consequences. In an alternative approach, you transfer your home into the trust at its market value and assume personal responsibility for the mortgage. You continue to enjoy the mortgage interest deduction, but your payments don't have any gift tax consequences.

When you set up a QPRT:

- ✔ You create a trust and transfer your home into the trust.

- ✔ The trust holds the home for a term of years, as few or as many as you choose.

- ✔ During that time, you retain the right to live in your home, rent-free, for the duration of the trust.

- ✔ You continue to pay any mortgage payments, property taxes, insurance, and costs of maintenance and repair.

- ✔ Capital improvements, such as an addition or a new swimming pool, are considered gifts to the trust, in the amount of their fair market value.

- ✔ At the end of the trust's term, the trust beneficiaries receive ownership of your home. All appreciation in the value of the home following its transfer into the trust is free of gift and inheritance taxes.

In order to benefit from a QPRT you have to consider your probable life expectancy when you determine how long the trust will last. If you die before the trust expires, your home is treated as part of your estate. Your estate gets credit for any gift tax consequences from the original transfer of the home into your trust. The net effect is that you're back where you started, as if you never created the QPRT.

If you're alive at the end of the trust, your home passes to the beneficiaries of the trust. Your beneficiaries may permit you to continue to rent the home, but they don't have to. At this point in time, it's their home.

During the term of your QPRT, you have the right to sell your home and purchase a different home. You have two years from the date of sale to purchase the new home. If your home is sold while it is in your QPRT and the proceeds of the sale aren't used to purchase a new residence, the trust may similarly be converted to a GRAT (see preceding section).

A QPRT is only effective as long as you continue to reside in your home. If you move, the trustee can return ownership to you or convert the QPRT into a GRAT, described in the preceding section.

Trusts that own life insurance: Irrevocable life insurance trusts (ILITs)

An *irrevocable life insurance trust* (ILIT) allows you to pass life insurance proceeds to your heirs, tax-free. Here's how it works.

- ✔ You create a trust and transfer sufficient assets into the trust to purchase the desired life insurance policy. You can't serve as trustee.
- ✔ Your trustee purchases a life insurance policy of the type and value you desire.
- ✔ Upon your death, the proceeds of the life insurance policy are paid into the ILIT and are managed and distributed according to the terms of the trust.
- ✔ As the life insurance proceeds are never part of your estate, no estate taxes are payable on those proceeds.

As with any irrevocable trust, you need to be careful in your selection of a trustee. Pick a trustee you are confident will follow your wishes in relation not only to the purchase of life insurance, but also when administering the trust after it receives the insurance proceeds.

If you transfer an existing life insurance policy into the ILIT, the proceeds of the policy will be included in your estate if you die within three years of the transfer.

You can incorporate elements of a Crummey trust, described earlier in this chapter, to provide annual contributions to your ILIT to cover the cost of premiums while avoiding any gift tax consequences. As with any Crummey trust, you take the chance that your beneficiaries will withdraw the money, but the folly of doing so (and losing the benefit of the life insurance proceeds) is obvious.

These trusts can come under intense IRS scrutiny, so I urge you to have your ILIT drafted by a professional.

Trusts for multiple generations: Dynasty trusts (generation-skipping trusts)

A *dynasty trust* is a wealth management tool that provides for multiple generations of heirs, while avoiding estate taxes and generation-skipping transfer taxes. Taxes aren't saved when the trust is created, but they are saved as wealth is distributed to later generations of beneficiaries. When properly created and funded, no federal gift or estate taxes are owed on distributions made at the following times:

- ✔ During your lifetime
- ✔ Following your death
- ✔ When the trust ends, and its remaining assets are distributed

If you create and fund a dynasty trust during your lifetime, your gift tax exposure is the value of the assets you transfer into the trust. After the transfer, the assets appreciate without further gift or estate tax liability. You can also fund the trust at the time of your death, taking full advantage of the remainder of your unified gift and estate tax exemption.

Laws collectively known as the *Rule Against Perpetuities* limit the duration of a dynasty trust. Most often, these laws require that all trust assets be distributed within a life in being, plus 21 years, meaning within 21 years of the death of the last surviving named beneficiary of your trust. These laws vary by state, and their application can be exceedingly technical, so be careful.

Often, a dynasty trust will include spendthrift provisions to protect trust assets from claims by beneficiaries' creditors or ex-spouses. Spendthrift trusts are described earlier in this chapter.

A dynasty trust may also be combined with an ILIT so that the trust is funded with tax-free life insurance proceeds.

You can easily fall into one of many potential traps that can destroy a dynasty trust, such as the rule against perpetuities. Dynasty trusts are subject to a high rate of taxation on trust income, meaning that you'll get the most benefit from the trust if it's funded with tax-free investments. Giving a beneficiary too much authority over trust assets can create gift tax liability on distributions. To avoid these and other pitfalls, this type of trust should be created by an experienced professional.

Trusts to postpone estate taxes: Qualified terminable interest property trusts (QTIPs)

A qualified terminable interest property trust, or QTIP trust, is designed to help married people leave assets to their heirs, while delaying the payment of gift and estate taxes. The QTIP trust is often used to protect inheritances intended for children from a prior marriage, as the trust's assets never become part of your surviving spouse's estate and are ultimately distributed according to your instructions.

Your QTIP trust is created upon your death. As long as your spouse remains alive, the trust property may not be distributed to anybody other than your spouse. Although your spouse doesn't directly receive the trust assets, gift and estate taxes are deferred until the death of your spouse.

Your surviving spouse will receive all of the trust's income and may sometimes also use the trust's assets, but you can impose significant limits on your spouse's ability to access and control the trust's assets. The trust's assets are also shielded from your spouse's creditors.

When your spouse dies, taxes are paid, and the trust's assets are distributed consistent with the terms of the trust instrument.

If you intend to create a QTIP trust, you need to be absolutely sure that your executor knows how to make a timely QTIP election following your death or have your probate lawyer ready to step in. If your estate makes a mistake or misses the deadline for making a QTIP election, your estate may lose all of the benefits of this trust.

Trusts for your pet

You expect to outlive your beloved pet, so how do you make sure that your pet is properly cared for? An increasingly popular way is to make your pet the beneficiary of a trust. (A sample trust instrument is available on the CD.)

Most states now formally recognize your ability to create a trust for your pet, and that number is growing. In the remaining states, your pet trust is non-binding and may potentially be set aside if challenged in court.

You may have heard that Leona Helmsley left $12 million to her dog, Trouble. When the dog dies, any remaining balance will go into her charitable trust. She left the care of her dog to a family friend, and many other people have an incentive to see that the money isn't misused. Most pets aren't that lucky.

The biggest safeguard for your pet, and perhaps the *only* safeguard, is your choice of a suitable trustee. Your pet can't complain about mistreatment, abuse, or neglect or monitor or report misuse of trust assets. In states where the trustee isn't bound to the terms of your trust, nothing may stop your trustee from simply pocketing the money.

Although you can use an institutional trustee or have the trust pay for periodic investigation of your pet's living conditions, in most cases, that route will not be cost-effective.

Deciding Which Trust Is Right for You

You can choose from many different types of trust, some of them very specialized, and combine them in interesting and innovative ways. For specialized needs, particularly if cost isn't an issue, the range of choices can seem endless. If cost is an issue, be careful. Some trusts are expensive to set up, and some are very expensive to administer.

Where does that leave you? If you've read this chapter, you're a lot more informed about your options, but what do you actually need? For some people, the answer is nothing. For most others, a simple revocable living trust is sufficient. For you? The following sections help you figure that out.

Serving your personal needs

When you're trying to take care of yourself, the revocable living trust is probably your first and best choice. Why?

- You pick your own trustee.
- Upon your incapacity, your trustee can assume responsibility for managing the assets of your trust.
- You define your trustee's powers. They can be as narrow or as broad as you wish.

In contrast, if you have no plan for your incapacity, your estate may end up being managed by a court-appointed guardian or conservator in a manner the court deems suitable. (Chapter 14 contains a lot more information on incapacity planning.)

A charitable remainder trust can offer you both a steady source of income and tax advantages during your lifetime.

You can utilize trusts as part of your business succession strategy to help you transfer business ownership to your successors. Chapter 4 discusses business succession in more detail.

Serving the needs of your family

Most trusts are designed to benefit your heirs, and it thus follows that most trusts can be set up to serve the needs of your family. The issue is more one of specialization. What are the specific needs of your family members, and what trusts will serve those needs?

Minor and dependent children

Most trusts can include provisions governing the distribution of your gifts to your children. Common trust provisions benefiting children:

- ✔ Place the children's assets under the supervision of a responsible trustee
- ✔ Defer part or all of their inheritance until they reach adulthood, or provide for gifts to be received in periodic installments after they reach adulthood
- ✔ Provide for the children's support and education during their minority, perhaps also providing for college expenses

You can implement these provisions through your revocable living trust or even through a testamentary trust that is created and funded at the time of your death.

Chapter 5 contains more suggestions for providing for your children.

Disabled dependents

The most useful trust for a recipient of public assistance is a special needs trust, described earlier in this chapter. This type of trust pays for modest comforts of life that your beneficiary probably will not otherwise be able to afford.

You can find more information on special needs planning in Chapter 5.

Second marriages

If you're worried about keeping your assets out of your combined marital estate or providing for your new spouse's financial well-being while protecting your children's inheritances, how creative do you want to be?

✔ You can place your assets into a revocable living trust before you marry to keep them separate from the marital estate, perhaps also executing a prenuptial agreement, whereby your new spouse waives any claim to trust assets.

✔ You can use bypass trusts and their A/B variants to provide for the support of your spouse, while ensuring that your children from a prior marriage receive a considerable inheritance.

✔ You can place your assets in trust, allowing your spouse to benefit from them for a specified number of years before they're distributed to your children. For example, you can provide for your second spouse to live in your home for seven years after your death, but anticipate that after that time, your spouse will have recovered financially and perhaps be in a new relationship, such that your children should inherit your home.

✔ You can create an ILIT to provide life insurance benefits to your children, while leaving the bulk of your estate to your spouse.

That's just scraping the surface of the many trusts that can help you structure your assets for the long-term benefit of your selected heirs.

Financially irresponsible beneficiaries

If your beneficiaries aren't good with money, have troubled marriages, or don't have a long enough track record with money that you're comfortable leaving them large bequests, you can utilize a spendthrift trust to limit their access to their inheritance and also to shield it from creditors and legal claims.

Spendthrift trust provisions may be added to most trusts. So pick the trusts that will distribute your assets the way you want and then look into adding spendthrift provisions.

Thinking about the tax man

Throughout this chapter, I discuss trusts that can help you save taxes, particularly estate taxes, gift taxes, and capital gains taxes. The most effective trusts for avoiding taxes are

✔ **Irrevocable:** Once your money goes in, it stays in.

✔ **Complicated:** A trust may seem deceptively simple, but the devil is in the details, and small mistakes can erase tax benefits.

✔ **Cautious:** To ensure compliance with tax laws, trusts shielding you from taxes are best drafted by an estate planning lawyer.

When I'm talking about estate taxes, I'm talking about estates worth millions of dollars. I'm talking about potential tax exposure of hundreds of thousands of dollars, or more. And I'm looking at state and federal tax agencies that want your money and may seek to invalidate your trust in order to get it.

Being wealthy doesn't mean that you like to pay money to lawyers. It probably means that you're careful with your money and avoid unnecessary expenses.

Yes, by reading this chapter, you can get a good idea of the trusts that can benefit you. You can try to create those trusts yourself. But you'll save a lot of time and aggravation by getting a professional to help you choose, draft, and fund your trusts. And when you use estate planning professionals, you have the reassurance that if *they* make a mistake you can make a claim against their firm or malpractice insurance coverage.

Taxes are discussed more fully in Chapter 6. Common tax traps are outlined in Chapter 20.

Chapter 13

When You Already Have a Trust

In This Chapter

▶ Putting assets into your trust

▶ Updating your trust

▶ Revoking your trust

*A*fter you draft your trust (see Chapters 11 and 12), you still have more work to do. You need to put money and assets into your trust. You need to periodically review your living trust and change it if it's no longer consistent with your estate planning goals. At times, you may even need to revoke your trust.

Creating the Trust Isn't the End of the Story

If you're using a living trust as part of your estate, the goals of your trust probably include incapacity planning and avoiding probate. If you're using other trusts, your goals are most likely to avoid taxes, plan for the succession of your business, provide for a disabled relative, or protect your beneficiaries from creditors or bad financial choices.

To ensure that your wishes are carried out, you must

- ✔ Fund your trust, by transferring into the trust the assets you want it to hold, manage, and ultimately distribute
- ✔ Periodically review your revocable trusts to confirm that they remain consistent with your estate planning goals and wishes

Even with all the benefits of a trust, putting all your assets into one isn't realistic — and may not even be desirable. Trusts also don't communicate your wishes to a probate court. Even if you have a sound, comprehensive trust, you also need to have a will.

Transferring Assets into Your Trust

You know the advantages of creating a trust. You've drafted your trust and signed the trust agreement. But you're not done yet. Now you must transfer assets into your trust.

Think of your brand new trust as a box. It's carefully constructed to hold your assets just the way you want and to keep them safe. But no matter how carefully made, your trust starts out empty. It doesn't hold any assets until you put them into it.

Anything you choose not to transfer into your trust will remain part of your estate, and the distribution of those assets will normally occur through a probate court.

When transferring assets into your trust, the first question you face is one of timing:

- ✔ You can transfer assets into your trust during your lifetime.
- ✔ You can use your will to transfer assets into your trust.

A will that puts estate assets into an existing trust is called a *pour over will.* You can also use your will to create a *testamentary trust,* a new trust created by your will to hold specified assets.

Real estate

The transfer of real estate is usually the most complicated transaction when funding a trust. To transfer real estate, take the following steps:

1. **Execute and file a quitclaim deed transferring title of the real estate from yourself to the trust.**

   If you want to transfer your interest in real estate that has multiple owners, all owners must cooperate in this process.

2. **Update your insurance policies to reflect that your trust is now the owner of the real estate.**

   You may need to obtain a new title insurance policy.

3. **Lease your real estate back from your trust.**

   This step, however, isn't necessary if you have a revocable living trust.

Forgetting to fund a trust

Believe it or not, even estate planning professionals sometimes forget to fund a trust. I recall a case where a large law firm had drafted an elegant trust that carefully laid out its client's estate plan, but neglected to transfer so much as a penny into the trust.

What happened? The client's estate was distributed pursuant to a will that predated the trust and did not fully reflect the client's wishes.

The law firm was sued for malpractice, but that didn't undo the damage. Faced with substantial legal costs, and the difficulty of proving both what the deceased client would have transferred into the trust and how the transfer would have affected her heirs' inheritances, the estate accepted a modest settlement.

If your real estate has a mortgage, review the language of the mortgage before transferring the real estate into a trust. Your mortgage may include a *due on sale* clause that will be triggered by the transfer, requiring you to pay off the mortgage balance. Get your lender's consent *before* you transfer the real estate. Fortunately, these clauses don't apply when you transfer your primary residence into your own revocable living trust.

If you're transferring your primary residence into your own revocable living trust, don't worry about homestead exemptions or tax valuations, as a transfer into your own living trust won't affect your exemptions or tax assessment. For other real estate or transfers into other types of trusts, be sure to consider the tax consequences of transfer, including reassessment and transfer taxes.

Financial accounts

If you want to transfer a bank account, money market account, or brokerage account into your trust, the simplest process is for the trust to open a new account and then transfer the account balances from the old account into the new account. If you prefer to transfer the existing account, contact your bank or brokerage for the required forms.

To transfer securities held in your own name (for example, stocks and bonds) into your trust, you will have to identify the transfer agent for the security. The transfer agent will provide you with paperwork to complete. You will return the completed paperwork with your certificates, and the transfer agent will reissue the certificates in the name of the trust.

You will not ordinarily transfer your personal checking accounts into your trust. Doing so needlessly complicates your day-to-day financial transactions.

Other assets

If you want to make your trust the beneficiary of a life insurance policy, annuity, or retirement account, contract the company that issued the policy or holds the account for change of beneficiary forms.

You can transfer items of personal property to your trust by executing an assignment or bill of sale, conveying the property to your trust.

Normally, you will not transfer your vehicles, boats, or furniture into your trust. Obtaining car insurance for a vehicle owned by a trust may be costly or difficult.

Reviewing Your Trust

You should review your revocable living trust every year, along with the rest of your estate plan. If that's too much for you, try not to go more than two or three years without revisiting your trust. Over time, it's inevitable that your life, and thus your estate plan, will change. For example, you'll have new heirs, you may want to reduce or eliminate certain gifts, or heirs will die. Your trustee may pass away or may no longer be a suitable choice. There may be changes in your estate or in the law that affect the distribution of property. To keep your trust effective and out of probate court, you need to keep it up to date.

Common changes include

- ✔ Adding or removing beneficiaries
- ✔ Designating a different trustee or successor trustee
- ✔ Designating beneficiaries for an asset you've added to the trust
- ✔ Changing the distribution of trust assets

Does the trust still serve your needs?

You may have drafted your trust to address specific estate planning needs, but later find that your needs have changed. For example:

✔ Your trust provides extensively for the management of your business in the event of your incapacity or death, but you have since sold your business or transferred ownership to your successors.

✔ The most significant asset in your trust was your home, but you have since sold your home to move into a condo or retirement community.

In most cases, if you conclude that you'll benefit from a living trust, you will continue to benefit from having a trust even as your needs change. But you may need to substantially revise or rewrite your trust to reflect changes in your needs.

Does the trust still fulfill your goals?

At various stages in your life, you may have different goals that you want to achieve through your estate plan. As time goes by, your needs and those of your family will change. These changes may occur in countless ways. For example:

✔ Your trust carefully plans how you'll provide for your minor children, pay for their education, and distribute an inheritance to them during their early adulthood. Now, though, they've finished school and are adults, and you're still alive and kicking.

✔ Since you drafted your trust, your eldest daughter has developed a drug dependency. Previously, you were going to simply leave her a lump sum of money, but now you want to protect her inheritance from being squandered on drugs or lost to bill collectors.

✔ When you entered your second marriage, you carefully structured your trust to maintain certain assets as separate property in case of divorce. But now you're not worried about divorce, and you want to be more generous with your spouse in your estate plan.

Through the periodic review of your estate plan, you can identify changes in your goals and amend your trust to reflect your current wishes.

Changing the name of your trust

Many people name their revocable living trusts after themselves. But what if you change your name? Do you have to change the name of your trust? The short answer is no. Your trust will remain effective under your old name.

If you want to change the name of your trust anyway, remember that you must also change the ownership of trust assets to reflect the new name of the trust. This process may involve quite a bit of paperwork, but isn't too difficult.

Is the trust adequately funded?

Changes in your estate may leave your trust without the assets you expected it to hold.

- ✔ Financial setbacks may deplete your savings or investments.
- ✔ You may have sold the house that was once the principal trust asset so that you could move into a smaller home or retirement community.
- ✔ Other trust assets may have been lost, sold, or destroyed.

When you're unable to fund the trust as you originally intended or reductions in its assets frustrate its purpose, you need to consider whether to amend or revoke the trust or to transfer additional assets into the trust.

Amending Your Trust

After you review your estate plan, you may want to change certain provisions of your revocable living trust. Fortunately, amending a trust is relatively easy (unless, of course, it's an irrevocable trust, which you can't change). You can execute an amendment to the trust, completely rewrite the trust, or, in some cases, revoke the trust and transfer its assets back to yourself.

Adding new property to a living trust shouldn't require amendment. A well-drafted trust anticipates that you'll continue to add property to the trust over your lifetime.

Your approach to amendment may be affected by the simplicity or complexity of the changes you want to make. For smaller changes, a simple amendment may suffice. For more complicated changes, you may choose to completely rewrite the trust or even to revoke it.

If you've registered your trust with a government office or probate court, remember to also register your amendments.

If you want to change your trust, keep the following points in mind:

- ✔ You can amend your trust by executing a supplemental document that changes the terms of the existing trust instrument.
- ✔ You can restate the trust, replacing the entire old trust with new trust language. Restatement will normally void all previous amendments to your trust.
- ✔ You can revoke the trust and transfer its assets back to yourself. If you choose, you can later create a new trust for some or all of those assets.

What if you have an irrevocable trust?

You can't change or revoke an irrevocable trust. Once you create the trust and transfer assets into it, the deal is done.

The obvious response to this revelation is, "Why create an irrevocable trust in the first place?" The leading purpose of irrevocable trusts is tax planning and tax avoidance, and those goals often require that you surrender both ownership and control of the trust's assets. Despite the loss of control, the capital gains tax and estate tax savings to yourself and your heirs may be substantial.

 Don't try to change your trust by less formal means, such as by crossing off language or writing notes in the margins. Similarly, don't attempt to remove a page from a trust and replace it with an updated page. You may render part or all of your trust invalid, create confusion as to your intent, or trigger litigation over whether the changes were in fact made by you.

After amending your trust, you may refer to the trust by the date of the most recent amendment (for example, The Jones Revocable Living Trust, As Amended On July 14, 2009).

Restating a Trust

When you *restate* a revocable trust, although the trust continues to hold its assets, you create an entirely new trust instrument to govern the operation of the trust and eventual distribution of its assets. (You can't restate an irrevocable trust.) This approach to amendment has several advantages:

- ✔ If you're making substantial changes to your trust, referring back and forth between the amendment and the original language can be complicated and confusing.

- ✔ If you amend your trust more than once, subsequent amendments may also affect prior amendments, adding to the complication and possible confusion.

- ✔ Sometimes trust language may become dated or irrelevant or may not reflect changes in the law. Restatement allows you to clean house.

- ✔ Due to the complexities, it's often easier to restate a trust than to amend it. If you're using a lawyer, restating your trust may also be cheaper.

After restating your trust, you may refer to the trust by the date of the restatement (for example, The Smith Revocable Living Trust, As Restated On July 14, 2009).

Revoking a Trust

When you create a revocable trust, as may seem obvious, you reserve to yourself the power to revoke it at any time. But before you revoke your trust, consider your continuing estate planning goals.

✔ When your revoke your trust, you must transfer ownership of all trust assets back to yourself. If you intend to create a new revocable living trust, you will save yourself a lot of work by amending or restating the trust.

✔ Restatement reduces the chance that you will accidentally forget to transfer an asset back into the trust — it's already there.

If you create a revocable living trust during your marriage or jointly with your spouse, you will want to revoke the trust upon divorce.

When a trust is revocable, as long as you remain competent, you may revoke your trust. You may even provide within a revocable trust that in the event of your incapacity, your trustee may revoke the trust.

Even when you create a living trust with your spouse, you can unilaterally revoke the trust. This step returns ownership of trust assets to you and your spouse, in the manner in which they were owned before you created the trust.

The process of revoking a trust is relatively simple:

1. **Transfer ownership of the trust assets out of the trust and back to yourself.**

2. **Execute a revocation of living trust form and keep it with your legal documents.**

If you've distributed copies of your trust to your trustee or any other people, you may want to inform them of the revocation and recover those copies.

What Happens If You Die?

Once you die, your trustee will manage and distribute trust assets pursuant to the terms of your trust. (If something happens to your trustee, your successor trustee will take over, or a probate court will appoint a successor.) That may mean immediately distributing your estate, or it may mean holding your assets for years while making periodic distributions of assets or trust income.

This process ordinarily occurs independently of the probate court, meaning that no public record of your trust exists.

Can you avoid probate?

The principal benefit of a revocable living trust is probate avoidance. The assets within your trust don't become part of your probate estate. But you can't completely avoid the probate court.

- ✔ No matter how many of your assets are held by your trust, there will always be some assets that aren't included. It's cumbersome to have your trust own certain assets, such as automobiles. You also have the risk that an asset wasn't properly transferred into the trust and remains part of your estate.

- ✔ Somebody has to prepare your final income tax returns and estate tax returns. The assets in your living trust are counted toward your estate when calculating estate taxes.

- ✔ You will have some property that isn't owned by your trust, even if they're only your clothes, personal effects, and the money in your wallet.

The probate court will oversee the final accounting of your estate, submission of tax returns and payment of taxes, and the distribution of any assets that aren't included in your trust. Your trust should make the probate process a lot faster and cheaper, but you can't completely avoid the probate court.

Should you also have a will?

Even if you have a trust, you absolutely should have a will as well. Your will is the failsafe tool for your estate plan, governing distribution of your assets when something else goes wrong. Having a will also has other benefits:

- ✔ Through your will, you pick the personal representative of your estate.

- ✔ If you have minor children, you use your will to designate your preferred caretakers for your children and their assets.

- ✔ Your will describes how any assets remaining in your estate will be distributed among your heirs. You're probably not concerned about your clothing undergarments, but what about your wedding ring? The balance of your checking and savings accounts? The brokerage account you forgot to transfer into your trust?

If you don't have a will, the court will choose the administrator of your estate and won't know your wishes when appointing guardians for your children. Anything that remains in your estate will pass according to your state's laws of intestate succession.

Part IV

Carrying Out the Intent of Your Will and Trust

The 5th Wave   By Rich Tennant

What's the chance of settling this without getting attorneys involved?

HARVARD LAW SCHOOL ALUMNI PICNIC

ANTS, GNATS AND BEES

In this part . . .

This part explains why you need to plan for your incapacity, and the benefits of creating a durable power of attorney, healthcare proxy, and living will. You find out how retirement accounts and life insurance figure into your estate plan. After seeing the ways you can own real estate, you discover how to put your home into a living trust or add your heirs to the title of your property, along with the risks and benefits of each approach.

Chapter 14

Planning for Your Incapacity

. . . .

. . . .

*A*s a result of age, illness, or accident, you may find yourself still alive but unable to care for yourself or make decisions. The good news is that you can help yourself and reduce the stress on your family by documenting your wishes and selecting people who will act on your behalf before — if ever — you're incapacitated. In this chapter, I talk about living wills, health-care proxies, and financial powers of attorney, which all can help you plan for your incapacity.

Planning for Incapacity Has Many Benefits

Why do you need to plan for incapacity? You probably already know the answer:

✔ **Aging is unavoidable.** We're all growing older, and with advanced age comes the risk that you'll lose your physical and mental capacity.

✔ **Illnesses are unavoidable.** While most illnesses are followed by a full recovery, some result in temporary or permanent incapacity.

✔ **Accidents are unavoidable.** While most accidents are minor, disaster can strike anyone at any age.

You're reading this chapter, so you've already done the hardest part of incapacity planning: recognizing that bad things can happen to you. Now you can take the steps necessary to ease the burden on yourself and your family, should disaster strike.

You avoid guardianship and conservatorship proceedings

A *healthcare proxy* (healthcare power of attorney) identifies a trusted person as your medical advocate who can make medical decisions on your behalf when you're unable to do so yourself. If you don't create a healthcare proxy, when a medical crisis arises or your health deteriorates, your family may have to go to court in order to obtain guardianship over you. Similarly, without a durable power of attorney, your family may have to petition the court to appoint a *conservator* (sometimes called a guardian of the estate) to manage your money and property. The people chosen by the court may not be the people you prefer, people you find objectionable, or even complete strangers. Your estate will bear the cost of court proceedings and may have to pay fees to the people managing your care and your assets during your period of disability or, if you don't recover, the rest of your life.

You get to choose who cares for you

When you execute a healthcare proxy and *durable power of attorney* — the document that authorizes somebody to manage your legal and financial affairs — you get to select the people who hold those powers. You can be reasonably certain that the people you select will respect your wishes. These individuals are authorized to act on your behalf without seeking court approval or providing reports or accountings to a court. Although bond requirements can often be waived, the holder of your financial power of attorney does not have to post a bond as a condition of providing that service.

Don't let fear of probate court dictate your choices

Having a healthcare proxy and durable power of attorney will allow most people to avoid probate proceedings relating to their incapacity. But if you lack the time to complete those documents, or do not know who to designate to represent your interests, the probate court is there to protect you. Guardianship and conservatorship proceedings are relatively straightforward, and are often initiated by people who care about you. Court-appointed guardians and conservators act subject to judicial oversight, and submit periodic reports and accountings to the court to document their actions.

If you're in a domestic partnership and become ill or incapacitated, healthcare providers and financial institutions may treat your partner as if you have no family relationship. Difficulties can arise even if your state permits registered domestic partnerships, particularly during travel to other parts of the country. A healthcare proxy and financial power of attorney can keep your partner in the picture.

You ensure that your wishes are followed

When you create a living will, healthcare proxy, or financial power of attorney, you get to

- ✓ **Nominate somebody you trust:** You pick the people who will be assisting you with your choices or making choices on your behalf.
- ✓ **Grant powers:** You describe what authority you want to grant over your property and your person.
- ✓ **Define limits:** You define the limits on the choices that these appointees can make.

These three documents help ensure that your wishes for your property and personal care are respected.

Drafting a Living Will

An *advance directive* is a document that provides instructions for what you want to happen in the future if you become unable to make or communicate your own decisions. A complete estate plan includes an *advance medical directive*, also known as a *living will*. Your *living will* describes the care you desire and the limits you want to place on your care during the final stages of your life.

Living wills provide instructions for your medical care when you're unable to speak for yourself. A typical living will addresses situations where you have a terminal illness or are in a permanent vegetative state or coma.

If you have a living will, your loved ones don't have to guess your wishes or argue over what course of treatment they believe you would choose. In the Terry Schiavo case, a woman's husband and parents battled for years over whether she should be kept alive with a feeding tube. Their dispute dragged through the courts and ended up broadcast in the national media. Although media coverage is unlikely, litigation over medical care options is not uncommon. You can help avoid this type of conflict by having a living will that describes your actual wishes.

Contrary to popular belief, a living will can do more than help you avoid being kept alive against your wishes. You can describe what treatments you desire to receive and even request the maximum level of intervention consistent with medical standards of practice. For example, you can state that if you're not expected to recover from an illness, you don't want to be placed on life support or fed through a feeding tube. Or if you wish, you can state that you *want* your life extended through life support and intubation. You can use your living will to request care and treatment that you believe will protect your comfort and dignity.

The most common situations where people require assistance making medical decisions, or require somebody to make decisions for them, do not come at the end of life. They involve patients who have lost capacity to understand their day-to-day needs and their treatment options, due to conditions such as Alzheimer's disease or dementia. A living will does not help you in these circumstances. In those situations, you also need a healthcare proxy. (For more on this topic, see the section "Looking into Other Advance Directives," later in this chapter.)

When your caregivers interpret your living will or decide which medical treatments are excluded by the living will, you always risk a misunderstanding. You can help avoid misunderstanding by making sure that your family and caregivers understand what you want. (See the section in this chapter on "Discussing your wishes.") You should also be careful to make your instructions clear. While a living will usually rules out treatment serving solely to prolong life, the same treatment may be justified on the basis that it will increase your comfort or has the potential to improve your level of consciousness or ability to communicate with your family. When these ambiguities arise, the person who holds your healthcare proxy can choose treatment options most likely to be consistent with your wishes.

The principal advantages of having a living will are as follows:

- ✔ **Your wishes are known.** In the event of a health crisis, your family can provide for your care without the stress of guessing what you would have wanted.

- ✔ **Your wishes are clearly recorded.** Although your doctor will follow your oral instructions, a living will reduces the chance of miscommunication and increases the likelihood that your wishes will be accurately conveyed to other medical providers.

- ✔ **You get peace of mind.** When you create a living will, your wishes are much more likely to be followed.

Life-prolonging alternatives

Although your living will can be crafted to inform your caregivers of your wish to prolong your life, a common perception of the living will is that it's about giving up care during your final days of life. Alternative documents, called *will-to-live* forms or *life-prolonging procedures*

forms, focus on the continuation of care during your final days.

National Right to Life offers will-to-live forms on its Web site at www.nrlc.org. Under Issue Info click Euthanasia and look for the links under the heading Will to Live Project.

Discussing your wishes

After you put your pen to paper and recorded your wishes in a living will, you may think you're done — but you're not. Unless you discuss your living will with the people involved with your care, you risk that your wishes may be misinterpreted or ignored.

Don't forget the following people when you discuss your living will:

- ✔ **Your family:** Of course, talk to your family about death. Even the young and healthy avoid these topics, thinking that they can be put off to the future. Yet even with a living will, the best way to ensure that your wishes are respected is to share them with your family and to address their concerns. You can't anticipate every possible future, but your intentions are most likely to be followed if your family understands your values, wishes, and desired quality of life.

  You can expect that your family will want you to be comfortable and well cared for, but that doesn't mean that they'll want to make the decision to "pull the plug." Your family may insist that your living will does not clearly state your wishes and argue for additional treatment despite your wishes. Although your doctors are obligated to follow your instructions instead of risking a confrontation, they may defer to your family's demand for an expansive reading of the treatment authorized by your living will. (After all, they don't want a lawsuit!) Discussing your wishes with your family makes it more likely that they will respect them.

- ✔ **Your medical advocate:** Even the best living wills can be ambiguous, and the holder of your healthcare proxy is the person authorized to clarify your intentions when you are no longer able. You want to be certain that your medical advocate understands your motives and goals for end-of-life care. By discussing your wishes with your medical advocate, you can *both* be confident that your wishes will be followed.

- ✔ **Your doctor:** Before you execute your living will, discuss your ideas with your doctor. Your doctor can help ensure that healthcare professionals will understand your instructions. If you have a medical condition, your doctor can talk to you about your treatment options so that you can decide whether you want to mandate a particular course of treatment. Your doctor may also alert you to provisions in your living will that may cause some health facilities to reject it. Although the issue doesn't arise often and a medical facility should warn you on admission that they have moral objections to your living will, by that time, you may not be able to arrange for alternate care.

Executing a living will

The best starting place for creating a living will is to use a form that has been pre-approved for your state. You can also benefit from looking at living wills that, although not in the standard format, demonstrate how people modify that format to better reflect their wishes and desires. State living will forms and additional customized examples are provided on the accompanying CD. You can customize your living will to suit your needs.

To complete a standard-form living will, simply follow the instructions that accompany the form. You provide information about yourself and your wishes and then execute your living will in front of witnesses or a notary public.

Follow the witnessing instructions for your state. Most states require that two disinterested witnesses sign your living will, meaning that these witnesses should not have any stake in your medical care and should not be receiving anything from your estate. Your witnesses should also be adults who are competent to testify in court. You can use a friend as a witness as long as they're not inheriting anything from your estate.

Your living will is interpreted under the laws of the state where you receive medical care. Although in most cases state laws will be very similar, if you move to another state, you should review your living will.

Moral objections to living wills

Doctors may have moral or religious objections to carrying out the instructions in your living will. This situation is most likely to happen with end-of-life care where your living will describes treatment choices that the doctor sees as accelerating death. If you discuss your wishes with your doctor and your doctor objects to your choices, you may want to change doctors.

The doctor's objections will depend upon your medical condition, as well as the types of treatment that you want to avoid. Your primary care physician can help you anticipate which health-care facilities are likely to take issue with your living will, and you can take that information into consideration when drafting your health-care proxy or choosing where to receive your medical care.

Distributing copies of your living will

You should keep your original living will at home. Provide copies to the following parties:

- ✔ Your medical advocate
- ✔ Any family members you want to know of your wishes
- ✔ Any other people you want to know of your wishes
- ✔ Your personal physician
- ✔ If applicable, the medical facility where you're receiving treatment

Discussing your living will with your family helps ensure that they understand your wishes and won't fight against them if something happens to you.

In order for your living will to be effective, your healthcare provider must know about it and have a copy. You should ask that the copy you provide be included in your chart.

If you're not currently receiving medical treatment and are drafting your living will as a precaution, you'll want your living will to be provided to any treatment facility you later enter. Your facility is most likely to receive a copy if you make sure that your doctor and family possess copies of your living will.

Reviewing your living will

As your life circumstances change, your wishes for the final stages of your life may change as well. You should review your living will every few years to make sure that it remains consistent with your wishes.

Your most recent living will is the one that is legally binding, but you must take care that nobody will inadvertently rely upon a copy of a prior version.

To update your living will, or if you no longer want a living will, you should do the following:

- ✔ Destroy your old living will and all copies.
- ✔ Notify your medical advocate of your decision.
- ✔ Provide written notice to any healthcare providers who possess your old living will and, if you're updating it, provide them with copies of the new living will.

If you're unable to revoke your living will in writing, perhaps due to a stroke or spinal cord injury, you can tell your medical advocate, family members, and doctors that you've changed your mind. They will follow your wishes, but you must be careful to be sure that your instructions reach the people who will be relying upon your living will, and that your new wishes are understood.

Looking into Other Advance Directives

Although the most common advance medical directive is the living will, you can create advance directives for other medical situations. For example, if you are undergoing surgery, you may want to create an advance directive describing what you want to happen during any period of incapacity, such as when you're under anesthesia and unable to make or communicate medical decisions. The process for enacting this type of advance directive is the same as the process for creating a living will, described in this chapter in the section "Drafting a Living Will."

Healthcare proxies

Thanks to advances in medical care, you can expect to live longer lives than your ancestors did and to be significantly more active in your advanced years. At the same time, the medical technology exists to keep people alive long past the point where your ancestors would have died. This capability raises difficult questions of quality of life. For example:

- ✔ You may be confined to bed.
- ✔ You may be unable to feed yourself.
- ✔ You may not be able to bathe or groom yourself.
- ✔ You may require assistance to go to the toilet.
- ✔ You may not be aware of who you are.
- ✔ You may lose your ability to recognize friends and family.
- ✔ You may be unable to communicate.
- ✔ You may require invasive surgery to be kept alive.
- ✔ You may require major medical treatment, such as dialysis or chemotherapy.
- ✔ You may require artificial life support to be kept alive.

A *healthcare proxy* designates an individual, your *medical advocate,* who will make medical decisions on your behalf in the event that you become incapable of making those decisions. This person may sometimes be referenced as your *healthcare agent* or *medical proxy.* (The CD contains worksheets for planning and preparing your healthcare proxy.) See next section for more on your medical advocate.

You have the right to direct your own health care, and your healthcare proxy helps ensure that your wishes are followed.

Don't wait until you're about to enter a hospital for treatment before executing a healthcare proxy. Create your proxy when you have the luxury of time to think about what you desire and can discuss your wishes with your family, friends, and physician.

Your medical advocate

Your medical advocate doesn't have any control over your medical care while you're competent to make those choices yourself. Upon your incapacity, your medical advocate gains enormous power over your medical care. When you're not capable of communicating your wishes to your doctors, your medical advocate communicates with your doctors to express how you want to be treated.

Your medical advocate should be

- An adult
- Someone willing to serve in this capacity
- Someone available to authorize medical care if the need arises
- Someone who will work to fulfill your wishes, even under pressure from your other friends and family members

Many people select their spouse or one of their adult children as their medical advocate. Others select a close personal friend. Some people want to designate their personal physician, although this option isn't generally recommended and is forbidden by law in many states. If a physician serves as your medical advocate, that physician can't participate in your treatment.

When selecting your medical advocate:

- If possible, choose a medical advocate who resides near you so that in the event of your incapacity, he can visit you and consult with your doctors.
- Choose somebody who is aware of your personal values and beliefs and who you trust to act in accord with those beliefs.
- Choose somebody you trust to assert your wishes, even in the face of opposition from your family.
- If you can, designate a backup medical advocate, in case your first choice is unavailable or declines to serve in that capacity.
- As you get older, consider designating a medical advocate who is younger than you.

Some people are tempted to appoint joint medical advocates. If both advocates are authorized to act independently, this decision can result in healthcare providers receiving conflicting instructions. Where consent of both advocates is required, delay can result if one of the advocates can't be located. Having more than one person that you trust to be your medical advocate is a wonderful problem to have, but you're best off naming one person as your advocate and the other as a successor.

You should be comfortable discussing your health and medical needs with your medical advocate, and your advocate should be willing to discuss those issues with you. Topics to discuss include

- ✔ What do you believe constitutes artificial life support, and what are your feelings on being kept alive artificially?
- ✔ What level of surgical intervention is acceptable in order to keep you alive?
- ✔ What level of consciousness or ability to communicate do you consider to be essential to your quality of life?
- ✔ What level of capacity for self-care, including capacity to attend to your own personal hygiene, do you consider to be essential to your quality of life?

Your discussions should leave you reasonably confident that your medical advocate will carry out your wishes, even in unanticipated circumstances.

You can reassure your advocate that

- ✔ A medical advocate will not be held liable for medical decisions made in good faith.
- ✔ Serving as a medical advocate will not result in responsibility for the cost of your medical care.

It's crucial that you select a medical advocate that you trust to carry out your wishes. If you don't have a person you trust with these decisions, you should consider not having a medical advocate. While this decision may force a court action in the event of your incapacity, any court-appointed guardian will be supervised by and answerable to the court.

Special instructions: Your wishes for your care

Your medical advocate is obligated to respect your wishes when making medical decisions on your behalf. Absent a good faith belief of a change in circumstances or that your wishes had changed, to the maximum extent possible your medical advocate should follow your instructions as written.

You should address the following questions in your healthcare proxy:

✔ **When do you want the proxy to take effect?** You should describe the circumstances under which the healthcare proxy will take effect. Possible triggering events include

- Terminal illness

- Serious personal injury

- Significant brain damage with no expectation of recovery

- Being in a coma without an expectation that you will awaken

- Being in a persistent vegetative state with no reasonable expectation of improvement

- Total inability to care for yourself with no expectation of recovery

You can define as many or as few triggering circumstances as you desire.

✔ **Where do you want to live?** While your medical needs may take priority, you can define your preferred living circumstances in your healthcare proxy. When describing your preferences for your living arrangement:

- You can describe a preference for where you want to receive care, including care at home, in a nursing home, or in a rehabilitation center. For end-of-life care, you can express a preference for hospital, nursing home, hospice, or in-home care.

- You can designate a doctor or medical facility as preferred or to be avoided.

- You can grant your medical proxy broad discretion to select or discharge facilities and care providers.

- You can choose to authorize your medical advocate to move you to another city or state for treatment or to be with your family.

✔ **What type of medical treatment you desire?** Healthcare proxies are sometimes depicted as describing only the circumstances under which healthcare will be withdrawn. A healthcare proxy is much more flexible than you may realize, and you can use it to define the type of care you want to receive and your preferences when medical treatment may interfere with the quality of your life. For example:

- **Pain management:** You can express your pain management preferences, including whether you want to maximize pain relief even if it may interfere with your consciousness and awareness, or if you'll accept a greater amount of pain in order to remain more aware of your surroundings.

- **Side effects of medication:** You can describe side effects of medication that, if possible, you want to avoid, such as drowsiness, nausea, or hallucinations.

- **Acts or omissions that may shorten or prolong life:** You can specify what treatments you'd like in your final days of life, from a demand for any life-saving measure available to a request for an absolute minimum of medical intervention beyond your basic comfort.

- **Medical conditions:** You can also provide a context for treatment, such that you might desire life-prolonging care if you're reasonably mentally competent, but not if you're experiencing severe brain damage, dementia, or late-stage Alzheimer's disease.

Use your healthcare proxy to help your healthcare providers understand what you regard as quality of life and appropriate comfort care.

Medical treatment you don't want

If you don't define limits, your medical advocate can make any medical decision that, but for your incapacity, you could make for yourself. You can use your healthcare proxy to list treatments that you don't want to receive. Some common objections include

- ✔ Use of a respirator
- ✔ Use of dialysis
- ✔ Use of a feeding tube
- ✔ Resuscitation following cardiac arrest
- ✔ Invasive diagnostic procedures
- ✔ Blood transfusions or use of blood products

If you have personal, moral, or religious objections to certain medical treatments, you may want to describe your beliefs in relation to those treatments.

If you want to make healthcare providers and paramedics aware that they should not administer CPR, in addition to your healthcare proxy, you can execute a *Do Not Resuscitate (DNR) order.* You should be able to obtain the DNR form from your doctor or hospital, and it may require your doctor's signature. Once executed, you should keep the original DNR order on your person or in a conspicuous location so that paramedics will see it if they respond to your home. You may be able to obtain a DNR medical alert bracelet, which will help make paramedics aware of your wishes.

Instructions for organ or tissue donation

Your healthcare proxy can include instruction as to organ or tissue donation. You can also specify how your organs or tissues may be used, including for medical treatment, medical research, or education. You can also limit the use of your tissues and organs or express that you don't want to be a donor.

If you don't want to be an organ or tissue donor, you should state your opposition. Your silence about organ donation isn't an instruction against donation and thus doesn't prevent donation.

Executing a Healthcare Proxy

In most states, you must sign your healthcare proxy in front of two witnesses. Some states instead require you to sign before a notary. Still others require both witnesses and notarization.

Executing a healthcare proxy is a major decision. You should discuss your healthcare proxy with your family, friends, and physician before signing it. Don't sign your healthcare proxy until you're certain that it describes what you want from your care.

Distributing copies of your healthcare proxy

You should keep your healthcare proxy in a convenient, accessible location. Don't keep the original in a safe deposit box or other location where people won't be able to obtain it if you become incapacitated. You may choose to carry a copy with you in your wallet or purse.

You should provide copies of your healthcare proxy to

- Your medical advocate and alternate medical advocate
- Your personal physician
- Family members and close friends who you want to be informed of your wishes
- Any hospital or clinic where you will receive treatment

You can also provide a copy to your lawyer. If you're active in a religion, you can choose to provide a copy to your church leader.

Revoking a healthcare proxy

As with any estate planning document, you should periodically review your healthcare proxy to make sure that it remains consistent with your wishes. Unless otherwise specified, your medical proxy is indefinite in its duration.

If you change your mind about having a healthcare proxy or want to change its terms or the designated medical advocate, you will need to revoke your proxy. You can do so by

- Providing oral notice
- Giving written notice
- Executing a new healthcare proxy

 To be sure that your revocation is effective, either destroy the old healthcare proxy or clearly label it as Revoked. You should provide notice of the revocation to your medical advocate, your physician, any person who helped you draft your healthcare proxy, and any person who possesses a copy of your proxy. If you've executed a new healthcare proxy, you can distribute copies of the new document.

You can also provide within your healthcare proxy for its automatic termination, as in the following circumstances:

- **The passage of time:** You can choose to have your healthcare proxy expire at a particular date or after a specified number of years.

- **Divorce or separation:** If you've designated your spouse as your medical advocate or as the alternate, you may want to include a provision terminating the healthcare proxy upon divorce or separation. In most states, divorce will automatically terminate the ex-spouse as a medical advocate or alternate. In some states, termination also occurs upon legal separation from your spouse.

You can also indicate that you don't want an event such as divorce to end your medical proxy so that your former spouse can continue to serve even if state law would otherwise have terminated the proxy.

Designating Your Financial Powers of Attorney

A *power of attorney* is a legal document you can use to grant legal authority to another person. When you execute a power of attorney, you're called the *principal.* The person to whom you grant legal authority is called your *attorney-in-fact,* your agent, or your proxy. Your power of attorney defines the powers of the agent, as well as any limits you want to place on that person's authority.

A durable power of attorney remains valid even after the principal becomes legally incapacitated. The durable power of attorney authorizes your agent to manage your estate in the event of your incapacity, without going to court. Although your durable power of attorney appears to give your agent immediate power over your assets, as long as you remain competent your agent must follow your instructions. (The CD contains worksheets for planning and preparing your durable power of attorney.)

The authority granted by a durable power of attorney terminates upon your death. If you want your agent to handle matters after your death, such as funeral arrangements, payment of bills, or the distribution of inheritances to your heirs, use your will to designate that person as executor of your estate.

A *nondurable power of attorney* becomes invalid if you lose mental capacity. This type of power of attorney is typically granted for a specific purpose — for example, during the principal's temporary absence from the country — or for a specific purpose, such as to sign legal documents on behalf of the principal in a specified legal transaction. You should include a termination provision, specifying a date upon which the power of attorney will expire.

A *springing power of attorney* doesn't become effective until a specified condition has been met. For example, a springing durable power of attorney may provide that it becomes effective only upon a determination by a physician that the principal is mentally incompetent.

Financial institutions may be hesitant to accept a springing power of attorney, due to uncertainty as to whether the principal has truly been determined mentally incompetent. Not all states permit springing durable powers of attorney.

Selecting power of attorney

Your agent should be a legally competent adult. Your agent will have a great deal of control over your assets and ordinarily serves without any oversight. As with your healthcare proxy, you should select somebody who you trust. Frequent choices are a spouse or domestic partner, relative, or close friend. In making your selection, consider the following:

✔ Do you trust this person with your assets?

✔ Is this person willing to serve?

✔ Does this person have the time to serve?

✔ Is this person capable of performing the tasks necessary to manage your estate?

✔ Will distance make it inconvenient for this person to manage your estate?

✔ Is this person likely to have financial interests that compete with or are in conflict with your own?

✔ Does this person's financial history reflect financial stability or money problems?

✔ Are you comfortable discussing the power of attorney with this person?

You should also designate an alternate agent in case your first choice becomes unwilling or unable to serve your estate. If no designated person is available to serve as agent, your power of attorney will fail.

Some people designate more than one agent. Joint appointments aren't permitted in all states. If you choose this approach you must indicate in the power of attorney whether your attorneys-in-fact may act independently or if they must agree prior to taking action. When you appoint joint attorneys-in-fact, you create a risk that they may not cooperate or communicate, or will make decisions in conflict with each other. Where joint consent is required, obtaining signatures from both attorneys-in-fact may result in delay.

Any attorney who works in this area can share horror stories about attorneys-in-fact who looted the estate they were supposed to safeguard. If you're unable to find somebody you believe is sufficiently trustworthy and capable of managing your assets, you should consider other options, including requiring your agent to post a bond or foregoing a power of attorney in favor of the appointment of a conservator by a court.

Deciding between durable powers of attorney or periodic renewal

Historically, states required that powers of attorney be periodically renewed in order to remain valid. The durable power of attorney is recognized in all states and doesn't require renewal. However, not all states recognize springing durable powers of attorney.

As a practical matter, you should periodically review your power of attorney and, as necessary, execute an updated version for several reasons:

✔ Some third parties may hesitate to accept a power of attorney that was executed many years before.

✔ Your wishes are likely to change over time.

✔ You should periodically review your choice of agent.

Drafting your durable power of attorney

A durable power of attorney usually gives very broad powers to the agent. In drafting your power of attorney, you have enormous flexibility in granting and limiting the powers of your agent and in instructing your agent as to your goals and wishes.

Some financial institutions may require that you use their power of attorney forms in order for them to recognize the authority of your agent. Check with your financial institutions to see whether they require the use of their form and, if so, complete and execute their forms in addition to your own power of attorney.

Determining which powers to grant

You choose the powers you grant to your agent. You'll likely choose to grant broad powers, but you have the option of providing narrow authority. Commonly granted powers include the authority to

- Manage your expenses and pay your bills
- Manage your real and personal property
- Manage your bank accounts and engage in banking transactions
- Manage your retirement accounts
- Access your safe deposit box
- Collect government benefits
- Invest your money
- Purchase insurance and annuities
- Pay taxes
- Make legal claims
- File and pursue lawsuits
- Purchase and sell real estate
- Maintain and improve real estate

You may also choose to grant authority to

- Operate your business
- Amend trust instruments
- Make personal use of certain assets of your estate

- Hire people to take care of you
- Appoint a successor agent
- Make gifts

You can authorize your agent to plan for the receipt of government benefits, such as Social Security, Medicare and Medicaid.

If you have a revocable living trust, you can authorize your agent to amend your trust. If you want to grant your agent that authority, you should explicitly grant the authority in your power of attorney document.

All powers you grant will end at the time of your death.

Placing limits on the authority of the agent

Your agent operates under a number of restrictions. Your agent

- May not make, amend, or revoke your will
- May not enact a healthcare proxy for you
- May not utilize the assets of your estate for personal benefit unless you have authorized the use
- May not receive payment for services performed for your estate unless authorized by you
- In some states, including Georgia and Florida, may not delegate the powers of the agent to other people

Your agent is restricted from using your assets for personal benefit. You should state in your power of attorney whether you authorize your agent to

- Make personal use of specific property or assets of your estate
- Personally benefit from transactions performed on behalf of the estate
- Borrow money from your estate at a customary rate of interest

If you authorize your agent to make gifts, be aware that the power to make gifts is easily abused. If you don't want your agent to be able to make gifts or donations from your assets, you should include that restriction in the power of attorney document.

If you want to grant gift-giving authority, you should specify any limits you want to place on who may receive a gift and the amounts that may be given. For example:

✔ You may limit gifts to members of your family, or to specified charities.

✔ You may limit the type of gifts that may be given — for example, birthday or Christmas presents.

✔ You may choose to permit gifts only to the extent necessary to achieve tax or Medicaid planning goals.

✔ You may forbid gifts that could increase tax exposure for your estate or potentially affect your eligibility for public benefits.

If you want your agent to be eligible to receive gifts, you should state that in your power of attorney.

Compensating the agent

You're not required to compensate your agent for time spent managing your estate, and many attorneys-in-fact perform their services without charge. Unless you specifically provide for payment, the agent won't be compensated for services performed for your estate.

If you specify an amount of compensation, the agent will receive the compensation you describe. You can, for example, specify compensation at an hourly rate or specify sums to be paid for specific services.

If you grant compensation but don't specify an amount, the agent will be entitled to reasonable fees for services provided. If services are performed while you remain competent, you and your agent should seek to agree on the fee to be paid. If not, a court may need to determine what fee is reasonable under the circumstances.

You can provide for your estate to reimburse your agent for the reasonable cost of services required by your estate. Such expenses may include

✔ Investment advice

✔ Professional trust or asset management

✔ Property management services

✔ Accounting and tax preparation services

Keeping records

Your agent should maintain records of your income, assets, expenditures, and financial transactions performed on your behalf. If you want to impose additional requirements, such as a periodic accounting of the estate, you can include that requirement in the power of attorney.

You can provide for compensation of your agent and reimbursement of expenses associated with any special recordkeeping or accounting requirements you impose.

Executing power of attorney

Depending upon your state, you must sign the power of attorney in the presence of two witnesses, a notary public, or both. Your witnesses should be legally competent adults. Consider having your power of attorney notarized even when it isn't required, as notarization can help convince third parties to accept your power of attorney.

You're required to sign one copy of your power of attorney and can designate that copies have the same authority as the original. Executing multiple originals is nonetheless common. Some organizations, such as financial institutions, will require that your agent provide them with an original copy of your power of attorney. Even if it will eventually be returned, it's important that your agent not be placed in the position of having to surrender his last or only original copy in order to gain authority over your accounts.

If you believe that somebody may challenge your mental capacity to execute a power of attorney, obtain a letter from a physician that confirms that you're mentally competent and are able to understand the power of attorney document.

Revoking a power of attorney

You should periodically review your power of attorney to make sure that it remains consistent with your wishes and to verify your choice of agent as well as of any successors. Review is appropriate after major changes in your life circumstances, such as divorce.

You can revoke your power of attorney by

- ✔ Incorporating a specific date of termination into the original grant document
- ✔ Providing notice to the agent or successor that you're terminating their authority
- ✔ In some states, by filing a formal notice of revocation with the recorder of deeds in the city or county where you live

Revocation will also occur

- ✔ If your designated agent and successors are unwilling or unable to serve
- ✔ In some states, if your agent is your spouse and the power of attorney doesn't provide otherwise, upon initiation of divorce proceedings
- ✔ Upon your death

When revoking a power of attorney, you should provide written notice of revocation to

- ✔ Your agent
- ✔ Every person who possesses a copy of your power of attorney
- ✔ Any bank or financial institution where your agent may have used the power of attorney
- ✔ If applicable in your state, the recorder of deeds in the city or county where you live, and in any county where you own real estate

Your notice should request that recipients return to you any copies of the power of attorney that are in their possession.

If you're revoking the authority of your agent, send notice of revocation by certified mail, with a return receipt requested.

Chapter 15

Those Cushy Retirement Funds

• •

• •

*I*f you're like most people, you're putting money into retirement savings accounts so that you can support your lifestyle after you retire. This chapter outlines the most common types of retirement savings accounts and the benefits of tax-deferred savings. You find out how to change your beneficiary and the importance of keeping records when you change your beneficiary.

You may want to leave your retirement accounts to your spouse, another beneficiary or beneficiaries, or even a charity. At times, you may want your retirement funds to go into a trust fund or into your estate. This chapter helps you understand the advantages and disadvantages of each of those choices, including income and estate tax consequences.

Exploring Retirement Savings Accounts

Retirement savings accounts come in a variety of forms. The type (or types) you have will depend upon what your employer has made available, whether you chose to take advantage of those savings opportunities, whether you opened any retirement savings accounts of your own, and whether you took advantage of your retirement savings options during any periods of self-employment.

You have a lot to gain by contributing to retirement savings accounts. Beyond the obvious:

- ✔ Your contributions grow tax-free.

- ✔ The earlier you start saving, the more years your savings will continue to compound and grow.

- ✔ Your contribution of pretax dollars may result in immediate income tax savings.

- ✔ Your retirement savings accounts are usually shielded from your creditors.

- ✔ Withdrawals from retirement accounts funded with money that has already been subject to income tax are made free of income tax.

If you're not yet retired, you have the opportunity for additional retirement savings. Choosing the right account may help you maximize your returns.

Retirement savings accounts fall into three main categories:

- ✔ Retirement accounts anybody may use

- ✔ Employment-based retirement accounts

- ✔ Self-employed retirement accounts

The different types of retirement savings accounts have a lot of features in common, but you should be aware of the key differences:

- ✔ While most retirement savings accounts are tax-deferred, some are funded with post-tax dollars.

- ✔ Limits on contributions can vary significantly, depending upon the type of account and your income.

- ✔ Some retirement plans can be rolled over to a spouse or other designated beneficiary, giving them some or all of the benefits of tax-deferral. Other plans are more restrictive as to if and when they may be rolled over to a beneficiary.

You may be able to participate in more than one retirement savings plan. Be aware that your contributions to one plan may reduce the amount you're eligible to contribute to another plan or reduce the amount of your tax-deferment for another plan.

Under some circumstances, the IRS will waive penalties for early withdrawals from your retirement savings. For example, you may be allowed to withdraw money to pay for certain medical costs or disabilities, certain higher education expenses, or the purchase of a first home. Unless you're prepared to pay a penalty, you should be certain that your withdrawal won't trigger a penalty *before* you withdraw the funds.

Retirement savings accounts available to anyone

The two plans you've probably heard the most about are the Individual Retirement Account (IRA) and the Roth IRA. These plans are very similar, with this key difference:

- ✔ You fund your traditional IRA with pretax dollars and pay income tax on money when you withdraw it from the account.

- ✔ You fund your Roth IRA with post-tax dollars and don't pay income tax on your withdrawals.

Going traditional

As long as you're below the age of 70½ and have earned income, the traditional IRA is available to you. It has the following features:

- ✔ Contributions are tax-deductible, with taxes on contributions and interest deferred until you withdraw money.

- ✔ You may contribute earned income, up to $5,000 each year. That cap will be increased by a cost of living adjustment starting in 2009.

- ✔ It's no harder to start a traditional IRA than it is to open a bank account.

- ✔ Early withdrawals from an IRA, taken before you reach the age of 59½, are subject to a penalty.

- ✔ You must start taking withdrawals at the age of 70½ , whether or not you're retired.

- ✔ A traditional IRA may be rolled over only into another traditional IRA or a SEP-IRA or may be converted and rolled over into Roth IRA.

Choosing a Roth IRA

The Roth IRA is very similar to a traditional IRA, but your eligibility phases out based upon your income:

- ✔ Contributions are made with post-tax dollars. Your account balance grows tax-free, and you pay no income tax on withdrawals.

- ✔ The basic limit on contribution is $5,000. That cap will be increased by a cost of living adjustment starting in 2009.

- ✔ Roth IRA contributions are subject to income limits, and your maximum contribution is phased out as you exceed those limits.

✔ Early withdrawals from a Roth IRA, taken before you reach the age of 59½, are subject to a penalty.

✔ A Roth IRA may be rolled over only into another Roth IRA.

If you've reached the age of 50, you can make a catch-up contribution to either a traditional or Roth IRA, which means that in 2008, your contributions are capped at $6,000 instead of $5,000. Regardless of your age, contributions to your Roth IRA remain subject to income limits.

Employment-based retirement savings accounts

The most common employer-sponsored retirement plan is the 401(k) plan. Employers often contribute to these plans on behalf of employees, perhaps matching an employee's contribution. Here's what you need to know:

✔ Contributions are made with pretax dollars, with taxes on contributions and interest deferred until you withdraw money.

✔ As of 2008, you can contribute $15,500 per year to your 401(k) account. If you're over age 50, that amount increases to $20,500. Starting in 2009, these amounts are subject to cost of living increases.

✔ You may borrow against the balance of your 401(k) account.

✔ When you change jobs, you can normally roll your 401(k) over into your new employer's retirement plan or into an IRA.

✔ You must ordinarily start taking withdrawals after you reach the age of 70½, whether or not you're retired.

A relatively new variation of the 401(k) plan is the Roth 401(k). The key difference is that the Roth 401(k) is funded with after-tax earnings. Your balance grows tax-free. Once you reach the age of 59½, you can make withdrawals without penalty and without owing any income tax. You can also avoid the requirement that you take withdrawals at age 70½ by rolling your Roth 401(k) into a Roth IRA.

If you work for an educational institution, museum, or nonprofit organization, your employer may offer a 403(b) plan. These accounts are very similar to 401(k) plans. The primary difference is that some employers offer poor oversight of investment options, resulting in excessive fees or poor returns for employees.

If you work for the government or for certain tax-exempt organizations, you may participate in a 457(b) plan. These plans are again extremely similar to 401(k) plans. 457(b) plans also have special catch-up rules, permitting employees to catch up for years in which they weren't able to make the maximum contribution to their plan. Government employees may reap special advantages from these plans, by being exempted from penalties for early withdrawal upon their retirement, even if they retire before the age of 59½.

Additional retirement savings plans that may be offered by employers include profit-sharing plans, in which the employer gives participating employees a share of its profits, and SIMPLE IRA plans, in which the employer facilitates the employee's participation in an account analogous to a traditional IRA.

Self-employed retirement savings accounts

The most common savings plans used by self-employed people are the Keogh plan, the Solo 401(k), and the Simplified Employee Pension plan (SEP IRA).

These plans may also be used to benefit employees of small businesses. If you have employees, in order to take advantage of your own retirement savings options, you may also be required to contribute to your employee's retirement plans. As a small employer, you should discuss your options and obligations with your accountant or a retirement planning professional.

All of these plans cap contributions, with solo 401(k) plans offering the most generous caps on tax-deductible contributions. Under present rules, if you're 50 or older, you may qualify to make higher catch up contributions to each of these retirement plans.

Keogh plan

A Keogh plan, sometimes called an HR 10 plan, is available to sole proprietors and business partnerships. You can set up a Keogh plan as either a defined benefit plan or a defined contribution plan:

- In a **defined benefit plan,** you receive a predetermined benefit at the end of the plan.
- In a **defined contribution plan,** your contributions are defined by the plan and your benefits are determined by the balance of your account at retirement.

The key aspects of a Keogh plan are as follows:

- Contributions are made with pretax dollars, with taxes on contributions and interest deferred until you withdraw money.

✔ Contribution limits are more generous than the limits for standard IRAs, with the contribution limit for 2008 being set at $46,000 or 100 percent of your eligible compensation, whichever is less. Even if you contribute a greater amount, your tax-deductible contribution is limited to 25 percent of your eligible compensation as defined by your plan. For self-employed people, your eligible compensation will typically be your net earnings for services provided to your business after your retirement contribution is deducted. (Investment income isn't eligible.)

✔ Keogh plans can be costly and cumbersome to create and maintain, particularly as compared to a SEP IRA.

✔ Early withdrawals from a Keogh plan, taken before you reach the age of 59½, are subject to a penalty.

✔ If you own more than 5 percent of your business, you must start taking withdrawals from your account no later than April 1 of the year after you reach the age of 70½, whether or not you're retired.

SEP IRA

The Simplified Employee Pension Plan (SEP IRA) is intended for self-employed people and small businesses. These plans are very similar to conventional IRAs, but have much higher contribution limits.

✔ Contributions are made with pretax dollars, with taxes on contributions and interest deferred until you withdraw money.

✔ Contribution limits are more generous than the limits for standard IRAs, with the contribution limit for 2008 being set at the lesser of $46,000 or 25 percent of your compensation.

✔ SEP IRAs are easy to create and maintain.

✔ Early withdrawals from a SEP IRA, taken before you reach the age of 59½, are subject to a penalty.

✔ You must start taking withdrawals from your account no later than April 1 of the year after you reach the age of 70½, whether or not you're retired.

Solo 401(k) plan

A Solo 401(k) plan is very similar to any other 401(k) plan. If you're able to make large contributions to your plan, a solo 401(k) permits contributions significantly larger than those permitted under Keogh plans and SEP IRAs. Here's what you need to know:

✔ Contributions are made with pretax dollars, with taxes on contributions and interest deferred until you withdraw money.

✔ Based upon 2008 limits, you may contribute up to 100 percent of the first $15,500 of your compensation. You may further contribute up to 25 percent of your compensation income or 20 percent of your self-employment income.

- Solo 401(k) plans are more cumbersome to create and maintain than a SEP IRA, although the process isn't particularly complicated or expensive if you don't have employees.

- You may be able to borrow money from your Solo 401(k) plan.

- Early withdrawals from a Solo 401(k), taken before you reach the age of 59½, are subject to a penalty.

- You must start taking withdrawals from your account no later than April 1 of the year after you reach the age of 70½, whether or not you're retired.

If you hire a full-time employee who isn't your spouse, expect that you will have to include your employee in your Solo 401(k) plan. That will end its status as a solo plan and make administration of the plan much more complicated.

Putting Off the Tax Man

Most retirement savings accounts allow for tax-deferred savings, which doesn't mean that you never pay taxes on your retirement savings. It means that although you don't pay income tax on your money at the time you put it into your account, you pay income tax on the money you eventually withdraw from the account.

Tax deferral gives you an upfront benefit by reducing your taxable income. Your investment grows tax-free, so it compounds more rapidly than a taxable investment. But tax deferral doesn't help you in the event of economic downturn, such that your savings don't grow or even shrink in value.

When evaluating the benefits of tax-deferral, you also need to estimate what your tax rate will be at the time you make withdrawals. If your tax rate isn't likely to go down when you retire, consider investing some of your retirement savings in accounts that aren't tax-deferred.

Moving Assets from One Tax-Deferred Investment to Another

A *rollover* is the tax-free transfer of assets from one tax-free or tax-deferred retirement account into another. After the rollover, your savings continue to grow in the new account on a tax-deferred basis.

During your lifetime, you may have to roll over your retirement savings when you change jobs. If you're required to roll over your accounts and don't do so in a timely manner, usually 60 days, your account balance is taxed as income.

Rollover may occur in two ways:

- ✔ A *direct rollover*, or plan-to-plan transfer, occurs when the eligible funds are directly transferred from your employer-sponsored plan to the new qualifying retirement savings account.

- ✔ An *indirect transfer* occurs when your employer-sponsored plan issues you a check for the account balance. You then have a limited amount of time to transfer part or all of that money into your new qualifying retirement savings account.

If you have to roll over your account due to a change of employment, your employers may assist you with the process through a direct rollover.

If you're rolling over your self-employed retirement accounts or are becoming self-employed, avoid mistakes: Discuss the process with a retirement planning professional.

When you die, your account beneficiary may also seek to roll over any balance of your retirement accounts. Not all accounts are eligible for rollover, so you should discuss this point with your retirement planning professional.

When permitted, rollover is easiest if your beneficiary is your spouse. Normally, once the rollover into your spouse's account is complete, the IRS treats the money as if it was contributed by your spouse. With IRA accounts, it's also possible for your IRA to be treated as if it was the surviving spouse's account.

Rules are different for nonspouse beneficiaries. Although recent legislation attempted to make retirement account rollovers easier, the IRS has interpreted the legislation very narrowly. As a consequence, eligibility to roll over your account to anybody other than a spouse, including your domestic partner, children, or grandchildren, is subject to the rules of the account. Even if your account presently permits a nonspouse rollover, those rules may later change, disqualifying your beneficiary from the benefits of rollover. If your account doesn't permit nonspouse rollover, your beneficiary will be forced to withdraw the entire balance within a few years after your death.

Rules may apply requiring your nonspouse beneficiary to start withdrawing funds from the account and to withdraw all funds within the space of a few years. For an IRA, that normally means that the nonspouse has to start taking withdrawals from your rolled over funds by December 31 of the year following your death and withdraw all funds within five years.

Be aware of the many potential traps in rolling over a retirement account to a nonspouse. A mistake can make the money immediately taxable. If you intend to designate a nonspouse beneficiary for your retirement accounts, consult a retirement planning professional to make sure that it's done correctly.

Designating a Beneficiary

Whatever retirement savings account you choose, you'll have to name a beneficiary for your account. Your beneficiary will receive the account balance upon your death, without its going through probate. He may also be able to benefit from rollover rules and continued tax deferral (see the preceding section).

Selecting your beneficiary

Choosing a beneficiary for your retirement account isn't much different from choosing a beneficiary for your insurance policies or other assets (see Chapter 16). If you're married, you'll probably name your spouse as your primary beneficiary.

You're not limited to selecting a single beneficiary. You can designate more than one person as your primary beneficiary. If you designate multiple beneficiaries, you should also designate the percentage of your account that you want to go to each beneficiary.

Pitfalls of beneficiary designation forms

Under a standard beneficiary designation form, your alternate beneficiaries don't qualify to receive anything from your account while any of your primary beneficiaries remains alive. If you designate your children as your primary beneficiaries and your grandchildren as alternate beneficiaries, your grandchildren don't automatically receive the share of their deceased parent.

Your beneficiary designation form may also not remind you of the possibility of choosing a charity as your beneficiary, even though such a designation may produce significant tax advantages for your estate.

If the standard form doesn't suit your needs, contact the plan administrator to see whether it has an alternate form that will accommodate you. If not, designate your beneficiaries the way you want, return the form, and confirm with the plan administrator that your beneficiary designation has been accepted and processed.

When you designate a beneficiary other than your spouse, you need to consider the rollover rules for your account. You also need to consider the tax consequences of your designation. Think about the following questions:

- ✔ Does your plan permit rollover by a nonspouse?
- ✔ Will your gift trigger estate tax liability for your estate?
- ✔ How quickly will the recipient have to withdraw funds from a tax-deferred account, and what are the income tax consequences?
- ✔ If you leave your account to your grandchildren, will you trigger generation-skipping taxes (see Chapter 6)?

If you have substantial retirement savings that you believe will be passed on to an heir other than your spouse, it makes sense to discuss your plan with a tax professional. You can name a trust as beneficiary, but you again need to be careful about tax consequences. Some specially designed trusts, such as the IRA inheritor's trust, are designed to stretch out the income distributions so as to minimize income taxes, while also offering asset protection benefits to your beneficiaries. If you're considering using a trust as a beneficiary, consult an estate planning professional.

You should keep a copy of your beneficiary designation forms with your financial records. That way, in the event of confusion about your beneficiary designation after your death, your personal representative has clear record of your choice. All bureaucracies make mistakes, and that includes the one holding your retirement savings account. If your estate is unable to establish that you submitted the change of beneficiary form prior to your death, your savings account will likely pass to the prior beneficiary.

You should periodically verify your beneficiary designation with the institution that holds your retirement savings account. That way, if any information is lost from your account, you'll discover the omission and be able to correct the error.

Loss of rollover rights to your spouse's account

As a general rule, any money remaining in your retirement accounts may be rolled over into your spouse's retirement account, without being treated as a withdrawal, allowing your estate to avoid paying income taxes on your tax-deferred savings and maximizing the benefit of those savings to your spouse.

When you designate somebody other than your spouse, these advantages are lost. Thus, if you can choose between leaving the nonspouse the retirement account or a gift of approximately equal value, in most cases you're better off keeping your spouse as your primary beneficiary and giving the nonspouse the alternate bequest.

Limits on who you may select as a beneficiary

States are concerned that upon your death, you might impoverish your spouse, which is why they restrict your ability to cut your spouse out of your will. The same applies within the context of retirement accounts. You should expect that you're required to designate your spouse as the sole beneficiary of your qualified retirement plan. Even if that designation isn't a requirement, your spouse may have an interest in your retirement plan under the community or marital property laws of your state.

If you want to designate a beneficiary other than your spouse, you may have to get your spouse's consent. If consent is required, your spouse can sign a waiver form permitting you to designate somebody else.

Why it's wise to select alternate beneficiaries

The primary reason to designate an alternate beneficiary is that your beneficiary may not survive you. Although unusual, sometimes your beneficiary will decline your gift. If you don't designate an alternate beneficiary, your retirement account will go into your estate, with the following consequences:

- ✔ Inclusion of your retirement account in your estate will probably trigger a large income tax bill and possibly even estate taxes.

- ✔ In states where your personal representative or the attorney for your estate are paid a percentage of the value of your estate, this event may significantly inflate their fees when your estate is probated.

Changing your beneficiaries

Changing beneficiaries is usually as simple as filling out a form, and returning it to the plan administrator or the institution where your account is held. If your plan is employment-based, ask your plan administrator for a form. Otherwise, ask the institution holding your retirement savings account.

Don't simply send a letter asking that your beneficiary be changed. Use the approved form and follow the instructions accompanying the form. Otherwise, your change of beneficiary may not be successful or may be subject to challenge by the original beneficiary. After you submit the change of beneficiary, verify that the form has been received and processed.

Maintaining Control Over Your Accounts

If you want to maintain control over your retirement account funds after your death, you can do so by designating either your estate or a trust fund as your beneficiary.

Some trust funds, such as the IRA inheritor's trust, try to preserve some of the benefits of tax deferral while limiting your heirs' access to the funds. Forming specialized trust funds for the purpose of avoiding or delaying taxes can be complex and is best done with the help of an estate planning professional.

If you're not concerned about the tax consequences to your estate, you're free to designate any trust, including your revocable living trust, as the beneficiary of your account. After taxes are paid, distribution of the remaining funds will be subject to any restrictions and conditions you have incorporated into your trust. (For more information on drafting your trust, see Chapter 11.)

Similarly, once the money is part of your estate, you can make conditional gifts through your will so that your heirs don't receive their bequest until your conditions are met. (For more information on placing conditions on testamentary gifts, see Chapter 8.)

The Tax Consequences of Putting Your Retirement Savings into Your Estate

If you designate your estate as the beneficiary of your retirement account, the balance of that account will go into your taxable estate. This can also happen if you don't name an alternate beneficiary, and your primary beneficiary dies before you do. Your estate will then owe income taxes on any tax-deferred balance and may also owe estate taxes.

If you don't designate a beneficiary, depending upon the terms of the account, your spouse may be treated as your beneficiary, or the balance may go into your estate with the same result.

Naming a nonspouse as your beneficiary will save your estate from paying income tax on your retirement account balance, but it won't keep the balance out of your taxable estate.

If your spouse is the beneficiary of your retirement account, the balance will pass to your spouse free of estate taxes. Your spouse can then take advantage of rollover rules to avoid paying income tax. But remember, the balance of your retirement account then becomes part of your spouse's estate and may be subject to estate taxes upon the death of your spouse.

You may also consider designating a tax-exempt organization as your beneficiary. Due to its tax exemption, the organization won't pay any income tax on your gift, and the balance of your account won't be included in your taxable estate.

Chapter 16

Life Insurance: Making Sure It Doesn't Backfire

. . . .

In This Chapter

▶ Understanding different types of life insurance

▶ Owning a life insurance policy

▶ Choosing your beneficiary

▶ Avoiding estate taxes

. . . .

*L*ife insurance can be a powerful tool in your estate plan. Even though it's probably not mentioned in your will or living trust, your life insurance can torpedo your estate plan.

When planning your estate, you need to understand the different types of life insurance and which type best suits your needs. You must also consider how ownership of the policy and your choice of beneficiary can affect your estate and create possible estate tax liability. You should also think about how your will or trust, as well as a probate court, handle insurance proceeds.

Taking a Look at the Different Types of Life Insurance

You know you need insurance, but what happens when you talk to your insurance agent or financial planner? You're presented with an assortment of options, and knowing which ones fit your needs is hard.

For most life insurance policies, you have to pass a medical screening when you apply, answering questions about your health and possibly obtaining a medical examination. If you have serious medical problems, you may be disqualified from life insurance, or it may become unaffordable. You can find life insurance policies that don't require health information, but they'll provide a limited death benefit.

Your premiums are affected by factors including your health history, your family's health history, your age, and whether you're a smoker. You may be asked about lifestyle choices and whether you participate in high-risk activities, such as skydiving, auto racing, rock climbing, or flying.

Premiums are normally paid on a periodic basis, usually monthly or annually. You may be able to find *single premium insurance*, where you pay a lump sum premium when you open the policy and aren't required to make any additional premium payments.

You can purchase your own separate life insurance policy, or you can purchase a joint policy with your spouse. If you buy a joint policy, you can choose between a *first-to-die policy,* which pays a death benefit when one of you dies, or *second-to-die* (also called *last survivor*) insurance, which pays a death benefit only after both you and your spouse die.

Life insurance falls into two broad categories: term life and permanent life insurance. A *term life insurance* policy provides coverage for a fixed period of time. *Permanent life insurance* accumulates value and (assuming premiums are paid) provides an eventual payout or death benefit. The three types of permanent life insurance are whole life, universal life, and variable life.

For estate planning purposes, permanent life insurance is usually your best option.

When planning your estate, consider the following factors when purchasing life insurance:

- ✔ The benefit of cash value accumulation and the opportunity to borrow against your policy or withdraw cash
- ✔ Your ability to later transfer ownership to another person or to a trust
- ✔ Whether the policy will remain in effect and also remain affordable throughout your lifetime

The following sections go through the types of insurance in more detail.

Term life

Term life insurance provides you with a death benefit during the period of time that your policy is in effect. If you die during the period of coverage, your beneficiary receives the death benefit (the value of the policy). If you don't die during the period of coverage, your coverage expires.

Your premium goes to the insurance company's expenses and profit, as well as to pay benefits to other insured people who die within the period of coverage. As you get older, your premium may increase. A term life policy has no value after your coverage expires.

Your death benefit may be fixed (level) throughout the term of your policy, or it may decrease over the term of your policy. Decreasing term life insurance may be appropriate if your financial needs will diminish over time.

Your term life policy may be renewable or nonrenewable. If your policy is renewable, you automatically qualify to continue the policy when your current term expires. If your policy isn't renewable, you must qualify for a new policy in order to continue coverage.

Some term life policies are *convertible,* meaning that you're allowed to convert the policy to whole life or variable life without answering health questions, as long as your policy remains in effect.

Whole life

A whole life policy provides insurance coverage for your whole life, rather than for a specific coverage period. It has the following characteristics:

- ✔ Your premium is greater than the cost to the insurer of providing your insurance coverage. The extra amount you pay goes into a cash value account.

- ✔ Your cash value account is invested by your insurance company and grows in value. You don't control how your money is invested.

- ✔ During your life, you can borrow against your cash value account, or you can surrender part or all of your policy and receive a payout from your cash value account. If you surrender insurance coverage, you terminate part or all of your death benefit.

- ✔ When the policy reaches its maturity date, the insurance company will pay the accumulated cash value to you. This amount is equal to your death benefit.

The maturity date for your policy will probably be age 100, or possibly an even greater age.

Universal life

Universal life insurance is very similar to whole life coverage, except you get greater flexibility in making premium payments. Your policy will usually define minimum and maximum premiums you may contribute, but you can pay any premium you choose within that range.

If you pay greater premiums, the cash value of the policy should grow faster, and you may also be able to increase your death benefit. However, you may have to undergo a medical screening in order to increase your coverage. If the value of your cash value account drops below a certain threshold, your policy may lapse.

Universal life policies may offer an enhanced benefit option, at an additional cost. If you choose this option, your beneficiary will receive both the death benefit from your policy and the accumulated cash value of your policy. Thus, if you have a $1 million death benefit and have accumulated $250,000 in cash value at the time you die, your beneficiary receives $1.25 million.

Variable life

A traditional variable life insurance policy is similar to whole life insurance. (See the "Whole life" section earlier in this chapter.) The key difference is that you choose how the money in your cash value account is invested. Your variable life policy has a fixed premium for the life of the policy. Your policy may offer a minimum guaranteed death benefit. If the cash value of your account exceeds a specified threshold, your death benefit increases.

You can also choose variable universal life insurance. As with universal life insurance, you choose the amount of your premium within a range specified in your policy. You can borrow against your policy and make cash withdrawals. Withdrawals may reduce the face value of your policy and may also be taxed. The policy will have a fixed death benefit, and you may be able to choose an enhanced death benefit.

Like whole life insurance, if the value of the cash value account drops below a certain threshold, your policy may lapse. Following a period of years defined by the policy, many variable universal life insurance policies guarantee a minimum death benefit without regard to the performance of your investments.

Variable life insurance policies often have very high management fees as compared to other forms of permanent life insurance.

Deciding Who Owns the Life Insurance

Every life insurance policy has at least one owner, named insured, and beneficiary. If the policy doesn't identify a separate owner, the insured is the owner of the policy. The owner pays the premiums, chooses the beneficiary, and, unless the initial designation of beneficiary is irrevocable, may change the beneficiary. The beneficiary receives the proceeds of the policy when the insured dies.

You may not give much thought to who owns your life insurance policy. You bought it, so you own it, right? Actually, there's a good chance that you don't want to own your policy. If you own the policy, your life insurance proceeds are part of your estate and may be subject to estate taxes.

Before you get excited about giving away your policies, keep in mind the advantages of continued ownership:

- ✔ When you own your policy, you control it, and you choose your beneficiaries.
- ✔ You can borrow against the cash value of your policy.
- ✔ For some policies, you can choose an investment strategy.
- ✔ You determine how your beneficiaries will receive the proceeds of the policy, whether through a lump sum, annuity payout, or trust.

If you surrender ownership of your life insurance policy and become uninsurable, perhaps due to age or illness, you won't be able to obtain another policy.

The process of transferring ownership of an insurance policy is usually simple. You complete a simple form provided by your insurance company. But to avoid estate taxes:

- ✔ The transfer must be absolute, with your giving up all control of the policy, ability to change beneficiaries, and ability to borrow against its cash value.
- ✔ You must complete the transfer at least three years before you die.

If you don't satisfy those requirements, the insurance proceeds will be included in your estate.

Some policies permit you to designate a contingent owner. If you transfer ownership of the policy to your spouse, when your spouse predeceases you, the policy again becomes part of your estate. If you designate your children as the contingent owner, ownership of the policy instead goes from your spouse to them. You can also designate a trust as the contingent owner.

The following sections outline your ownership options.

Ownership by a spouse

As a general rule, ownership by your spouse is appropriate when your combined estates, including the life insurance proceeds, will not be subject to estate tax. Life insurance provides a simple mechanism to get money to your spouse that may be necessary to pay your debts, ongoing bills and expenses and support your children. If you transfer ownership of your life insurance to your spouse:

> ✔ Your spouse remains able to borrow against the cash value of your insurance.
>
> ✔ Your spouse maintains control over the beneficiaries.
>
> ✔ If you have variable life insurance, your spouse gets to choose the investment strategy.

Although your surviving spouse benefits from the unlimited marital deduction and pays no estate taxes on the insurance proceeds, their estate will be taxed when they die. Applying current tax rates, 45 percent of your insurance proceeds may end up going to the IRS. Thus, if you may have to pay estate tax, you should consider an alternative that keeps the value of the insurance proceeds out of your estates.

Ownership by a child or children

If you want to leave your life insurance proceeds to your adult children, you benefit from having them own the policy. As the policy isn't part of your estate, the proceeds go to your children free of estate tax. Direct ownership is simpler than ownership through a trust, which is described later in this chapter.

At the same time, your children have to pay the premiums for the policy. Although you can gift them the money for the premiums, taking advantage of your annual gift tax exemption, you can't pay the premiums directly. Direct payment will result in the IRS finding that you own the policy and including the proceeds in your estate. Thus, your children must be responsible enough to pay the premiums instead of pocketing or spending the money.

You should reconsider having your children own your policy if you don't want them to take and keep the life insurance proceeds. If you imagine them using the insurance proceeds to support your spouse or to pay certain debts of your estate, think again. Although many (perhaps most) children will abide by your wishes, the money is theirs. They're entitled to keep it.

Ownership by a qualified plan

A qualified plan is a type of retirement savings plan that provides for the deferment of tax and tax-free appreciation of assets held within the plan. These plans must meet legal criteria defined by federal tax law, generally Section 401(a) of the Internal Revenue Code.

Paying for life insurance through your qualified plan may seem like a good idea. After all, if you pay your premiums with pretax dollars or get a tax deduction, you enjoy substantial upfront savings. The downside is that your death benefit is subject to state and federal income tax.

Ownership by a trust

So you want to avoid estate taxes, but still maintain some amount of control over how your insurance benefits are used and distributed after your death? Then you need to consider having an irrevocable life insurance trust (ILIT) own your life insurance policy.

Note that word irrevocable: Once you create the ILIT and it acquires an insurance policy on your life, you can't change your mind. Don't expect that you'll be trustee of your own ILIT, as your ability to control the trust is considered to be an incident of ownership of the insurance policy, such that your ILIT is included in your estate. You also can't change the beneficiaries of an irrevocable trust, even if, for example, you divorce your spouse.

You can fund your ILIT by:

- ✓ Transferring an existing policy into your trust
- ✓ Buying a new policy

The transfer of an existing life insurance policy is subject to a federal restriction, such that if you die within three years of the transfer your life insurance, proceeds are counted as part of your estate. Thus, a transfer is best done when you're younger and healthy.

To purchase a new life insurance policy, you transfer money into your ILIT, and the trustee obtains the policy and pays the premiums. The trust is named as the owner of the new policy, not you. You can transfer additional funds into your ILIT for the premiums as they become due.

Your contributions to your ILIT are subject to gift taxes, but you can avoid them by keeping your contributions within your $12,000 annual gift tax exclusion. You can also apply part of your $1 million lifetime gift tax exemption.

ILITs are very effective tax avoidance tools, and the IRS is hostile to them. Also, administrative costs can be high. It's important to set up an ILIT correctly, so enlisting the help of an estate planning professional will help you avoid unnecessary expenses and withstand IRS scrutiny.

Designating Beneficiaries for Your Insurance Policy

When you fill out your insurance application, you'll find a blank space for you to designate your beneficiary. You may not have thought much about who to pick. If you're married, your first thought is probably to name your spouse as your primary beneficiary, and your children as contingent beneficiaries in case your spouse dies before you do.

But the choice is more complicated than you think. You need to consider factors such as the age of your beneficiary, how your choice may affect estate tax liability, and whether you want your beneficiary to receive a large lump sum payout.

Life insurance proceeds are often said to be tax free to your estate. This reference is to income tax. Unless you're careful, the proceeds of your life insurance policy will be subject to estate tax.

If you designate your spouse as beneficiary, your U.S. citizen spouse benefits from an unlimited marital deduction so that no estate taxes are owed on your insurance proceeds. You may also get a tax advantage and create an income stream for your surviving spouse if you direct the proceeds into a charitable trust. The following sections discuss the tax advantages and disadvantages of specific beneficiaries.

When choosing beneficiaries and contingent beneficiaries, sometimes you have to consider the unthinkable. In one case, a divorced mother and her three young children were killed in a car accident. The mother had named her children as the beneficiary of her life insurance. As you might expect, her children did not have wills, so the insurance proceeds became part of their intestate estate. Their legal heir was their father, who was way behind in his child support. Needless to say, that was not what the mother would have wanted. This outcome could have been prevented had she named a contingent beneficiary for her life insurance, or if her beneficiary were a trust created for the benefit of her children. With a trust, had the children survived, she could also have prevented her ex-husband from becoming the custodian of the insurance proceeds.

Spouse

Under the unlimited marital deduction, everything you leave to your U.S. citizen spouse is inherited free of estate taxes. Thus, when your spouse receives your life insurance benefits, no estate tax is due.

If you name your spouse as beneficiary, remember the following:

✔ Your spouse may die before you do.

✔ Your spouse's estate may have to pay estate taxes.

But don't overlook these potential pitfalls:

✔ The $10 million policy payout your spouse receives is tax-free, but when she dies, the tax man will be looking for a share.

✔ The proceeds are subject to the claims of your spouse's creditors.

✔ If your spouse remarries, her subsequent spouse can make claims against the money and may inherit part or all of the money when your spouse dies.

Naming an alternate beneficiary will ensure that your life insurance proceeds go to your intended recipient. But remember, your other beneficiaries don't enjoy the unlimited marital deduction, and your estate may owe taxes on the insurance proceeds.

Child or children

You get no estate tax benefit from leaving your insurance proceeds to your children. But if your estate (including the insurance proceeds) isn't large enough to owe estate taxes, or if you want to designate your children despite estate tax exposure, you may do so anyway. As with your spouse, once your children receive the money, it's subject to potential claims by their spouses and creditors.

Be careful about designating your minor children as life insurance beneficiaries. Your children will require a court-appointed guardian to manage their money until they reach the age of 18.

Also, don't forget that your estate pays your estate taxes, not your children. Make sure that your estate has the capacity to pay its taxes, including taxes on the life insurance payout.

Another individual

Perhaps you don't have a spouse or children. You can name any person you want as your life insurance beneficiary, including your parents, a sibling, or another relative. You can choose a friend, former teacher, or even somebody you randomly pick from the phone book. Whomever you choose, if your estate owes taxes, payment will be out of your estate's assets and not the insurance payout.

Using insurance to equalize inheritances

You may want to leave a large asset to a particular heir, but not be able to make similar bequests to your other heirs. Life insurance can help bridge the gap.

For example, you may have a child who has taken over the family business, and you want that child to inherit the business. You may have a child who has moved into your home to care for you, or who needs a stable residence, and intend to leave your home to that child. You can

use life insurance to provide an equivalent gift to your other children.

Life insurance may also be useful if you have remarried and have children from the prior marriage. You want to leave your home to your new spouse, or perhaps only a life estate in your home, but that means your children won't inherit the home for many years after your death. You can use life insurance to provide an immediate inheritance to your children.

Multiple beneficiaries

You have considerable flexibility in designating a beneficiary for your insurance. In addition to a specific individual, you can identify more than one person as co-beneficiaries of your policy. You can also designate a class of people, such as my children or my grandchildren, as beneficiary.

A trust

If you direct your life insurance proceeds into your living trust or a testamentary trust (one created by your will), your trust will manage those proceeds pursuant to your instruction. This approach can be particularly beneficial if:

- ✔ Your spouse needs help managing money.

- ✔ You want the proceeds to benefit your minor children, but prefer that the money be held and managed by your chosen trustee rather than a court-appointed conservator.

- ✔ You don't want your heirs to receive the payout from your policy in a single lump sum.

The proceeds will be part of your estate and subject to estate tax.

Another option is to name a charitable remainder trust as the beneficiary of your life insurance. You transfer ownership of assets into the trust, and it creates an income stream for a designated period of up to 20 years. If you create a charitable remainder trust for the benefit of your spouse, you guarantee your spouse an income during the term of the trust. Any income tax payable by your spouse is deferred until each payment is made.

Although a charitable remainder trust is irrevocable, if you use life insurance fund it at the time of your death, you can change your mind at any time during your life. When the trust ends or your spouse dies, the trust's assets go to a designated charity or charities. By virtue of that charitable donation, this trust can help you reduce your estate taxes, if your estate is likely to pay them. Chapter 12 discusses charitable remainder trusts in more detail.

 If you have a noncitizen spouse, you can use a qualified domestic trust (QDOT) to postpone estate tax. Your noncitizen spouse can receive distributions of income from the QDOT without paying estate tax. Any distributions of principal are subject to estate tax.

Your estate

Your life insurance proceeds become part of your probate estate if:

- ✔ You name your estate as your beneficiary
- ✔ You fail to name a beneficiary for your policy
- ✔ Your beneficiary, and any contingent beneficiaries, die before you, in some cases.

Life insurance can be useful to pay the financial obligations of your estate, including debts, funeral costs, costs of administration, income taxes, and estate taxes. Life insurance proceeds paid into your estate are applied by your personal representative to satisfy your estate's obligations. Any remaining funds are distributed to your heirs in accord with your will.

Possible estate tax issues

Life insurance proceeds paid into your estate will increase its size. In some cases, that increase will cause your estate to have to pay estate taxes. If the value of your estate already exceeds your estate tax exemption, your entire life insurance benefit may be taxed.

If you intend to purchase life insurance to cover estate tax, you should do so early. If your life insurance is owned by an ILIT for three or more years before your death, the proceeds of your policy aren't part of your estate. If you purchase life insurance within three years of your death, it's likely to be more expensive, and you can't avoid estate taxes. (For more information on ILITs, see Chapter 12).

 The interplay of life insurance with federal estate tax laws is complex. You must take care that your estate tax plan is effective and that it also achieves your personal estate planning goals. Consult with an estate planning professional.

Probate issues

If your life insurance benefits are paid into your estate, the proceeds are distributed in accord with your will. If you haven't executed a will or don't provide for the distribution of the proceeds within your will or through a residuary clause, the proceeds will be distributed under your state's intestate succession laws (as if you have no will). For more discussion of probate court proceedings, see Chapter 10.

You should designate beneficiaries and contingent beneficiaries for your insurance policies. In some cases, you may choose to designate multiple contingent beneficiaries. You should also include a residuary clause in your will, directing the distribution of any assets remaining in your estate after your bills have been paid and your specific bequests have been distributed.

Chapter 17

Your Castle: How It's Owned Makes a Huge Difference

You may own your home in a variety of ways, either alone or with others. Your home may take a number of forms, including a single-family dwelling, condo, co-op, boat, or manufactured home. You may also own your home with others, including your spouse or a domestic partner.

The type of home you own and the manner in which you own it may create tax concerns and influence whether you leave your home to your heirs through your will or through a trust. You face additional estate planning issues if you want your domestic partner to inherit your home.

In addition to your home, you may own other real estate. Your estate can face significant tax issues if you don't plan for inheritance of your vacation home, business or investment property, or farmland. You also may disrupt the operation of your business.

House, Condo, Co-op, or More: Exploring the Types of Residential Properties

If you're like most people, your home is your largest asset. When you consider mortgage payments, upkeep, insurance, and utility bills, it's also probably the source of your most significant expenses.

You have a great many housing options to choose from. Depending upon your budget and personal preferences, your primary choices are a single-family home, townhouse or row home, condominium, or co-op. You can also purchase a manufactured home or even live in a houseboat.

Most residential properties are roughly equal for estate planning purposes. The greatest difference comes from cooperative housing, where you can have significant restrictions on who may own your shares, or manufactured homes and houseboats, which are forms of personal property.

The single-family home

A single-family home is a housing unit that provides living space for one home or family. Single-family homes fall into two general categories:

- ✔ **Detached homes** don't touch any adjacent building and stand upon their own piece of land.
- ✔ **Attached homes,** such as row houses, townhouses, and duplexes, have an independent outside entrance and are separated from neighboring structures by walls that extend from the roof to the basement or foundation. You own the land under your home. You share at least one wall with your neighbors, so you may experience noise issues that you wouldn't have with a detached home.

Row houses and townhouses are often regulated by homeowner's associations. Owners pay monthly fees to the association. The fees may cover a broad range of services, including exterior maintenance, snow removal, and lawn care, or may be more narrowly focused on structural issues that affect adjoining homes, such as roof maintenance. The association may place restrictions on modification of the appearance of the external appearance of your home and yard.

A community of detached homes may also have a homeowner's association, which may maintain common areas or buildings, restrict changes to the exterior of your home, maintain private roads within the community, provide security, or perform similar tasks desired by the community.

Within the constraints of homeowner's association rules and local zoning ordinances, your home is your castle. For example, you can generally paint it whatever color you choose or, with appropriate building permits, install a pool or add an addition. You're typically responsible for all maintenance and yard work.

The condominium

When you buy a condominium, or condo, you're buying the interior space of a building, but not the exterior structure or the land upon which it sits. Condominiums can take the form of apartment blocks, townhouses, duplexes, or even detached homes.

A condominium community is governed by a condo association, pursuant to written bylaws. The condo owners ordinarily elect the association's board of directors.

Condo owners pay fees to the association, which are used to maintain the exterior structure, common areas and buildings, and any recreational facilities offered by the condominium community and to build a cash reserve for future needs. If cash reserves aren't sufficient, the condo association may charge a special assessment to cover certain expenditures, such as roof replacement.

The condo association performs all exterior maintenance, including lawn care, snow removal, and pool maintenance. The condo association may also provide heating, cooling, and water.

You're responsible for all interior maintenance for your home. You should expect to be forbidden from making any structural changes to your home (such as the removal of a wall) that the condo association hasn't approved.

Some condominium associations permit owners to rent their units to tenants. This policy can make a condo community resemble an apartment complex. Before you buy a condo, you should ask about rental policies and talk to members of the community about their experiences.

Condominiums often take longer to sell than single-family homes.

Housing cooperatives (co-ops)

A typical housing cooperative is a nonprofit corporation, organized for the democratic management of residential housing. The cooperative may restrict who may reside within the community (for example, a senior housing cooperative).

If you're a member of a housing cooperative, you own shares of the cooperative and get to vote in certain management decisions. Each month, you pay a fee, contributing to the co-op's operating expenses. Provided you abide by community rules, the shares give you the right to live within the cooperative, but you don't actually own real estate.

Your equity grows in one of three ways:

- ✔ In a leasing cooperative, the cooperative leases its premises. You thus have no equity in the real estate and get no equity growth. You may be entitled to a share of any cash reserves that accumulate during your period of ownership.
- ✔ In a limited equity cooperative, you're restricted in what you will receive for your shares. Often the limits are described in the co-op's bylaws.
- ✔ In a market rate cooperative, you're free to sell your shares for whatever a seller is willing to pay. Appreciation may be comparable to a condominium.

When your residence is a manufactured home or boat

A houseboat or manufactured home is a form of personal property, not real estate. If you put your manufactured home on real estate that you own, you should be able to convert the home to real estate so that it no longer requires its own separate title.

Depending upon the policies of your state, title to your manufactured home is probably issued by the state department of motor vehicles, in the same manner as a car, or by the department of housing. Boat titles are normally issued by a state's department of motor vehicles.

If a co-owner is named on the title to your manufactured home or boat, that person will ordinarily be treated as a joint tenant and will receive your ownership share when you die. Otherwise, you're ordinarily free to leave your interest in personal property to whomever you choose and may do so through either a will or trust.

Ownership of Your Residence

When you plan your estate, the manner in which you own your home will affect your estate plan. Some forms of ownership result in automatic inheritance by your spouse or co-owner. Others require that your property pass through probate.

Ownership by one person: Sole ownership

As the sole owner of your home, you have the general right to get a mortgage, refinance, sell your home, and leave your home to whomever you choose.

Yet even with sole ownership, your ability to choose your heir may be limited by marriage or family status:

- ✔ Some states will permit your wife to claim a life estate in your real property.

- ✔ Some states restrict your ability to leave your residence to anyone other than your surviving spouse or dependent children.

Chapter 8 discusses the impact of state law on your estate plan.

Ownership by two or more people

Leaving marital interests aside for the moment, as an individual, you can own real property with other people:

- ✔ **As tenants in common:** You own your share of the property independent of your co-owners' interest. Co-owners may own shares that differ in size. When you die, your share of the real estate is part of your estate and is distributed to your heirs.

- ✔ **As joint tenants:** You share equal ownership with two or more people with rights passing to surviving owners

Joint tenancy

To create a joint tenancy, the co-owners must share four *unities:*

- ✔ **Time:** The joint tenants' interest must be created at the same time.

- ✔ **Title:** All joint tenants must have the same title interest in the property.

- ✔ **Interest:** All joint tenants must share the same interest in the property.

- ✔ **Possession:** All joint tenants must have equal rights to possess the entire property.

If any one of these elements isn't present, the joint tenancy fails, and the owners become tenants in common.

A joint tenancy can be broken and become a tenancy in common if one of the joint tenants sells her interest in the property to a third party. Some states permit a joint tenant to break a joint tenancy by executing a document expressing that intention. In some states, a joint tenancy is broken if one joint tenant obtains a mortgage on the jointly owned property.

In a joint tenancy, each co-owner has a right of survivorship. When you die, your interest in the property automatically passes to the other co-owner (or owners).

Tenancy by the entirety

A *tenancy by the entirety* is a form of joint tenancy available only to married couples. Its creation requires all four unities described in the preceding section, in addition to the fifth unity of marriage. Not all states recognize tenancy by the entirety.

Unlike a regular joint tenancy, a tenancy by the entirety may be broken only with the consent of both parties or by divorce. In most states, after divorce, a tenancy by the entirety becomes a tenancy in common.

The biggest advantages of a tenancy by the entirety arise in collections or bankruptcy. A tenancy by the entirety can protect your property from the claims of your spouse's debtors and may provide significant protection of the property if one spouse files for bankruptcy protection.

Married couples purchasing real estate together will usually choose to own as joint tenants or, if allowed, tenancy by the entirety. If you're purchasing an investment property with a partner, you'd ordinarily choose to be tenants in common. If you choose to jointly own real estate with somebody other than your spouse, even a relative, you should consider entering a contract describing your respective rights to the property, payment of mortgage payments, taxes, maintenance, and other expenses, and what happens if one of you wants to sell the property.

Life estates

A *life estate* describes an ownership interest measured by the duration of the owner's life. The owner of a life estate is called a *life tenant,* and the people who receive title upon the life tenant's death are called *remaindermen.* A life estate is irrevocable.

If you create a life tenancy for yourself in your home and designate your children as remaindermen, normally:

- ✔ You have the exclusive right to the use and possession of your home.
- ✔ You're responsible for payment of routine maintenance, insurance, taxes, and the mortgage interest.
- ✔ Your remaindermen are responsible to pay the portion of the mortgage payment that is applied to principal.

Like a joint tenancy, title to your home passes to your remaindermen without going through probate.

Life estates are often used as an estate planning tool for second marriages, with the second spouse receiving a life estate and children from a prior marriage being designated as remaindermen.

Community property laws

In a community property state, if you purchase real estate during your marriage, your spouse has an automatic interest in the real estate. (Community property states are listed in Chapter 3.) The following exceptions commonly apply:

- ✔ Property that you receive as a gift or inheritance remains your separate property.
- ✔ If you purchase the property with your own resources, acquired before the marriage, you'll likely be able to claim it as separate property.

If you divorce, your spouse can claim a half-interest in all community property.

In some community property states, your surviving spouse has a right of survivorship. In other community property states, you're free to leave your half-interest to whomever you wish.

Special issues for domestic partners

Although some states are expanding the rights available to registered domestic partners, in most states, you're treated as unrelated to your domestic partner.

If your state doesn't grant property rights to domestic partners, you're not eligible for a domestic partnership, or you choose not to enter a domestic partnership, you can still jointly own a home. For example, you can own real estate as joint tenants, tenants in common, or even through a trust. But remember:

- ✔ You can't rely upon divorce laws and courts to separate your property if you break up.
- ✔ If you can't agree how your shared real estate will be divided, legal actions for sale or partition of real estate can be costly and time-consuming.
- ✔ If you don't create a plan for your partner to inherit your property, it may end up being inherited by your legal heirs, not including your domestic partner.

If your state doesn't offer property rights to domestic partners, I recommend that you enter into a contract for any shared real estate, including:

- ✔ How the costs of ownership, including the mortgage, utilities, insurance, and maintenance, are to be divided
- ✔ Who may remain in the home if you separate
- ✔ What will happen to the property if you break up, including how it will be sold and how the proceeds of the sale will be divided between you
- ✔ Any right to buy out your partner's interest in the property, and how that interest will be valued
- ✔ Your rights if your partner dies, and you end up jointly owning your home with your partner's heirs

Should Ownership of Your Home Be Held by Your Trust?

If your home is your largest asset, you want to avoid probate, and your living trust is the best tool for avoiding probate, you should immediately transfer your home into your living trust, right? Perhaps not. You may not want your home to be owned by your trust if:

- ✔ **You plan to sell your home.** Although your trust can sell your home, if you have short-term plans to sell your home, you may want to skip the step of transferring the property into the trust.
- ✔ **You may file for bankruptcy.** If your home is owned by your trust at the time of your bankruptcy, you may lose your homestead exemption. You'll need to transfer your house back out of your revocable living trust before you file bankruptcy.

Due to the nature of a revocable living trust, you can regain title to your home simply by transferring the home back out of the trust or by revoking the trust.

Needless to say, if you're considering transferring your home into an irrevocable trust, you need to be very confident that your plans and wishes for your home won't change.

The Drawbacks Of Adding Your Heirs to the Title

You may have heard that you can avoid the trouble of estate planning simply by adding your heirs to the title of your property. The rationale is this: If you add somebody to your property as a joint tenant, that person will automatically gain full ownership when you die. The same is true if you title property over to your heirs and retain a life estate.

You create serious risks for yourself by using a joint tenancy or life estate as a substitute for estate planning. You may also increase tax exposure for your heirs. Odds are, you're much better off using a living trust.

The cons outweigh the pros

Of course, adding your desired heir as a joint owner of your home brings potential benefits:

- **Probate avoidance:** Your child inherits your home without its going through probate.

- **Simplicity:** You can achieve joint tenancy or create a life estate simply by preparing and filing a quitclaim deed.

However, you can achieve the same benefits through a living trust. As a trust allows you to avoid the pitfalls of joint ownership, I encourage you to choose that alternative.

On the other hand, the dangers often exceed the benefits. For joint ownership, in the most common scenario, you add your child to the title of your home. These pitfalls apply to any joint owners you add:

- Your child may add her spouse to the title without your knowledge or consent.

- Your child gains equal rights to the use and enjoyment of your home.

- You expose your property to your children's creditors. If your child falls into debt, is sued after a car accident, or goes bankrupt, your child's creditors may try to take your home.

- You can't borrow against your home without your child's permission and possibly also the permission of your child's spouse. If you want to refinance, take out a home equity line to fund repairs or improvements, or want to use your home to finance your dream vacation, you need your child to cooperate.

✔ In most cases, you can't sell your home without your child's permission and possibly also the permission of your child's spouse. If you want to move into a smaller home, to a different state, or into a retirement community, your child can say no. You can bring a lawsuit against your child to force the sale of your home, but your child will be entitled to a share of the proceeds from the sale.

✔ Your child's spouse may try to claim an interest in your home. If your child divorces, your child's spouse may claim that the joint interest in the home is a marital asset and should be divided in the divorce.

You may have the idea that the joint title is only for convenience and add your child to the title with the understanding that the child will share the property equally with your other children when you die. Your child has no obligation to carry out your wishes— even if you spell out your wishes in your will — and in many cases, a child will keep the house despite a parent's wishes.

For life estates, the most common scenario involves your giving yourself and your spouse a life tenancy in your real estate, and adding one or more of your children as your remaindermen, designating them to receive the property when your life estates end. A life estate carries some of the main drawbacks of joint ownership:

✔ You should not expect to be able to borrow against your life estate.

✔ You can no longer sell your home without your children's cooperation and consent.

Possible tax consequences

The two leading tax concerns from adding an heir to your title are

✔ Increased capital gains tax exposure for your heirs (see Chapter 6)

✔ Potential loss of an estate tax exemption for your estate

When you add somebody to your title as a joint tenant with the right of survivorship, normally only half the value of the asset is stepped up at the time of your death (see Chapter 6). Thus, as compared to inheritance, the joint tenancy can significantly increase your heir's capital gains tax exposure.

Consider also what happens if your heir dies before you. The IRS will presume that the entire value of your home belongs in your heir's estate and, in some cases, you may have to fight hard to avoid having your heir's estate held liable for estate taxes on your home.

Estate tax exemptions

Did you own a home before you married? If you have a large estate and add your spouse as a joint tenant, you may lose your ability to take advantage of your estate tax exemption. Although your spouse will receive jointly owned property tax-free, all the property passing into your spouse's estate is potentially subject to estate tax.

If you place your separately owned home into a bypass trust, you can take advantage of your own estate tax exemption when you die while keeping your home out of your spouse's estate, potentially doubling the assets you and your spouse can leave to your heirs tax-free. See Chapter 6 for a greater discussion of the estate tax planning.

Possible Medicaid consequences

When you apply for Medicaid benefits, your homestead exemption shields your primary residence from being counted toward your Medicaid eligibility, provided you intend to return to your home, or if you have a spouse or minor child residing in your home.

Adding a joint tenant to your home, other than a spouse, within the 36-month period before you apply for benefits can make you ineligible during a penalty period based upon the value of your home and the ownership interest of your joint tenant.

If you receive Medicaid benefits, when you die your state will attempt to recoup the cost of those benefits from your estate. In some states, Medicaid recovery is made only against your probate estate. As your joint title holder receives ownership of your home without going through probate, you may be able to avoid Medicaid Recovery against your home by adding a joint title holder.

Don't assume that your joint owner will get this benefit. In many states, despite joint ownership, your home will be treated as if it's part of your estate and be subject to Medicaid recovery. State budget problems are inspiring states to be more aggressive about Medicaid recovery, so you can expect that practice to grow.

Leaving Real Property by Will or Trust

If you leave your real property to your heirs through your will or a living trust, you can maintain the advantages of joint ownership but avoid the many risks of that approach. Whether you use a will or revocable living trust:

✔ You can change your mind. You can revoke or amend your living trust or will as you please.

✔ You can protect the home from your heirs' creditors. For example, you can use an asset protection trust to leave your home to your child while protecting it from the reach of creditors or from the claim of a spouse in later divorce proceedings.

✔ You can create a bypass trust that keeps your home out of your spouse's estate and take advantage of both marital estate tax deductions.

✔ Your heirs receive a step up in basis, to the value of your home at the time of your death.

You may also consider irrevocable trusts, such as the qualified personal residence trust (QPRT), which may avoid some of the problems of joint ownership, but you can't change your mind once you transfer ownership of your home to an irrevocable trust. See Chapter 12 for a discussion of many popular varieties of trust.

Remembering Other Properties

Do you own land other than your primary residence? If so, don't forget to include it in your estate plan.

If your other property is located in another state, your use of a trust can simplify probate. If your real estate is held in a trust, no probate proceedings are necessary to pass your property to your heirs. If not, your estate is probated in your state of residence, but additional probate lawsuits must be filed in every state in which you own real property.

If you transfer any property other than your personal residence into a trust, beware of _due on sale clauses_ in your mortgages. If you don't have your mortgage lender's permission for the transfer, this clause permits your lender to accelerate the loan and demand full payment.

For any property you hold, you must consider how your estate plan will affect your estate's tax burden, control of the property, and exposure to creditors, as well as capital gains tax obligations for your heirs.

Vacation properties

You may feel a special attachment to your family's vacation property and envision many generations of your family continuing to enjoy the property. But be aware of common problems that may arise:

✔ One of the co-owners is unable or unwilling to contribute to expenses, such as maintenance, insurance, and taxes.

✔ One co-owner wants to sell the property, and the others don't, but the others can't afford to buy out his share.

✔ One co-owner wants to keep the property, but can't afford to buy out the other co-owners, who want to sell.

✔ Your family continues to grow, and your vacation home is no longer large enough for family gatherings, or disputes arise over scheduling access.

If you want to keep your vacation home within your family, discuss your plans with your heirs. You may discover that one of your children is much more interested in the vacation home than the others, so it makes more sense to simply leave the home to that child with your other children inheriting assets of equal value.

Investment properties

If you own investment property that you want to leave to your heirs, you need to consider the following:

✔ **Estate taxes:** Will the value of your investment property create estate tax liability for your estate?

✔ **Division of the property among your heirs:** Will you hold the properties in trust for your heirs? If you own multiple properties, will you distribute different properties among your heirs?

If your investment property is valuable and you expect to pay estate taxes, you should consider a Family Limited Partnership. (For more on Family Limited Partnerships, see Chapter 6.)

You can also utilize a trust to hold your investment property. You can define how the property will be managed, and how trust income will be distributed.

Be careful when distributing specific investment properties to your heirs. The relative values of any properties you own will change over time, including after your death. Consider how those changes may affect the value of your bequests:

✔ Differences that arise before you die can create resentment when your children inherit unequally.

✔ Even if the properties are exactly equal in value after you die, vagaries of the real estate market may cause their values to diverge.

The child who receives the less valuable property may harbor resentment against you and against the child who received the more valuable property.

Business real estate

What about real estate owned by your business, such as a retail store or office space? If you own the land from which your business operates or own an office condo, you need to consider that real estate when creating your estate plan.

The first question is whether the real estate is owned by the business itself or by you and either used or leased by the business. If you have a corporation, LLC, or similar entity that owns the real estate, your business succession plan will encompass that real estate.

If your business isn't incorporated or you own the real estate apart from your business, you need to make sure that you have an adequate estate and succession plan. If your business doesn't already own the real estate, consider these approaches:

- ✔ If the business will falter or fail if it has to move, and you have not yet done so, consider executing a formal lease to protect the right of the business to remain on the premises.
- ✔ Consider selling the real estate to your business, with due consideration to the capital gains tax issues that may arise.

Business real estate is otherwise not much different from other investment property.

Farmland

Estate planning for a farm is a complex process and is best done in consultation with an estate planning professional. Creating a succession plan for the family farm usually requires a broad spectrum of estate planning tools:

- ✔ A business succession plan and gifting strategy, to transfer ownership of the business to your heirs while minimizing estate and capital gains taxes. See Chapter 6 for a discussion of tax planning tools.
- ✔ Life insurance, to cover the farm's debts and estate taxes.
- ✔ Long-term care insurance, so that farm assets aren't depleted to pay for your nursing home care.
- ✔ The use of trusts and possibly a Family Limited Partnership, to help provide financial stability for your family and a smooth transition of farm management. (See Chapter 6 for more on the Family Limited Partnership.)

If you own farmland that isn't productive, consider also the prior discussion of estate planning for investment properties.

Whether or not your farmland is productive, if consistent with your goals, you should consider using an *agricultural conservation easement*. This easement reduces the value of farmland to your estate, while preventing it from being developed. You create restrictions on part or all of your farmland to protect resources such as wildlife habitat, water resources, scenery, or even to preserve it as productive farmland, and then sell or donate the easement to a qualified conservation organization or public agency.

Although agricultural conservation easements are usually permanent, they may also be created for a fixed number of years. The restrictions created by the conservation easement hold down the value of your land by making it unsuitable for non-agricultural use.

Part V
The Part of Tens

The 5th Wave   By Rich Tennant

"I can set you up with a Will or a Living Trust.
Curses are a little trickier."

In this part . . .

No *For Dummies* book is complete without the irrev-
erent Part of Tens. This reader favorite contains
lists to help you with common estate planning issues and
traps. You also get the inside scoop on how to make
estate planning choices and plan for taxes.

Chapter 18

Ten Common Will Mistakes

In This Chapter

▶ Avoiding having your will invalidated

▶ Keeping your bequests from failing

▶ Saving your estate (and heirs) time and money

f you're reading this chapter, you've more than likely done the hard work of creating an estate plan and have written a will that reflects your goals. But will a mistake undo all your hard work? Will your heirs receive the inheritances you intend for them? What if your heirs can't even find your will?

Some mistakes create confusion or cause specific bequests to fail. Some mistakes cause your assets to be distributed in a manner you would regard as unfair and very different from what you have written in your will. Worse, some mistakes can completely invalidate your will.

This chapter describes common mistakes and how to avoid them.

Not Updating Your Will

Over the course of your life, you will experience changes in your personal relationships, possessions, and finances. Your will is like a photograph – a snapshot of your estate and your plans at a particular moment in time. You should review your will as a matter of course, every few years, to confirm that it remains consistent with your wishes.

Chapter 8 covers the reasons why you may need to update your will. Any time you go through a major life change, such as marriage, divorce or remarriage, you should update your will to avoid the following complications:

✔ A divorce is unlikely to invalidate your entire will, but it should invalidate your ex-spouse's inheritance. If that happens, your ex-spouse's share will likely be distributed to your other heirs as if the ex-spouse died first. The result may be a distribution of your estate that is very different from what you intend.

✔ If you marry, your spouse will have inheritance rights under state law. If you don't provide for your new spouse, expect that the court will do so out of your estate, which will dramatically change the distribution of your estate.

✔ If you have a child or adopt a child, after you draft your will, the child's inheritance rights under law can be drastically different from what you would choose. In some cases, your new child may inherit significantly more than what your other children will inherit.

✔ If one of your heirs precedes you in death, have you provided for what will happen to their share of your estate? If not, you should update your will.

You should also review the people you designate as your primary and successor personal representatives. Have your relationships with those people changed? Are they likely to outlive you? Are you still certain that they're up to the task of administering your estate or that they'll be capable of doing so years from now, after you die? If not, consider designating somebody else.

Do you change the batteries in your smoke detectors every year? You can also make that the day you review your will.

Being Too Specific in Your Bequests

Although it may seem at first that you can't be too specific when writing your will, sometimes the opposite is true. Being too specific can be a big problem when

✔ Your assets or their values change.

✔ You list heirs you want to share in a bequest, and you omit a name or forget to amend your will to keep the list current.

✔ Your heirs change.

When you write your will, you may picture certain belongings going to a particular heir, or choose to leave specific parcels of real estate to your children. But what if the property is no longer part of your estate because you lost, sold, or broke it years before? Your bequest will fail, and your heir may take nothing.

If you make bequests of specific items or accounts, you should verify that you still have the asset you describe in your will. You should also consider any change in its value. If you do not, the person who was to receive that bequest may receive nothing at all or may receive something worth far less than you had intended.

If the value of the bequest has changed, your heir may receive an inheritance significantly greater or substantially less than you intended. (You wrote a will in 1999 leaving one child your eBay stock and one child your Pets.com stock, equal in value at the time. The eBay stock is now worth millions, and the Pets.com stock is worth nothing.)

Another common error is to forget that the value of your estate will change over time, and to make specific bequests based upon the current value of your estate. Usually your estate will increase in value, but sometimes its value will go down.

If your estate is currently worth $250,000, you may be tempted to write a will leaving $50,000 to your brother and the rest of your estate to your children. Yet due to a prolonged illness, $200,000 of your estate is consumed by medical costs and nursing home care. After your brother inherits his $50,000, your children are left with nothing.

If you instead leave your brother 20 percent of your estate, although your children still inherit far less than you currently expect, they won't be left with nothing. They'll still receive 80 percent of your reduced estate.

When you're leaving bequests to specific groups of people, such as your children or grandchildren, a will drafting error may omit a name, or a new grandchild may be born who is not included in your list. I know you're thinking, "I could never make such a huge mistake," but this mistake happens even in professionally prepared, carefully proofread wills.

Instead of naming individual heirs, consider making your bequest to the group. If you have four grandchildren, you can leave the gift "to my grandchildren" instead of "to Jack, Jill, and Emma." That way, the accidental omission of George won't keep him from inheriting. Also, your will won't need to be changed upon the birth of your fifth grandchild, Jacob.

Finally, keep in mind that a beneficiary of your will may die before you do. Consider designating a successor beneficiary for specific bequests that may otherwise become part of the residuary of your estate.

Forgetting to Address the Residuary of Your Estate

The *residuary* part of your estate is the amount left over after your bequests are distributed to your heirs. The two most likely sources are

- ✔ Assets you forgot to consider when you wrote your will.
- ✔ Property you acquired after you wrote your will.
- ✔ The remaining balance of funds you set aside for payment of your estate's bills, costs, and taxes.

If you make no provision, these leftovers will pass to your heirs under your state's laws of intestate succession, as if you had no will.

The solution is to always include a residuary clause that provides how you wish the residue of your estate to pass to your heirs.

Leaving Everything to Your Spouse

You want everything to go to your spouse when you die. You know that your gift to your spouse won't be subject to inheritance taxes. So what can go wrong? If you have a large estate, you're walking away from your estate tax exemption.

As of the time of this writing, your estate has a $2 million estate tax exemption, and your spouse's estate also has a $2 million exemption. If you both take advantage of your exemptions, you can leave $4 million to your heirs without incurring estate taxes. If you instead leave everything to your spouse, your spouse will benefit only from her $2 million exemption, and up to $2 million of your combined estate will unnecessarily be subject to taxation.

The bypass trust is a common tool to take advantage of both exemptions while allowing your spouse to benefit from your entire estate. I discuss this trust in Chapter 12.

Leaving Nothing to Your Spouse

The state doesn't want you to die and leave your spouse penniless. States have laws defining the amount a spouse is entitled to inherit from your estate, giving your spouse the option of choosing their legally defined inheritance instead of the bequest you define in your will. Usually, the amount your spouse may claim is between one-third and one-half of your estate.

If you leave your spouse too little, or nothing at all, you should expect your spouse to choose the larger inheritance allowed by law. That will wreak havoc with your other bequests.

If you intend to leave your spouse less than about half of your estate, you should ask a lawyer to advise you on your estate plan.

Including Items in Your Will That Pass Outside of Your Estate

Some of your assets never become part of your probated estate. Jointly held real estate will normally pass to the surviving owner without going through probate. The same is true for jointly held bank accounts.

Retirement savings accounts and pension plans with a designated beneficiary will pass to the beneficiary without going through probate. As long as you name a beneficiary other than your estate, the same is true for the proceeds of life insurance policies and annuities.

If an asset passes to a beneficiary outside of probate, you can't direct the inheritance of that asset through your will.

If you leave your $100,000 bank account to your son and your $100,000 life insurance policy to your daughter, but your son is the designated beneficiary of your life insurance policy, your bequest to your daughter will fail and your son will get both your bank account and the insurance proceeds.

Improper Witnessing of Your Will

I can't emphasize enough how important it is to properly execute your will. If you have gone through all the work of creating a will, the last thing you want to do is have it fail. Yet if you do not have your will properly witnessed, your will may be invalidated.

Common errors include

- **Having an heir (or heirs) witness your will.** Your witnesses should be impartial adults with nothing to gain from your estate.

✔ **Signing your will at a different time than your witnesses, or having your witnesses sign at different times.** Have everybody in the same room, and sign the will together.

✔ **Improper notarization.** If you execute a self-proving affidavit for your will so that your will is presumed valid by a probate court, improper notarization will cause the affidavit to fail. If you're in Louisiana and don't follow your state's laws for proper execution of a will before a notary, your entire will may fail.

Chapter 7 discusses the proper execution of wills.

Losing Your Will (or Making It Impossible to Find)

If you're drafting your own will, find a safe location for your will. If you keep your will at home, consider keeping it in a fire-resistant safe or lock box and make sure that your personal representative and heirs know where to find the key or combination.

I do not recommend storing your will in a safe deposit box. Your personal representative needs the original will, and it may be weeks before your estate has access to its contents. If you keep your original will in a safe deposit box, at least make a photocopy to keep at home in a location known to your personal representative and heirs.

When your original will is lost, although the process can be difficult, you may be able to probate a copy of your will. If you have a lawyer draft your will, often the law office will keep a copy of your will on file. As long as your personal representative or your heirs know who drafted your will, they can get a copy from your lawyer. Don't assume that your lawyer will preserve a copy of your will, as not all law offices do so.

Chapter 2 discusses the storage of your important documents in more detail.

Forgetting to Leave Good Financial Records

Your heirs know exactly where you keep your will. That's great. But now that your estate needs to find your savings accounts, retirement accounts, investments, creditors, and real estate holdings, where do they look? Where are your assets located? Do you have any insurance policies? Where did you store copies of your recent tax returns?

Make things easy on your heirs. Keep good financial records and make sure that your personal representative and heirs know where the records are stored.

If you keep even a set of simple records describing where your financial accounts are held and where your assets are located, it will be of considerable help to your personal representative and heirs as they probate your estate. List such assets and obligations as your savings and checking accounts, CDs, insurance policies, and credit cards. Remember to identify the financial institutions and account numbers.

Forgetting That Your Estate Needs Cash

Your estate will have bills to pay, including your own outstanding debts, funeral expenses, probate costs, taxes, and the fees of the professionals who perform work for your estate.

If your estate doesn't have liquid assets (cash, or assets readily converted to cash) available, some of your other assets will have to be sold to pay the bills. That sale can significantly disrupt your estate plan. You may specify in your will the order in which assets are to be sold to pay bills.

If you're concerned about your estate's liquidity, you should consider purchasing a life insurance policy sufficient to cover the debts of your estate.

Chapter 19

Ten Reasons to Have a Trust

*Y*ou have certainly heard of revocable living trusts, but you may not be aware of the full range of benefits you can obtain by using trusts in your estate plan, or of the full range of trusts you may choose from. Trusts can help you plan for incapacity, control distribution of inheritances, avoid probate, and avoid taxes.

This chapter describes the top ten ways a trust can help you plan and structure your estate. (For more on trusts in general, see Part III.)

You Avoid Probate

Trusts aren't submitted to probate court, and your trustee doesn't require probate court approval to carry out your wishes. Thus, your use of a trust can help your estate plan remain private.

When your estate passes through probate, a public record is made of your will and of your assets and their worth. Anybody can look up your probate court file and learn the intimate details of your estate. Some law firms and financial planners use probate records to identify heirs and target them with sales pitches.

Don't worry too much about privacy. Unless you're a celebrity, it's unlikely that anybody is going to have much interest in reading your will or reviewing a probate court's inventory of your assets. Also, even with a living trust, you won't completely avoid probate. You will have some assets that are not owned by the trust.

Although small estates may qualify for simplified probate, and probate laws and their complexity differ in each state, most estates go through a full probate process, which usually takes between six months and two years to complete. Particularly complicated estates may take longer. Distributing your assets through a trust should prevent this type of delay.

The more complicated your estate plan is, the more money you're likely to save by choosing a living trust in addition to a will. But keep in mind that trusts also have administration costs, and those costs can easily equal (and sometimes exceed) the cost of probate.

Do you want to have the distribution of your assets supervised by a court? A trustee has a great deal of discretion in managing (and thus in potentially mismanaging) your assets. Probate court supervision may help prevent your assets from being lost to mistake or misappropriation. At the same time, before you choose to forego a trust, don't forget to consider the costs of the probate to your estate.

You're Prepared for Incapacity

When you create a living trust, you structure your assets in the manner of your choosing. You choose your own trustee (and successor trustee), and when your trust comes into effect, the trustee manages your assets consistent with the terms of your trust.

In a living trust, your assets are already structured for your benefit, with a trustee and successor of your choosing. Although a durable power of attorney permits your agent to manage your financial affairs, the power of attorney will usually contain far less detail than a living trust. The detail of a living trust helps ensure that your trustee will know and follow your wishes and can make it more difficult for your trustee to misappropriate funds.

Your living trust may also provide for how your business interests are to be managed during your incapacity. If you own a small business, this provision can be crucial to keeping the business open in the event of an unexpected health crisis.

If you have both a living trust and a durable power of attorney, you can be pretty confident that your assets are protected and will be used as you intend in the event of your incapacity.

If you don't utilize a trust and rely only upon a durable power of attorney, you still leave the management of your estate to somebody else's discretion. Your assets may end up being managed by somebody appointed by a court. Also, sometimes a financial institution refuses to recognize a durable power of attorney. If your assets have been transferred into your trust, your trustee should not encounter that problem.

You Avoid a Will Contest

When you submit a will to probate, a *will contest* may occur. In a will contest, the person challenging your will attempts to demonstrate that at a particular point of time you weren't competent to execute your will, or that you were being pressured or tricked into signing a will you didn't really want.

While will contests are not common and are usually unsuccessful, they can delay the distribution of your estate. Your heirs may settle the contest, giving up part of their rightful inheritance just to save litigation costs and to be able to move on with their lives.

Challenging a living trust is much more difficult. The person bringing the contest must establish that you remained incompetent or that any duress or confusion continued not only when you executed the trust, but also at each point in time when you transferred assets into or out of your trust or made management or investment decisions relating to trust assets.

While a will contest can tie up your entire estate until the contest is resolved, your living trust becomes operational upon your death. Your trustee manages your assets the way you intended while the litigation continues, meaning that your surviving spouse and children benefit from your trust despite any litigation.

Some law firms will litigate a will contest on a contingency fee, taking as their fee a percentage of any money they obtain from the estate. This approach can make it "cheap" for somebody to contest your will, as no legal fees are paid up front. Trust litigation is much more costly and complicated. The person challenging your trust can expect to incur substantial legal fees.

You Protect Your Heirs

Sometimes your heirs will not have much experience with money or will be too young or otherwise unable to manage their own financial affairs.

Consider the following illustrations of when your heirs may benefit from the additional protection of a trust:

- ✔ If you've always managed the household finances, your spouse may benefit from having the family assets managed by a trustee. Discuss this issue with your spouse. You shouldn't underestimate your spouse's ability to learn how to manage a household budget.

- ✔ When leaving money to your children or grandchildren, you may want to limit their access to their inheritances until they're out of college. If you simply leave bequests by will, they get a lump sum inheritance usually when they reach adulthood. A trust lets you decide how and when they receive their inheritances.

✔ If your child has special needs and receives government benefits, a trust can protect their inheritance from being taken by the government as reimbursement for public assistance.

It makes sense to protect your heirs, but don't overprotect them. No matter how carefully you try to anticipate their future financial needs and problems, you can't predict the future. Tying up your bequests with conditions and contingencies may prevent your heirs from getting the full benefit of their inheritances or block their access to funds at times of need.

You Can Protect Estate Assets from Creditors and Lawsuits

Putting your assets into a living trust doesn't protect them from your creditors, but you can protect beneficiaries from their creditors. You can also avoid the dangers of adding your heirs as joint owners of your property and financial accounts.

If your child is in financial trouble, the bequest you leave may go directly to your child's creditors. You can protect your child's inheritance by using a spendthrift trust, which prevents your child from borrowing against the trust and protects the trust's assets against your child's creditors. (Spendthrift trusts are discussed in Chapter 12.)

You may be tempted to try to avoid the need for an estate plan by simply adding your children as joint owners of your real estate and bank accounts. But what if your child gets into financial difficulties or goes into bankruptcy? If your child is a co-owner, your child's creditors will pursue your home and your savings to pay your child's bills.

A revocable living trust provides benefits similar to having your child on the title, but your child's financial troubles won't jeopardize your estate. A transfer of title is extremely hard to undo, but you can amend or revoke your living trust any time you choose.

You Plan for Second (and Third, and Fourth) Marriages

If you don't have children, remarriage shouldn't complicate your estate. Rather than leaving your estate to your former spouse, it goes to your new spouse. But if you have children from a prior relationship or from more than one relationship, your estate is suddenly complicated. Without an estate plan, money you planned for your children to inherit may instead end up with your stepchildren.

In addition, the subsequent marriage may not be yours. If you die, your spouse may marry again. If your spouse dies or divorces, and the new spouse claims a share of their estate, what happens to your estate and to money you had hoped to go to your children? What if your spouse has children with the new spouse and chooses to leave your estate to them?

You can employ a trust to ensure that your spouse is well supported, but that the balance of your estate ultimately goes to your children. The Qualified Terminable Interest Property (QTIP) trust, also known as a marital trust, is used often for this purpose. With a QTIP trust, you can benefit from your assets during your life and support your spouse after your death, yet still control how your assets are distributed. This type of trust is discussed in Chapter 12.

You Plan for the Future of Your Business

If you own a business that you intend to leave to your heirs, trusts can help you avoid estate taxes and keep the business up and running after your death or incapacity.

The use of a revocable living trust can provide for the continued operation of the business during succession, without the interruption that may result from probate. If you want to get more complicated — and you probably do — trusts may

- ✔ Reduce the taxable value of your business interests to your estate.
- ✔ Help you give shares of the business to your children.
- ✔ Help maintain liquidity for the business in the event of your death.

 Business succession planning can be very complex. You will almost always benefit from having an experienced estate planning lawyer help create your succession plan (see Chapter 4).

You Can Transfer Real Property Located in Another State

A probate court in one state doesn't have authority over real estate located in another. Thus, when you own real estate in more than one state, probate proceedings become more complicated. To settle your estate, your personal representative will have to file an ancillary legal action (another probate case) in the state and county where the real estate is located. Ancillary actions are usually not complicated, but they create expense and delay the settlement of your estate.

Once you transfer your real estate holdings into a living trust, your trustee can manage your real estate across state lines. You thus avoid having to litigate probate issues in multiple states.

You Have Continuity of Investments

In probate, the assets of your estate may be temporarily frozen, with little or no active management of your investments while the probate process is completed. Your estate may liquidate your investments and distribute the proceeds as cash.

When you place your assets in a trust, your trustee can continuously manage your investments pursuant to the terms of the trust.

You Avoid Taxes

Trusts can help you avoid estate taxes. For example:

- ✔ The bypass trust (or A/B trust) is a common tool used to effectively double the estate tax exemption for a married couple.
- ✔ Charitable trusts can help you reduce your taxable estate while continuing to provide you with income.
- ✔ Insurance trusts can protect the proceeds of your life insurance from estate taxes.

Chapter 12 covers these trusts, as well as a number of others.

Although that list isn't intended to be comprehensive, you're probably wondering why your living trust is not included. The answer is simple: A basic living trust is primarily a tool for probate avoidance and has limited value for tax planning.

You can (and often should) incorporate tax-saving tools into your living trust — for example, by creating a bypass trust upon the death of a spouse — but you can also create a bypass trust with your will.

Chapter 20

Ten Tax Traps to Avoid When Planning Your Estate

● ●

In This Chapter

▶ Identifying estate tax traps

▶ Remembering your priorities when planning your estate

● ●

*W*hen you plan your estate, you plan how you're going to give your money to your heirs, not to the government. Yet if you have a substantial estate, failure to plan for taxes can result in a huge estate tax bill.

With planning, you can reduce your estate's tax liabilities and provide for the payment of any estate taxes owed without your heirs having to liquidate assets you intended them to inherit.

Not Planning Your Estate

You wouldn't be reading this book if you weren't intending to create an estate plan. Odds are, you also don't like the idea of paying lawyers or accountants to help you plan your estate. Some people don't like the idea of paying even $1 to a lawyer for help structuring an asset protection plan, even if it their estate will save $10 in taxes for every dollar they spend on planning.

I admit that I have sympathy for that position. It can be difficult to take money out of your wallet today in order to save taxes in the future, particularly when you won't even be alive to see the tax bill. You can easily say that your heirs are lucky to get anything, and that the estate tax is their problem.

Yet if your estate has to pay taxes, your entire estate plan may fall apart. The business you built, now managed by your child, may be encumbered by a significant loan necessary to pay estate taxes. The home you left to your child may have to be sold to pay the tax bill. Or perhaps the tax bill will be paid through the sale of heirlooms you hoped to keep in your family forever.

Your best approach is to plan your estate so that your assets are distributed in accord with your wishes, while accounting for the possibility of estate tax liability and providing for the payment of those taxes.

Focusing Too Much on the Estate Tax

I'm confident that you don't like the idea that the government may take a bite out of the assets you intend to leave to your heirs. I personally accept that paying taxes is a civic duty, but I don't know of anybody who feels a duty to pay taxes that can be lawfully avoided.

Nonetheless, the primary purpose of your estate plan is to leave your assets to your heirs. Tax planning can help ensure that your heirs receive the inheritances you intend, but too much tax planning can complicate your estate and their inheritances.

As you move from trying to minimize estate taxes to trying to completely avoid them, you may instead end up tying up your assets in a maze of trusts and restrictions that frustrate the primary goals of your estate plan.

Doubling the estate tax exemption with a bypass trust

An estate planning tool frequently used in larger estates is the *bypass trust,* through which a married couple can effectively double their exemption from estate taxes. While I highly recommend that you have a lawyer assist you in setting up a bypass trust, the potential cost savings is in the hundreds of thousands of dollars. Your spouse's inheritance from you is exempt from estate taxes, but the full value of your spouse's estate will be subject to estate taxes. If you leave all your assets to your spouse, they all potentially end up being subject to estate taxes.

If you and your spouse use a bypass trust, you place an amount, usually the value of the estate tax exemption at the time of your death, into a trust for the benefit of your children. While the trust must restrict your spouse's power to withdraw principal or redirect trust assets, you can direct the trust's income to your spouse. But because this money isn't included in your spouse's estate, your spouse's estate also benefits from the full estate tax exemption — and you've effectively doubled the exemption. See Chapter 12 for more detail on this trust.

Assuming that the Estate Tax Will Not Change

Ever since the passage of estate tax reform in 2001, the estate tax has been in a state of constant evolution. Each year brings new reductions, with the estate tax scheduled to be completely eliminated in 2010. And then in 2011, due to the budget trickery used to minimize the long-term financial impact of the reform, estate taxes revert back to the levels in effect prior to the 2001 tax cut.

Nobody expects that the reverse will occur. Congress will likely entertain a new reform bill that will impose an estate tax, but with much higher exemptions than existed in 2001. Estate tax opponents won't attempt to block a reform bill, as the consequence would be a full reversal of the estate tax.

The conventional wisdom is that very large estates should plan for the return of an estate tax, and that smaller estates (those held by 95 to 98 percent of all Americans) should expect to continue to be exempt from estate taxes. The greatest uncertainty is for estates valued between $1.5 million to $4 million, as the estate tax exemption is expected to fall somewhere within that range.

You can argue that this speculation is all guesswork, and the estate tax repeal will be made permanent. I will agree that even the best educated guesses can be wrong, but I will also remind you that nothing is permanent. No matter what happens prior to the 2011 estate tax reversion, another round (or more!) of estate tax reforms will likely occur during your lifetime.

Accept that an estate tax applies to larger estates and plan your estate with that in mind. Accept also that you may have to revise your estate in the future based upon unexpected changes in the nation's tax laws.

Trying to Guess How the Estate Tax Will Change

You can reasonably assume that the estate tax will change during your lifetime. After all, if you read the preceding section, I just told you that it's going to change. What you should not do is tie yourself up in knots trying to guess what the changes will be or try to plan your estate for every possible contingency.

You can't know the future. Plan your estate to the best of your ability based upon what you actually know or what you believe is reasonably certain to occur, and don't worry about the rest. If the law changes significantly during your lifetime, you can revise your estate plan.

Not Taking Advantage of Your Lifetime Gift Exclusion

At present, you can make lifetime gifts of up to $1 million under your lifetime gift tax exclusion. You may make individual gifts of up to $12,000 per year without triggering gift taxes. Gifts to your U.S. citizen spouse are not subject to gift tax and aren't counted toward these limits.

Your gift is valued at the time it's given, so the appreciation on your gift doesn't become part of your estate. The gift of stock worth $12,000 today may represent a reduction of your taxable estate by $25,000 or more a decade later. Two decades later, it may be $50,000 or more. Early gifting can effectively decrease your taxable estate by far more than the nominal $1 million lifetime exemption.

While gifts, once given, can't be taken back, for people with substantial estates gifts can be a very important part of the estate planning process.

Not Engaging in Business Succession Planning

If you're a business owner or own a significant share of a business, you may be making a comfortable living but not be paying much attention to how much the business is worth. When your estate is administered, the IRS will take a great deal of interest in the value of your business.

Here's a possible scenario . Your adult child joins your family business and gradually assumes a management role. Eventually, you retire, and your child takes over the business, achieving significant growth. You enjoy a healthy retirement income, and it never occurs to you to transfer any ownership interest to your child. Leaving aside the problems that can result if you have other children who will share in the inheritance of the business, the child who manages the business may suddenly have to deal with substantial estate tax obligations based upon the valuation of the business at the time of your death.

With a transition plan in place, your child (or children) can receive shares of the business during your lifetime, and the value of those gifts will be fixed as of the time they were given. While they won't get stepped-up basis in the share value at the time of your death, they will still benefit from the lower stock valuation at the time they received the gift. The lower value of the shares at the time of your gift can potentially save a great deal of estate tax and, if your child intends to retain ownership of the business, the potential increase in capital gains tax at the time any shares are sold should not be a significant concern.

You can also engage in a stock purchase plan, which allows your manager child or all your children to buy shares of the business from you, replacing income from the business with income from the stock purchase agreement. Be sure to take into consideration the capital gains taxes you may owe upon selling the shares.

Hiding Property Transfers and Gifts from the IRS

You know you're likely to owe estate taxes, but what if you give your assets away to your heirs before you die? You can add them to the deeds of your real estate, or make gifts of cash or other valuables in excess of the annual gift tax exclusion, and how will the IRS ever know?

The IRS will know, because your personal representative will report the gifts when completing the inventory of your estate for the probate court. The inventory is submitted under penalty of perjury, and you shouldn't be surprised that the possibility of jail can inspire a great deal of honesty. From your lifetime of tax returns, the IRS should have a pretty good idea of the assets that should be in your estate, and your executor will realize that lying about your history of gifts creates a serious personal risk.

You may be thinking about adding your heirs to the title of your property to avoid having it pass through your estate. With the exception of joint ownership by your spouse, where the IRS will tax only half the value of the jointly held asset, the IRS will presume that the entire value of the jointly held real estate is part of your estate.

> ## Be careful with jointly titled property
>
> You may have a good reason to own your property jointly with others, but joint title can create unexpected estate tax ramifications. Imagine, for example, that your daughter wants to buy a house, and you loan her the down payment. In order to protect your interest in the property, you decide that the home should be jointly titled to you and your daughter.
>
> When the IRS learns of the jointly held property, it won't just include the amount of the down payment in your estate. Even if your daughter
>
> has made all the tax, mortgage, and maintenance payments from the day the house was purchased, the IRS will seek to include the entire value of the joint asset in your estate. To avoid having her contribution subjected to estate taxes, your daughter must document to the IRS her contribution to the value of the property, providing evidence as bank records, cancelled checks, and other documentation the IRS requests.

Having Your Estate Be the Beneficiary of Your Life Insurance

Life insurance is generally said to pass outside your estate, meaning that life insurance proceeds do not have to pass through probate and don't have to be counted as part of your estate for the calculation of estate taxes. You can avoid taxes by transferring ownership of your policy to somebody else, and by making sure that your estate isn't the beneficiary of your policy. (See Chapter 16 for a more detailed explanation of how life insurance works.)

If you make your estate the beneficiary of your life insurance, your insurance proceeds become part of your estate, and the tax man is happy to take a share.

Changing beneficiaries is simple. Ask your insurance company for a designation of beneficiary form, complete and return it, and confirm that it has been received and processed by your insurer. But if your estate may have to pay estate taxes, designating a beneficiary is only half of the story.

To avoid estate taxes on the proceeds of your life insurance policies, you also need to transfer ownership of your policy away from yourself — to another person or entity, such as an irrevocable life insurance trust. (Life insurance trusts are discussed in Chapter 12). If premiums are due on your policy after the transfer, the new owners must pay the premiums. (You can use the annual gift tax exclusion to provide the owner with a gift of up to $12,000 per year, which they can use to pay the premium.) When you transfer ownership, you also give up your ability to directly make changes to the policy, including changing beneficiaries. You should obtain written confirmation of the ownership change from your insurance company.

If you transfer ownership of your life insurance from your estate within three years of your death, you risk having the proceeds included in your estate anyway. Gifts of life insurance policies made within three years of your death remain subject to federal estate tax.

Not Preparing Your Estate to Pay Any Estate Tax Owed

Assume that you have carefully composed an estate plan, and you expect that your estate will owe taxes. If your estate doesn't have cash on hand to pay the estate taxes, it may have to sell off the property you intend for your heirs in order to pay the tax bill.

If your estate holds substantial investment accounts or other savings, its ability to pay taxes may not be an issue. You may be content to have your investments liquidated to pay the estate tax. But if you don't wish for that outcome or don't have that type of liquidity, you may choose to purchase life insurance to cover your estate's tax bill.

You can create a life insurance trust and either transfer an existing life insurance policy to your trust or have your trust purchase a new policy. In order to avoid having the trust included in your estate, this trust must be irrevocable, meaning that once you create this trust, you can't change your mind. When a life insurance trust is done correctly, the insurance proceeds will not be subject to estate taxes, and your estate can use the money to pay the expenses of the estate, including taxes and administrative expenses, outstanding debts, and funeral costs.

Forgetting That Your Estate Will Grow Over Time

If you're like most people, your estate will continue to grow over the course of your life. As you accumulate more assets, this growth tends to accelerate.

Today, estate tax may look like a distant, unlikely possibility. Twenty or 30 years from now, your situation may be very different.

Some appreciation in your assets may be almost invisible. Your home or vacation property may substantially increase in value. Your business may grow, as will your retirement savings. If you forget to transfer your insurance policies to third parties or make an ineffective transfer, the insurance money is added to the pool. You may be on track to having a much larger estate than you had realized.

Periodically review your estate plan and be sure that you include a residuary clause directing assets not specifically described in your will to your desired heirs. And don't forget, tax avoidance strategies are best implemented early. If you own a business or may pay estate taxes, the sooner you implement your gifting strategy, business succession plan, and other tax strategies, the more tax you and your heirs are likely to avoid.

Part VI
Appendixes

The 5th Wave   By Rich Tennant

"That? That's form 1040DTX. In the unlikely event that anyone ever does figure out how to 'take it with them,' the federal government has in place a form and instructions on how to send back the appropriate amount of taxes due."

In this part . . .

This part contains information to help you understand state law requirements for executing a valid will, state inheritance taxes, and a form to help you compile personal and financial information for your estate plan. It also offers a list of the forms provided on the accompanying CD.

Appendix A

State Signing Requirements

This appendix summarizes the signing requirements for formal wills in all 50 states and provides an overview of how to properly execute a will. Although I strive for accuracy, the laws of some states may have changed since the time of publication.

When you execute your will, consider your state's requirements as the minimum you should do. For example:

- ✔ If your state requires two witnesses, consider using three.
- ✔ If your state permits you to use a minor as a witness to your will, instead use competent adults.
- ✔ If your state is among those that don't penalize a witness who is also an heir, choose witnesses who will not inherit under your will anyway.
- ✔ If a self-proving affidavit is optional in your state, execute one anyway.

A *self-proving affidavit* creates a presumption that the will was properly executed and that the signatures on the will are valid. The affidavit simplifies admission of your will to the probate court.

Alabama

To execute a valid will in Alabama:

- ✔ You must sign your will, or your will must be signed in your name by some other person in your presence and at your direction.
- ✔ Your will must be signed by at least two witnesses who either witness the signing of your will or witness you acknowledge the signature or your will.

Any person generally competent to be a witness may act as a witness to your will. No part of your will becomes invalid if will is signed by an interested witness.

Alabama recognizes self-proving affidavits.

Alaska

To execute a valid will in Alaska:

- ✔ You must sign your will, or your will must be signed in your name by some other person in your presence and at your direction.
- ✔ Your will must be signed by at least two witnesses within a reasonable time after they either witness the signing of your will or witness that you acknowledge the signature on your will.

Any person generally competent to be a witness may act as a witness to your will. No part of your will becomes invalid if an interested witness signs the will.

Alaska recognizes self-proving affidavits.

Arizona

To execute a valid will in Arizona:

- ✔ You must sign your will, or the will must be signed in your name by some other person in your presence and at your direction.
- ✔ Your will must be signed by at least two witnesses within a reasonable time after they either witness the signing or your will or witness that you acknowledge the signature or your will.

Any person generally competent to be a witness may act as a witness to your will. No part of your will becomes invalid if an interested witness signs your will.

Arizona recognizes self-proving affidavits.

Arkansas

To execute a valid will in Arkansas:

- ✔ You must sign your will at the end of the document, whether in your own hand, by *mark* (a mark, such as an X, made in lieu of a signature by a person who is illiterate or is physically unable to sign her own name), or by instructing somebody else to sign your name for you.

✔ In the presence of two or more attesting witnesses, you must declare to your witnesses that the instrument is your will and do one of the following:

- Sign your will.

- Acknowledge your signature already made.

- Sign by mark, with your name written near the mark and witnessed by a person who writes his own name as witness to the signature.

- In your presence, have someone else sign your name for you. The person signing your will must write his own name and state that he signed your name at your request.

Any person aged 18 or older and competent to be a witness may act as a witness to your will. Your will isn't invalidated if signed by an interested witness, but unless you have at least two other qualified disinterested witnesses to the will, the interested witness will inherit the lesser of your bequest or the amount the witness would have inherited had you died intestate.

Arkansas recognizes self-proving affidavits.

California

To execute a valid will in California:

✔ Your will must be signed

- By you

- In your name by some other person in your presence and by your direction

- By a conservator pursuant to a court order to make a will under Section 2580 of the California Probate Code

✔ Your will must be witnessed by being signed by at least two persons, present at the same time, who

- Witness either the signing of the will or your acknowledgment of the signature or of the will

- Understand that the instrument they sign is the your will

Any person generally competent to be a witness may act as a witness to your will. No part of your will is invalid if your will is signed by an interested witness.

However, unless you have at least two other subscribing witnesses to your will who are disinterested, the interested witness is presumed to have procured your bequest by means of duress, menace, fraud, or undue influence. If that presumption isn't overcome, the interested witness will inherit the lesser of your bequest or the amount the witness would have inherited had you died intestate.

California recognizes self-proving affidavits.

Colorado

To execute a valid will in Colorado:

✔ Your will must be signed by you or in your name by some other individual in your conscious presence and by your direction. *Conscious presence* requires the individual to be in physical proximity to you but not necessarily within your line of sight.

✔ Signed by at least two witnesses, either prior to or after the testator's death, each of whom sign within a reasonable time after he witnesses either your signing of the will as described in the preceding paragraph or your acknowledgment of that signature or acknowledgment of the will.

Any person generally competent to be a witness may act as a witness to your will. No part of your will becomes invalid if will is signed by an interested witness.

Colorado recognizes self-proving affidavits.

Connecticut

To execute a valid will in Connecticut:

✔ You must sign your will.

✔ Two witnesses must attest to your will, each of them signing in your presence.

Your bequest to somebody who serves as a witness to your will is ordinarily rendered void.

Connecticut recognizes self-proving affidavits.

Delaware

To execute a valid will in Delaware:

- ✔ Your will must be signed by you, or in your name by some other individual in your presence and by your direction.
- ✔ Two or more credible witnesses must attest to your will, each of them signing in your presence.

Any person generally competent to be a witness may act as a witness to your will. No part of your will becomes invalid if an interested witness signs your will.

Delaware recognizes self-proving affidavits.

Florida

To execute a valid will in Florida:

- ✔ You must sign your will at the end of the document, either by your own hand or by having another person subscribe your name to the will.
- ✔ In the presence of two or more attesting witnesses, you must declare to your witnesses that the instrument is your will and do one of the following:
  - Sign your will
  - Acknowledge your signature already made
  - Acknowledge that another person has subscribed your name to your will

Any person generally competent to be a witness may act as a witness to your will. No part of your will becomes invalid if will is signed by an interested witness.

Florida recognizes self-proving affidavits.

Georgia

To execute a valid will in Georgia:

> ✔ You must sign your will or by express direction have some other indi-
> vidual sign your will in your presence. You may sign by mark or by any
> name that is intended to authenticate the instrument as your will.
>
> ✔ Your will must be attested and subscribed in your presence by two or
> more competent witnesses. A witness to your will may attest by mark.

Any person generally competent to be a witness and age 14 or over may act
as a witness to your will. Another individual may not subscribe the name of a
witness, even in that witness's presence and at that witness's direction.

Georgia recognizes self-proving affidavits.

Hawaii

To execute a valid will in Hawaii:

> ✔ You must sign your will, or your will must be signed in your name by
> some other person in your presence and at your direction.
>
> ✔ Your will must be signed by at least two witnesses within a reasonable
> time after they either witness the signing of your will or witness you
> acknowledging the signature on your will.

Any person generally competent to be a witness may act as a witness to your
will. No part of your will becomes invalid if an interested witness signs your will.

Hawaii recognizes self-proving affidavits.

Idaho

To execute a valid will in Idaho:

> ✔ You must sign your will, or your will must be signed in your name by
> some other person in your presence and at your direction.
>
> ✔ Your will must be signed by at least two witnesses who either witness the
> signing of your will or witness you acknowledging the signature on your will.

Any person generally competent to be a witness may act as a witness to your will.
No part of your will becomes invalid if an interested witness signs your will.

Idaho recognizes self-proving affidavits.

Illinois

To execute a valid will in Illinois:

- ✔ You must sign your will, or your will must be signed in your name by some other person in your presence and at your direction.
- ✔ Your will must be attested in the presence of two or more credible witnesses.

If you leave property to a witness, or to the spouse of a witness, to your will, your bequest to the witness is void as to that witness, unless your will is witnessed by at least two other independent witnesses. However, the interested witness is entitled to receive the lesser of your bequest or the amount the witness would have inherited had you died intestate.

Illinois recognizes self-proving affidavits.

Indiana

To execute a valid will in Indiana:

- ✔ In the presence of two or more attesting witnesses, signify to your witnesses that the instrument is your will and:

  - Sign your will

  - Acknowledge your signature already made

  - Direct somebody within your presence to sign your name to your will

- ✔ Your attesting witnesses must sign your will in the presence of you and each other.

Any person competent to be a witness in the State of Indiana may serve as a witness to your will. If an heir serves as your witness and the will can't be proved without the testimony or proof of the signature of that witness, your bequest to that witness and those claiming under him is void. However, the interested witness is entitled to receive the lesser of your bequest or the amount the witness would have inherited had you died intestate.

Indiana recognizes self-proving affidavits.

Iowa

To execute a valid will in Iowa:

- ✔ You must

    - Sign your will or have somebody sign your name to the will within your presence and by your express direction

    - Declare that the will is in fact your will

- ✔ Two or more attesting witnesses must sign your will in the presence of you and each other.

Any person who is 16 years of age or older and who is competent to be a witness generally in the State of Iowa may act as an attesting witness to your will.

Iowa recognizes self-proving affidavits.

Kansas

To execute a valid will in Kansas:

- ✔ At the end of your will, you must sign your will or have somebody sign your name to the will within your presence and by your express direction.

- ✔ Two or more competent witnesses must attest and subscribe to your will in your presence, having seen you subscribe to your will or having heard you acknowledge the will.

Kansas recognizes self-proving affidavits.

Kentucky

To execute a valid will in Kentucky:

- ✔ You must sign your will or have some other person sign your will in your presence and at your direction.

- ✔ The subscription must be made or your will must be acknowledged by you in the presence of at least two credible witnesses, who must subscribe the will with their names in your presence and in the presence of each other.

Kansas recognizes self-proving affidavits.

Louisiana

Your notarial testament must be prepared in writing and dated. If you know how to sign your name and can read and are physically able to do both, then your notarial testament must be executed in the following manner:

1. In the presence of a notary and two competent witnesses, you must declare or signify to them that the instrument is your testament and shall sign your name at the end of the testament and on each other separate page.

2. In the presence of the testator and each other, the notary and the witnesses must sign the following declaration, or one substantially similar: "In our presence, the testator has declared or signified that this instrument is his testament and has signed it at the end and on each other separate page, and in the presence of the testator and each other we have hereunto subscribed our names this ____day of _____, ____."

Louisiana law also provides for the *notarial testament,* including, if needed, a notarial testament in Braille form, for

- ✔ A person who is literate and sighted, but unable to sign

- ✔ A person who is unable to read

- ✔ A person who is legally deaf, or deaf and blind

The formalities prescribed for the execution of a testament must be observed, or the testament is absolutely null.

Witness qualifications are as follows:

- ✔ A person can't be a witness to any testament if he is insane, blind, under the age of 16, or unable to sign his name.

- ✔ A person who is competent but deaf or unable to read can't be a witness to a notarial testament under Louisiana Civil Code Article 1579.

The fact that a witness or the notary is a beneficiary of the will doesn't invalidate the testament. A legacy to a witness or the notary is invalid, but if the witness would be an heir in intestacy, the witness may receive the lesser of his intestate share (the amount the witness would have inherited had you died intestate) or the legacy in the testament. A person may not be a witness to a testament if that person is a spouse of a legatee at the time of the execution of the testament. The fact that a witness is the spouse of a legatee doesn't invalidate the testament; however, a legacy to a witness' spouse is invalid if the witness is the spouse of the legatee at the time of the execution of the testament.

Generally, if the legacy is invalidated and if the legatee would be an heir in intestacy, the legatee may receive the lesser of his intestate share or legacy in the testament. Any testamentary terms or restrictions placed on the legacy shall remain in effect.

Notarization is mandatory.

Maine

To execute a valid will in Maine:

- ✔ You must sign your will, or your will must be signed in your name by some other person in your presence and at your direction.
- ✔ Your will must be signed by at least two witnesses, each of whom witnessed either your signing or your acknowledgement of the signature or of the will.

Any person generally competent to be a witness may act as a witness to your will. Your will isn't invalid if an interested witness signs it.

Maine recognizes self-proving affidavits.

Maryland

To execute a valid will in Maryland:

- ✔ You must sign your will, or somebody else must sign your will on your behalf.
- ✔ Your will must be attested and signed by two or more credible witnesses in your presence.

Maryland doesn't have a statute setting forth a format for self-proved wills. However, even if not properly witnessed, Maryland's laws permit submission of a will for probate based upon the verified statement of a person with personal knowledge of the circumstances of execution of the will, whether or not that person was a witness to the will.

Massachusetts

To execute a valid will in Massachusetts:

- ✔ Your will must be signed by you or by a person in your presence and by your express direction.
- ✔ Your will must be attested and subscribed in your presence by two or more competent witnesses.

Any person of sufficient understanding is deemed to be a competent witness to a will, notwithstanding any common law disqualification for interest or otherwise. However, a bequest to a subscribing witness or to the husband or wife of such witness is void unless your will has two other subscribing witnesses who aren't similarly benefited by the will.

Massachusetts recognizes self-proving affidavits.

Michigan

To execute a valid will in Michigan:

- ✔ You must sign your will, or your will must be signed in your name by some other individual in your conscious presence and by your direction.

- ✔ Your will must be signed by at least two individuals, each of whom signed within a reasonable time after witnessing either the signing of your will or your acknowledgment of that signature or acknowledgment of your will.

An individual generally competent to be a witness may act as a witness to a will. The signing of a will by an interested witness doesn't invalidate the will or any provision of it.

Michigan recognizes self-proving affidavits.

Minnesota

To execute a valid will in Minnesota:

- ✔ Your will must be signed by you, be signed in your name by some other individual in your conscious presence and by your direction, or signed by your conservator pursuant to a court order under section 524.5-411 of the Minnesota Statutes.

- ✔ Your will must be signed by at least two individuals, each of whom signed within a reasonable time after witnessing either your signing of your will or your acknowledgment of the signature or acknowledgment of your will.

An individual generally competent to be a witness may act as a witness to a will. The signing of a will by an interested witness doesn't invalidate the will or any provision of it.

Minnesota recognizes self-proving affidavits.

Mississippi

To execute a valid will in Mississippi:

- ✔ Your will must be signed by you, be signed in your name by some other individual in your presence and by your express direction.
- ✔ Your will must be attested by two or more credible witnesses in your presence.

If you leave property to a witness to your will and the will can't be proven without the testimony of that witness, your bequest to the witness is void. However, the interested witness is entitled to receive the lesser of your bequest or the amount the witness would have inherited had you died intestate.

Mississippi recognizes self-proving affidavits.

Missouri

To execute a valid will in Missouri:

- ✔ You must sign your will, or your will must be signed by another person by your direction and in your presence.
- ✔ Your will must be attested by two or more competent witnesses who subscribe their names to the will in your presence.

Any person competent to be a witness generally in the State of Missouri may act as attesting witness to a will. If an heir serves as your witness and the will can't be proved without the testimony or proof of the signature of that witness, your bequest to that witness and those claiming under him is void. However, the interested witness is entitled to receive the lesser of your bequest or the amount the witness would have inherited had you died intestate.

Missouri recognizes self-proving affidavits.

Montana

To execute a valid will in Montana:

- ✔ You must sign your will, or your will must be signed in your name by some other individual in your conscious presence and by your direction.

✔ Your will must be signed by at least two individuals, each of whom signs within a reasonable time after having witnessed either your signing of your will or your acknowledgment of the signature or acknowledgment of your will.

An individual generally competent to be a witness may act as a witness to a will. The signing of a will by an interested witness doesn't invalidate the will or any provision of it.

Montana recognizes self-proving affidavits.

Nebraska

To execute a valid will in Nebraska:

✔ You must sign your will, or your will must be signed in your name by some other individual in your conscious presence and by your direction.

✔ Your will must be signed by at least two individuals, each of whom witnessed either your signing or your acknowledgment of the signature or of your will.

Any individual generally competent to be a witness may act as a witness to your will. No part of your will is invalid because your will is signed by an interested witness. However, unless you have at least one disinterested witness to a will, an interested witness to a will inherits the lesser of your bequest or the amount the witness would have inherited had you died intestate.

Nebraska recognizes self-proving affidavits.

Nevada

To execute a valid will in Nevada:

✔ You must sign your will, or your will must be signed by an attending person at your express direction.

✔ Your will must be attested by at least two competent witnesses who subscribe their names to your will in your presence.

All bequests to a subscribing witness are void unless you have two other competent subscribing witnesses to your will.

Nevada recognizes self-proving affidavits.

New Hampshire

To execute a valid will in New Hampshire:

- ✔ You must sign your will, or your will must be signed by some other person at your express direction in your presence.
- ✔ Your will must be signed by two or more credible witnesses, who shall, at your request and in your presence, attest to your signature.

Any bequest to a witness to your will, or to the spouse of a witness, is void unless you have two other competent subscribing witnesses to your will.

New Hampshire recognizes self-proving affidavits.

New Jersey

To execute a valid will in New Jersey:

- ✔ You must sign your will, or your will must be signed in your name by some other individual in your conscious presence and at your direction.
- ✔ Your will must be signed by at least two individuals, each of whom signed within a reasonable time after each witnessed either the signing of your will or your acknowledgment of that signature or acknowledgment of your will.

Any individual generally competent to be a witness may act as a witness to a will and testify concerning its execution. A will isn't invalidated if signed by an interested witness.

New Jersey recognizes self-proving affidavits.

New Mexico

To execute a valid will in New Mexico:

- ✔ Your will must be signed by you or in your name by some other individual in your conscious presence and by your direction
- ✔ Your will must be signed by at least two individuals, each of whom signs in your presence and in the presence of each other after each witnessed the signing of your will.

An individual generally competent to be a witness may act as a witness to your will. The signing of your will by an interested witness doesn't invalidate your will or any of its provisions.

New Mexico recognizes self-proving affidavits.

New York

To execute a valid will in New York:

- You must sign your will at the end of the document, or your will must be signed at its end in your name by another person in your presence and by your direction.

- Your signature must be affixed to the will in the presence of each of the attesting witnesses or shall be acknowledged by you to each of them to have been affixed by you or at your direction. You may either sign in the presence of the attesting witnesses or acknowledge your signature to each attesting witness separately.

- During the ceremony or ceremonies of execution and attestation, you must declare to each of the attesting witnesses that the instrument to which your signature has been affixed is your will.

- You must have at least two attesting witnesses who, within one 30-day period, both attest to your signature, as affixed or acknowledged in their presence, and at your request, sign their names and affix their residence addresses at the end of the will. It's presumed that this 30-day requirement has been fulfilled unless evidence is produced to rebut that presumption. The failure of a witness to affix his address doesn't affect the validity of the will.

If another person signs your will on your behalf, that person must sign his own name and affix his residence address to your will. That person doesn't count as a witness.

If you leave a bequest to a witness to your will, your bequest to the witness is void as to that witness unless your will is witnessed by at least two other independent witnesses, and even then it's valid only if the will can be proved without the testimony of the interested witness. However, the interested witness is entitled to receive the lesser of your bequest or the amount the witness would have inherited had you died intestate.

New York recognizes self-proving affidavits.

North Carolina

To execute a valid will in North Carolina:

- ✔ You must, with intent to sign your will, do so by signing the will yourself or by having someone else in your presence and at your direction sign your name thereon.

- ✔ You must signify to the attesting witnesses that the instrument is your instrument by signing it in their presence or by acknowledging to them your signature on your will, either of which may be done before the attesting witnesses separately.

- ✔ The attesting witnesses must sign the will in your presence but need not sign in the presence of each other.

Any person competent to be a witness generally in the State of North Carolina may act as a witness to a will. If you leave a bequest to a witness or to the spouse of a witness, and you don't have at least two other witnesses to the will who are disinterested, the interested witness and spouse and anyone claiming under them take nothing under the will, and the will is void in relation to their interests.

North Carolina recognizes self-proving affidavits.

North Dakota

To execute a valid will in North Dakota:

- ✔ You must sign your will, or your will must be signed in your name by some other individual in your conscious presence and by your direction.

- ✔ Your will must be signed by at least two individuals, each of whom signs within a reasonable time after witnessing either the signing of your will or your acknowledgment of the signature or acknowledgment of your will.

Any person generally competent to be a witness may act as a witness to a will. No provision of your will is rendered invalid because the will is signed by an interested witness.

North Dakota recognizes self-proving affidavits.

Ohio

To execute a valid will in Ohio:

> ✔ You must sign your will at the end, or your will must be signed at its end by some other person in your presence and at your express direction.
>
> ✔ Your will must be attested and subscribed in your presence, by two or more competent witnesses, who saw your subscribe, or heard you acknowledge your signature.

Your witnesses must be at least 18 years of age.

Oklahoma

To execute a valid will in Oklahoma:

> ✔ You must subscribe to your will at the end of the document, or some other person, in your presence and by your direction must subscribe your name at the end of your will.
>
> ✔ The subscription must be made in the presence of the attesting witnesses or be acknowledged by you to them to have been made by you or by your authority.
>
> ✔ You must, at the time of subscribing or acknowledging you will, declare to the attesting witnesses that the instrument is your will.
>
> ✔ You must have two attesting witnesses, each of whom must sign his name as a witness at the end of your will at your request and in your presence.

Your bequests to a subscribing witness to your will are void unless you have two other competent subscribing witnesses to your will.

Oklahoma recognizes self-proving affidavits.

Oregon

To execute a valid will in Oregon:

> ✔ In the presence of the witnesses, you must
>
>   • Sign the will
>
>   • Direct one of the witnesses or some other person to sign your name on the will, also having that person sign his own name on the will and write on the will that the signer signed at your direction
>
>   • Acknowledge a signature previously made on the will by you or at your direction

✔ At least two witnesses shall each

- See you sign the will or hear you acknowledge the signature on the will

- Attest the will by signing their names to it

A will attested by an interested witness isn't thereby invalidated

Oregon recognizes self-proving affidavits.

Pennsylvania

To execute a valid will in Pennsylvania, you must sign your will at the end of the document.

✔ If you're unable to sign your name, you may subscribe to your will by making your mark in the presence of two witnesses who sign their names to the will in your presence.

✔ If you're unable to sign your name or to make your mark for any reason, a will to which your name is subscribed in your presence and by your express direction shall be as valid as though you had signed your name, provided that you declare the instrument to be your will in the presence of two witnesses who sign their names to it in your presence.

Pennsylvania recognizes self-proving affidavits.

Rhode Island

To execute a valid will in Rhode Island:

✔ You must sign your will, or your will must be signed by some other person for you in your presence and by your express direction.

✔ The signature must be made or acknowledged by you in the presence of two or more witnesses present at the same time.

✔ The witnesses must attest and must subscribe the will in your presence, but no form of attestation shall be necessary, and no other publication shall be necessary.

Rhode Island recognizes self-proving affidavits.

South Carolina

To execute a valid will in South Carolina:

- ✔ You must sign your will, or your will must be signed in your name by some other person in your presence and by your direction.
- ✔ Your will must be signed by at least two persons each of whom witnessed either the signing or your acknowledgment of the signature or of the will.

If you leave a bequest to a witness or the spouse of a witness, unless you have two other disinterested witnesses to your will, the witness or spouse may inherit only up to the amount of the share of your estate they would have received had you died intestate.

South Carolina recognizes self-proving affidavits.

South Dakota

To execute a valid will in South Dakota:

- ✔ You must sign your will, or your will must be signed in your name by some other individual in your conscious presence and by your direction.
- ✔ Your will must be signed in your conscious presence by two or more individuals who, in your conscious presence, witnessed either the signing of your will or your acknowledgment of the signature.

An individual generally competent to be a witness may act as a witness to a will. The signing of a will by an interested witness doesn't invalidate the will or any provision of it.

South Dakota recognizes self-proving affidavits.

Tennessee

To execute a valid will in Tennessee:

✔ In the presence of at least two witnesses, you must signify to the attesting witnesses that the instrument is your will and

- Sign the will

- Acknowledge your signature, already made

- At your direction and in your presence have someone else sign your name

✔ The attesting witnesses must sign in your presence, and in the presence of each other

Any person competent to be a witness generally in this state may act as attesting witness to a will. No will is invalidated because it's attested by an interested witness, but, unless your will is also attested by two disinterested witnesses, any interested witness shall forfeit any inheritance greater than what the witness would have received had you died intestate.

Tennessee recognizes self-proving affidavits.

Texas

To execute a valid will in Texas:

✔ You must sign your will, or your will must be signed by another person for you by your direction and in your presence.

✔ Two or more credible witnesses above the age of 14 years must attest to your will and must subscribe their names to your will in their own handwriting in your presence.

If you leave a bequest to a witness, and the will can't be established without the testimony of that witness, the bequest to the witness is void. However, the interested witness is entitled to receive the lesser of your bequest or the amount the witness would have inherited had you died intestate.

Texas recognizes self-proving affidavits.

Utah

To execute a valid will in Utah:

✔ You must sign your will, or your will must be signed in your name by some other individual in your conscious presence and by your direction.

✔ Your will must be signed by at least two individuals, each of whom signs within a reasonable time after witnessing either the signing of the will or your acknowledgment of the signature or acknowledgment of the will.

An individual generally competent to be a witness may act as a witness to a will. The signing of a will by an interested witness doesn't invalidate the will or any provision of it.

Utah recognizes self-proving affidavits.

Vermont

To execute a valid will in Vermont:

✔ You must sign your will, or your name must be written by some other person in your presence and by your express direction.

✔ Your will must be attested and subscribed by two or more credible witnesses in your presence and in the presence of each other.

If you leave a bequest to a witness or the spouse of a witness, the bequest is void unless you have three other competent witnesses to the will.

Virginia

To execute a valid will in Virginia:

✔ You must sign your will, or your will must be signed by some other person in your presence and by your direction, in such manner as to make it manifest that the name is intended as a signature.

✔ Your signature must be made or the will acknowledged by you in the presence of at least two competent witnesses, present at the same time.

✔ The witnesses must subscribe the will in your presence, but no form of attestation shall be necessary.

No person is incompetent to testify for or against your will solely because that person has an interest in your will or estate.

Virginia recognizes self-proving affidavits.

Washington

To execute a valid will in Washington:

- ✔ You must sign your will, or your will must be signed by some other person under your direction in your presence.

- ✔ Your will must be attested by two or more competent witnesses, who must either subscribe their names to the will or sign an affidavit meeting statutory requirements, while in your presence and at your direction or request.

No part of your will is invalid because it's signed by a witness to whom you have left a bequest. However, it's presumed that the gift was a result of fraud unless you have two other witnesses to your will.

Washington recognizes self-proving affidavits.

West Virginia

To execute a valid will in West Virginia:

- ✔ You must sign your will, or your will must be signed by some other person in your presence and by your direction, in such manner as to make it manifest that the name is intended as a signature.

- ✔ The signature must be made or the will acknowledged by you in the presence of at least two competent witnesses, present at the same time.

- ✔ Your witnesses must subscribe the will in your presence and in the presence of each other.

If you leave a bequest to a witness or the spouse of a witness, the bequest is normally void. The exception? If your witness or spouse would be entitled to an intestate share of your estate, your bequest is saved up to the amount of the intestate share.

West Virginia recognizes self-proving affidavits.

Wisconsin

To execute a valid will in Wisconsin:

- ✔ You must sign your will, alone or with another person assisting you with your consent, or in your name by another person at your direction and in your conscious presence.

- ✔ Your will must be signed by at least two witnesses who sign within a reasonable time after any of the following:

  - Your signing of your will in the conscious presence of the witness

  - Your implicit or explicit acknowledgement of your signature on the will, in the conscious presence of the witness

  - Your implicit or explicit acknowledgement of the will, in the conscious presence of the witness

Your witnesses may observe your signing or acknowledgement at different times.

Any person who, at the time of execution of the will, would be competent to testify as a witness in court to the facts relating to execution may act as a witness to the will. If you leave a bequest to a witness or to the spouse of a witness, the bequests are invalid to the extent that their aggregate value exceeds what the witness or spouse would receive if you die intestate. However, that limitation doesn't apply if you have two other disinterested witnesses to your will, or if sufficient evidence is produced to demonstrate that you intended the full transfer to take effect.

Wisconsin recognizes self-proving affidavits.

Wyoming

To execute a valid will in Wyoming:

- ✔ You must sign your will, or your will must be signed by some other person in your presence and by your express direction.
- ✔ Your will must be witnessed by two competent witnesses.

Any person generally competent to be a witness may act as a witness to your will. If you leave a bequest to a witness, unless you have at least two other qualified disinterested witnesses to the will, the interested witness will inherit the lesser of your bequest or the amount the witness would have inherited had you died intestate.

Wyoming recognizes self-proving affidavits.

Appendix B

State Inheritance Taxes

S tates have traditionally imposed two forms of taxes on estates:

✔ **Estate taxes:** Taxes paid by your estate, based upon the total size of your estate. Traditionally, every state has imposed an estate tax. For the most part, these taxes were covered by a federal estate tax exemption and didn't raise the tax burden on estates.

✔ **Inheritance taxes:** Taxes based upon the size of your bequest to a particular heir and your heir's relationship to you. Only a few states impose inheritance taxes.

Your estate may also file federal, state, and local income tax returns for your last year of life, and another set of tax returns for income earned by your assets during the administration of your estate. Those income taxes aren't affected by estate tax reforms.

This appendix guides you through the taxes you need to pay based on where you live. If you want to see the laws of your state in more detail, the Web site of CCH Incorporated (www.cch.com) summarizes state estate and inheritance tax laws . Click CCH Websites, CCH Financial Planning Toolkit, and then Estate Planning. Then scroll down toward the bottom of the page where you'll find a link to Estate Taxes.

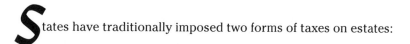

The Impact of Federal Estate Tax Reform

Prior to 2001, the federal estate tax law included a credit for state estate taxes paid, up to a specified dollar limit. States were able to tax estates up to the amount of the federal limit without raising the overall tax bill of the estate. This type of tax is known as a *pick-up tax*. As of 2001, all states imposed estate taxes up to the federal limit, and most imposed no further estate taxes.

With the passage of the estate tax reform law in 2001, the federal estate tax credit was phased out. As a consequence of that law, states can no longer impose estate taxes without increasing the tax burden on estates. Most states chose not to impose an additional tax burden, and some repealed their existing estate taxes.

Because most states haven't changed their laws, if the 2001 estate tax legislation expires in 2010 and the federal estate tax credit returns, most states will immediately start collecting pick-up taxes. A few states have repealed their pick-up taxes along with their state estate tax laws, but it is reasonable to assume that they will quickly pass legislation to take advantage of any federal estate tax credit. Although pickup taxes don't increase your estate's total tax bill, your personal representative will have to prepare and submit an additional tax return.

States That Don't Tax Estates

The following states do not presently impose either inheritance or estate taxes:

Alabama	Alaska	Arizona	Arkansas	California
Colorado	Delaware	Florida	Georgia	Hawaii
Idaho	Michigan	Mississippi	Missouri	Montana
Nevada	New Hampshire	New Mexico	North Dakota	South Carolina
South Dakota	Texas	Utah	Virginia	West Virginia
Wisconsin	Wyoming			

Most of these states have dormant pick-up taxes that will come back into effect if the 2001 estate tax legislation expires in 2010. (For more information, see the preceding section.)

States That Impose Only Inheritance Taxes

The following states impose inheritance taxes, but do not impose estate taxes:

Indiana	Iowa	Kentucky	Louisiana
Nebraska	Pennsylvania	Tennessee	

Most states either exempt close relatives from inheritance taxes or offer different tax rates and exemption levels based upon how closely related your heir is to you.

States That Impose Only Estate Taxes

The following states impose estate taxes, but do not impose inheritance taxes. The threshold for estate taxation is provided for each state. (Estates valued at or above the described threshold are subject to estate tax.)

- Connecticut: $2 million
- Illinois: $2 million
- Kansas: $1 million
- Maine: $1 million
- Massachusetts: $1 million
- Minnesota: $1 million
- New York: $1 million
- North Carolina: $2 million
- Ohio: $338,333
- Oklahoma: $1 million
- Oregon: $1 million
- Rhode Island: $675,000
- Vermont: $2 million
- Washington: $2 million

If the federal estate tax repeal becomes permanent, estate tax laws of Illinois and Vermont are scheduled to expire in 2010. Kansas and Oklahoma have passed legislation repealing their estate taxes as of January 1, 2010.

States That Impose Both Estate and Inheritance Taxes

Two states impose both estate taxes and inheritance taxes:

- Maryland: Estate tax threshold, $1 million
- New Jersey: Estate tax threshold, $675,000

Appendix C

Estate Planning Worksheet

• •

In This Appendix

▶ Setting your priorities

▶ Identifying your assets

▶ Choosing your beneficiaries

• •

*T*he following questionnaire can help you plan your estate and bequests and guide the creation of your estate planning documents. You should add additional lines and spaces as needed.

Estate Plan

Your estate plan encompasses your entire estate and how you want to leave your assets to your heirs.

Personal information

Your name: _____

Other names, nicknames: _____

Date of birth: _____ Social Security Number: _____

Place of birth: _____ Citizenship: _____

Home address: _____

Employer: _____ Occupation: _____

State of residence: _____ Length of residence in state: _____

Marital status: _____ Prior marriages: _____

Goals and priorities

What are your priorities for your estate plan? (Examples: providing for the education of your minor children, providing for the care and comfort of your spouse.)

_____

_____

Do you have any special concerns as you plan your estate? (Examples: providing for the future needs of a disabled child, disinheriting an heir.)

_____

_____

Family information

Please provide information about your family.

Your spouse

Spouse's name: _____

Other names, nicknames: _____

Date of birth: _____ Social Security Number: _____

Place of birth: _____ Citizenship: _____

Home address: _____

Employer: _____ Occupation: _____

State of residence: _____ Length of residence in state: _____

Date of marriage: _____ Place of marriage: _____

Prior marriages: _____ Children from prior marriages: _____

Your children

Name: _____ Age: _____

Address: _____

Is this a child from a prior marriage? _____ Adopted? _____

Is this child's education complete? _____ Special needs? _____

Do you want your child to inherit equally with your other children? _____

If your child dies before you, do you want their share go to their spouse, to their children (your grandchildren), or to your other surviving children? ____

_____

Name: _____ Age: _____

Address: _____

Is this a child from a prior marriage? _____ Adopted? _____

Is this child's education complete? _____ Special needs? _____

Do you want your child to inherit equally with your other children? _____

If your child dies before you, do you want their share go to their spouse, to their children (your grandchildren), or to your other surviving children? ____

_____

Name: _____ Age: _____

Address: _____

Is this a child from a prior marriage? _____ Adopted? _____

Is this child's education complete? _____ Special needs? _____

Do you want your child to inherit equally with your other children? _____

If your child dies before you, do you want their share go to their spouse, to their children (your grandchildren), or to your other surviving children? ____

_____

Your spouse's children (stepchildren)

Name: _____ Age: _____

Address: _____

Is this child's education complete? _____ Special needs? _____

Do you want your spouse's child to inherit equally with your children? _____
_____

If your spouse's child dies before you, do you want their share go to their spouse, to their children (your stepgrandchildren), or to your other surviving children? _____

Name: _____ Age: _____

Address: _____

Is this child's education complete? _____ Special needs? _____

Do you want your spouse's child to inherit equally with your children? _____
_____

If your spouse's child dies before you, do you want their share go to their spouse, to their children (your stepgrandchildren), or to your other surviving children? _____

Grandchildren

Name: _____ Age: _____

Parent: _____ Special needs? _____

Name: _____ Age: _____

Parent: _____ Special needs? _____

Name: _____ Age: _____

Parent: _____ Special needs? _____

Name: _____ Age: _____

Parent: _____ Special needs? _____

Your parents

If you want, also list any stepparents.

Mother: _____ Still alive? _____

Father: _____ Still alive? _____

Your spouse's parents

Mother: _____ Still alive? _____

Father: _____ Still alive? _____

Your brothers and sisters

Name: _____ Still alive? _____

Address: _____

Name: _____ Still alive? _____

Address: _____

Your spouse's brothers and sisters

Name: _____ Still alive? _____

Address: _____

Name: _____ Still alive? _____

Address: _____

Assets

Please describe your family's assets and how they're owned (solely by you, jointly with your spouse, or by your spouse).

Personal assets

Description	Location	Ownership	Value
Cash (bank accounts, CDs, money market accounts, and so on.)			
Investments (stocks, bonds, mutual funds, brokerage accounts, stock options, and so on.)			
Home furnishings			
Jewelry			
Antiques			
Artworks			
Collections (coins, stamps, and so on)			
Other:			
Other:			

Titled property

Description	Lender	Loan Balance	Ownership	Value
Car				
Boat				
Other:				

Real estate

Description	Address	Owner-ship	Cost Plus Improve-ments	Mortgage Balance(s)	Market Value
Primary residence					
Other:					

Have you ever lived in a community property state? (Arizona, California, Idaho, Louisiana, Nevada, New Mexico, Texas, Washington, Wisconsin) _____

_____

If yes, do you own a home or real property within that state? _____

Insurance policies and annuities

Type of policy (whole life, term life, and so on): _____

Insurance company: _____

Insured: _____ Owner: _____

Primary beneficiary: _____ Contingent beneficiary: _____

Death benefit: _____ Cash surrender value: _____

Balance of outstanding loan: _____ Annual premium: _____

Type of policy (whole life, term life, and so on.): _____

Insurance company: _____

Insured: _____ Owner: _____

Primary beneficiary: _____ Contingent beneficiary: _____

Death benefit: _____ Cash surrender value: _____

Balance of outstanding loan: _____ Annual premium: _____

Retirement plans

Please describe your retirement plans, including your IRAs, Keogh plans, deferred compensation plans, pensions, and 401K plans.

Plan Type	Where Held	Beneficiary Designation	Your Contri- bution	Loan Balance	Present Value

Business interests

Business name: _____

Address: _____

Business form (sole proprietorship, partnership, corporation, LLP, LLC, and so on.): _____

Ownership (you, spouse, children, other): _____

Original investment(s) (by you, spouse, children, other): _____

Approximate present value of your business: _____

Additional assets

Please describe any other assets that are part of your estate.

Intellectual property (patents, trademarks, copyrights): _____

Mortgages or leases: _____

Loans you have made: _____

Trusts: _____

Expected inheritances: _____

Other assets: _____

Debts

Please describe your debts.

Nature of Debt	Creditor's Name and Address	Amount Owed
Home mortgage		
Bank loan		
Credit cards		
Car loans		
Other:		
Other:		
Other:		

Bequests

Please describe the specific bequests you want to make in your will and trust.

Item (Describe)	Beneficiary	Alternate Beneficiary	By Will or by Trust
Example: Stamp collection	Son Michael	Cousin Fred	Will

Please be sure that all your specific bequests are carried over into the will and trust planning sections of this questionnaire, later in this appendix.

Special needs heirs

If any of your heirs are disabled, how do you want to provide for them? (Example: provision for basic care, provision for extra care and comfort to supplement government benefits):

_____

_____

_____

Alternate beneficiaries

If you survive all members of your family, who do you want to receive your estate? (In addition to a person, you can designate an educational institution, organization or charity.)

_____

_____

_____

Your advisors

Please identify your personal and financial advisors.

- ✔ Accountant: _____
- ✔ Lawyer: _____
- ✔ Insurance agent: _____
- ✔ Physician: _____
- ✔ Investment counselor: _____
- ✔ Stockbroker: _____
- ✔ Other: _____

Estate planning documents

Where do you store original copies of your estate planning documents?

Will: _____

Trust: _____

Durable power of attorney: _____

Healthcare proxy: _____

Living will: _____

Insurance policies and annuities: _____

If you have a safety deposit box, please describe its location and the name under which it is held: _____

Do you have a prior will or trust? _____

Do you have a prenuptial agreement with your spouse? _____

The following information will help you prepare your will.

Personal representative

Who will serve as your personal representative?

Name: _____

Address _____

Work Phone _____ Home Phone _____

First Alternate:
Name: _____

Address _____

Work Phone _____ Home Phone _____

Second Alternate:
Name: _____

Address _____

Work Phone _____ Home Phone _____

Do you want to require your personal representative to post a bond, to protect your estate from financial misconduct or mistakes? (The cost of the bond is paid by your estate.)

Guardian for minor children

Who do you select to serve as guardian of your minor children? If you want, you can designate different individuals to serve as guardians for the personal care of your children and guardians of their property.

Name: _____

Address _____

Work Phone _____ Home Phone _____

First Alternate:
Name: _____

Address _____

Work Phone _____ Home Phone _____

Second Alternate:

Name: _____

Address _____

Work Phone _____ Home Phone _____

Bequests

Referencing your planned bequests from the general form, please describe the specific bequests you want to make in your will:

Item (Describe)	Beneficiary	Alternate Beneficiary

Please describe the division of the residuary of your estate.

Beneficiary	Alternate Beneficiary	Percentage*

*The percentages should sum to 100 percent.

Special Distributions: Do you want to distribute funds from your estate before your entire estate is settled?

Description: _____ Heir: _____

Description: _____ Heir: _____

If an heir named in your will dies before you, how do you want your estate to distribute the bequest to that heir? (Example: *per capita,* divided equally among a class; *per stirpes,* divided equally among the heir's children; or treat the bequest as part of the residuary.)

_____

Estate taxes

Have you previously given taxable gifts (currently gifts to a recipient, valued in excess of $12,000 in a single year). If so, please describe them.

Description	Recipient	Year Given	Amount

If you filed gift tax returns for any of the gifts, you should keep copies of the tax returns with your will.

For items passing by will, how would you like estate taxes to be paid?

❑ Estate taxes should be paid from the residue of the estate.

❑ Each gift should "pay its own share" of estate taxes.

❑ Other: _____.

For items passing **outside** of your will, how would you like estate taxes to be paid:

❑ Estate taxes should be paid from the residue of the estate.

❑ Each gift should "pay its own share" of estate taxes.

❑ Other: _____.

Disinheritance

Are you disinheriting or intentionally omitting any heirs?

Name: _____

Name: _____

Trust provisions

Are you creating a trust with your will (a testamentary trust)? If so, describe the trust and your choice(s) of trustee(s) and successor(s):

_____

_____

_____

Are you funding a trust with your will (a pour over will)? If so, please identify the trust:

_____

Funeral and burial arrangements

You may provide information about your funeral and burial in your will or in a separate document. If you use a separate document, keep it with your will.

Cemetery lot: If you own a cemetery lot, what is the cemetery name and location?

_____

Funeral ceremony: What type of funeral do you want, how elaborate should it be, and where should the service be held?

_____

_____

_____

Memorial service: What type of memorial service do you want, and how formal should it be?

_____

_____

_____

Readings: Would you like a specific poem, scripture, song, quotation, or other reading?

_____

_____

Invitations: Are there any people you would like to have invited to your funeral and memorial service?

_____

_____

_____

Disposition of your body: Would you prefer burial, cremation, or another disposition?

_____

_____

Donations: Do you wish to donate organs or your body for transplant, research, or education?

_____

_____

Living Trust

The following information can help you prepare your living trust, if you choose to create one.

Trustees and alternates

During your lifetime, who will serve as the trustee? You, your spouse, you and your spouse, or somebody else?

_____

_____

Who will serve as trustee after your death(s):

Name: _____ Successor or cotrustee _____

Address: _____

Work phone: _____ Home phone: _____

First successor or cotrustee:

Name: _____ Successor or cotrustee _____

Address: _____

Work phone: _____ Home phone: _____

Second successor or cotrustee:

Name: _____ Successor or cotrustee _____

Address: _____

Work phone: _____ Home phone: _____

Do you wish to require your trustee to post a bond? _____

If you designate cotrustees, how do you want disputes to be resolved between the trustees? (For example., arbitration, drawing cards, coin toss.) _____

_____

Property to transfer into trust*

Using the list of property you created for your overall estate plan, list the property you intend to transfer into your trust. Your trust isn't complete until you transfer that property into your trust. After you transfer ownership into your trust, check to indicate that the transfer is complete.

Description	Check When Transfer Is Completed
Example: Marital Home, 1234 Sisyphus Drive, Toledo Ohio	√

* Your personal automobile is not typically transferred into your living trust.

Disinheritance

Are you intentionally omitting any heirs from your trust?

Name: _____

Name: _____

Distribution of trust assets

Referencing your planned bequests from the general form, please describe the specific distributions you want to make from your trust:

Item (Describe)	Beneficiary	Alternate Beneficiary

What conditions do you want to place on the trust? (For example, "Income starts at age 21, one-third of principal at age 25, and the rest at age 30.") Are there special circumstances when the principal may be used or distributed?

❑ All distributions should be made upon the death of the surviving grantor.

❑ Distributions to children should be held in trust until they reach age of

❑ Other: _____

Please describe the division of the residuary of your trust.

Beneficiary	Alternate Beneficiary	Percentage*

*The percentages should sum to 100 percent.

Conditions on distribution

What conditions do you want to place on the trust? For example, "Income starts at age 21, one-third of principal at age 25, and the rest at age 30.") Are there special circumstances when the principal may be used or distributed (for example, to provide for educational expenses, or "at the discretion of the trustee to provide for support, education, and medical care")?

_____

_____

Special concerns

Do you need to address any other special issues in your trust? For example, do you need to include a spendthrift provision to protect a child from creditors?

_____

_____

Durable Power of Attorney

In the event of your disability, your durable power of attorney designates the person (your agent) who can manage your financial affairs on your behalf.

Choice of agent

Who will serve as trustee after your death(s):

Name: _____ Successor or cotrustee _____

Address: _____

Work phone: _____ Home phone: _____

First successor agent:
Name: _____ Successor or cotrustee _____

Address: _____

Work phone: _____ Home phone: _____

Second successor agent:

Name: _____ Successor or cotrustee _____

Address: _____

Work phone: _____ Home phone: _____

Powers granted

In addition to managing your personal financial affairs, do you want to grant additional powers to your agent?

❏ The power to make gifts.

❏ The power to manage your business.

❏ Other: _____

Preferences for the sale of property

If your agent needs to sell some of your property in order to provide for your care or to protect the value of your estate, what are your preferences? Do you prefer any certain people as buyers?

_____

_____

Healthcare Proxy

Your healthcare proxy designates a medical advocate to make treatment decisions for you, if you're unable to make or communicate those decisions yourself. You can designate your spouse as your medical advocate.

Choice of medical advocate

Who do you want to serve as your medical advocate?

Name: _____

Address: _____

Work phone: _____ Home phone: _____

Successor:

Name: _____

Address: _____

Work phone: _____ Home phone: _____

Consulting with others:

Do you want your medical advocate to consult with other people (for example, a relative, your primary care physician) when making decisions for you? If so, please identify the people and describe when they should be consulted:

_____

_____

Care provider preferences:

Which healthcare facilities and providers do you prefer for your medical care and treatment?

_____

_____

Which healthcare facilities and providers do you want to avoid for your medical care and treatment?

_____

_____

Living Will

Please describe the medical care you desire during the last stages of your life.

❑ I wish for doctors to make all available efforts to extend my life.

❑ I wish for doctors to follow generally accepted medical standards and to provide all medical treatments within those standards.

❑ I do not want my life prolonged if I have a diagnosis or must undergo a treatment checked in the next section.

When should treatments cease

Under what circumstances do you wish doctors to **stop** life-extending treatments:

❑ You receive a diagnosis of an incurable condition that will soon result in death.

❑ You experience loss of consciousness or coma with doctors finding with reasonable medical certainty that you won't regain consciousness.

❑ The risks or side effects of treatment outweigh the medical benefits.

❑ Your life can be sustained only through artificial life support.

❑ Other: _____

Additional comments and explanation:

_____

_____

Treatments that may prolong life

If you're diagnosed with a terminal condition, which treatments do you choose *not* to receive:

❑ Having your life artificially prolonged by machine

❑ Blood transfusions

❑ Organ transplants

❑ Nutrition and hydration by feeding tube

Additional comments and explanation:

_____

_____

Comfort and pain relief

Please indicate the circumstances under which you choose not to receive care that, although not life-extending, contributes to your comfort:

❑ I wish to receive care to improve my comfort and pain level even if the treatment hastens death.

❑ I wish to receive care to improve my comfort and pain level unless the treatment hastens death.

❑ I wish to avoid treatments that interfere with my mental capacity to the point that I have difficulty understanding or communicating with other people.

❑ I wish to avoid treatments that carry harmful side-effects.

❑ Other: _____

Additional comments and explanation:

_____

_____

Place of death

If possible, where would you like to receive your end-of-life care? (Example: at home, in a hospice, in a specific nursing home or hospital.)

_____

Appendix D

About the CD

System Requirements

Make sure that your computer meets the minimum system requirements shown in the following list. If your computer doesn't match up to most of these requirements, you may have problems using the software and files on the CD. For the latest and greatest information, please refer to the ReadMe file located at the root of the CD-ROM.

- ✔ A PC running Microsoft Windows 98, Windows 2000, Windows NT4 (with SP4 or later), Windows Me, Windows XP, or Windows Vista
- ✔ A Macintosh running Apple OS X or later
- ✔ An Internet connection
- ✔ A CD-ROM drive
- ✔ Microsoft Word

If you need more information on the basics, check out these books published by Wiley Publishing, Inc.: *PCs For Dummies,* by Dan Gookin; *Macs For Dummies,* by David Pogue; *iMacs For Dummies* by David Pogue; *Windows 95 For Dummies, Windows 98 For Dummies, Windows 2000 Professional For Dummies, Microsoft Windows ME Millennium Edition For Dummies,* all by Andy Rathbone.

Using the CD

To install the items from the CD to your hard drive, follow these steps.

1. **Insert the CD into your computer's CD-ROM drive.**

   The license agreement appears.

   Note to Windows users: The interface won't launch if you have <u>autorun</u> <u>disabled</u>. In that case, click Start⇨Run (For Windows Vista, choose Start⇨All Programs⇨Accessories⇨Run). In the dialog box that appears, type D:\Start.exe. (Replace D with the proper letter if your CD drive uses a different letter. If you don't know the letter, see how your CD drive is listed under My Computer.) Click OK.

   Note for Mac users: The CD icon will appear on your desktop, double-click the icon to open the CD, and double-click the Start icon.

2. **Read through the license agreement and then click the Accept button if you want to use the CD.**

   The CD interface appears. The interface allows you to install the programs and run the demos with just a click of a button (or two).

What You'll Find on the CD

The forms and worksheets referenced are located on the CD and work with Macintosh and Windows 95/98/NT/Vista and later computers. These files contain forms to create a will, living trust, living will, durable power of attorney, and healthcare proxy. Here are the forms you can find in each folder:

- ✔ **Worksheets:** Estate Planning Worksheet; Trusts Worksheet; and Wills Worksheet.

- ✔ **Trusts:** Revocable Living Trust – Individual; Revocable Living Trust – Married Couple; Revocable Living Trust – Individual with A-B Trust; Pet Trust; Assignment of Property to Trust; Reversal of Assignment of Property to Trust; and Revocation of Trust.

- ✔ **Incapacity Planning:** Living Will; Healthcare Proxy; and Durable Power of Attorney.

- ✔ **Wills:** Married with Children; Married without Children; Single with Children; Single without Children; Domestic Partnership with Children; Domestic Partnership without Children; and Self-Proving Affidavits.

General instructions that apply to all forms are included as well. Each folder also contains detailed instructions.

Troubleshooting

I tried my best to compile forms and worksheets that work on most computers with the minimum system requirements. Alas, your computer may differ, and some may not work properly for some reason.

The two likeliest problems are that you don't have enough memory (RAM) for the programs you want to use, or you have other programs running that are affecting installation or running of a program. If you get an error message such as `Not enough memory` or `Setup cannot continue`, try one or more of the following suggestions and then try using the software again:

- **Turn off any antivirus software running on your computer.** Installation programs sometimes mimic virus activity and may make your computer incorrectly believe that it's being infected by a virus.

- **Close all running programs.** The more programs you have running, the less memory is available to other programs. Installation programs typically update files and programs; so if you keep other programs running, installation may not work properly.

- **Have your local computer store add more RAM to your computer.** This step is, admittedly, drastic and somewhat expensive. However, adding more memory can really help the speed of your computer and allow more programs to run at the same time.

Customer Care

If you have trouble with the CD-ROM, please call the Wiley Product Technical Support phone number at (800) 762-2974. Outside the United States, call 1(317) 572-3994. You can also contact Wiley Product Technical Support at **http://support.wiley.com**. John Wiley & Sons will provide technical support only for installation and other general quality control items. For technical support on the applications themselves, consult the program's vendor or author.

To place additional orders or to request information about other Wiley products, please call (877) 762-2974.

Index

• *M* •

Wiley Publishing, Inc.
End-User License Agreement

INESS, CAREERS & PERSONAL FINANCE

0-7645-9847-3

0-7645-2431-3

Also available:

- Business Plans Kit For Dummies
0-7645-9794-9
- Economics For Dummies
0-7645-5726-2
- Grant Writing For Dummies
0-7645-8416-2
- Home Buying For Dummies
0-7645-5331-3
- Managing For Dummies
0-7645-1771-6
- Marketing For Dummies
0-7645-5600-2

- Personal Finance For Dummies
0-7645-2590-5*
- Resumes For Dummies
0-7645-5471-9
- Selling For Dummies
0-7645-5363-1
- Six Sigma For Dummies
0-7645-6798-5
- Small Business Kit For Dummies
0-7645-5984-2
- Starting an eBay Business For Dummies
0-7645-6924-4
- Your Dream Career For Dummies
0-7645-9795-7

ME & BUSINESS COMPUTER BASICS

0-470-05432-8

0-471-75421-8

Also available:

- Cleaning Windows Vista For Dummies
0-471-78293-9
- Excel 2007 For Dummies
0-470-03737-7
- Mac OS X Tiger For Dummies
0-7645-7675-5
- MacBook For Dummies
0-470-04859-X
- Macs For Dummies
0-470-04849-2
- Office 2007 For Dummies
0-470-00923-3

- Outlook 2007 For Dummies
0-470-03830-6
- PCs For Dummies
0-7645-8958-X
- Salesforce.com For Dummies
0-470-04893-X
- Upgrading & Fixing Laptops For Dummies
0-7645-8959-8
- Word 2007 For Dummies
0-470-03658-3
- Quicken 2007 For Dummies
0-470-04600-7

OD, HOME, GARDEN, HOBBIES, MUSIC & PETS

0-7645-8404-9

0-7645-9904-6

Also available:

- Candy Making For Dummies
0-7645-9734-5
- Card Games For Dummies
0-7645-9910-0
- Crocheting For Dummies
0-7645-4151-X
- Dog Training For Dummies
0-7645-8418-9
- Healthy Carb Cookbook For Dummies
0-7645-8476-6
- Home Maintenance For Dummies
0-7645-5215-5

- Horses For Dummies
0-7645-9797-3
- Jewelry Making & Beading For Dummies
0-7645-2571-9
- Orchids For Dummies
0-7645-6759-4
- Puppies For Dummies
0-7645-5255-4
- Rock Guitar For Dummies
0-7645-5356-9
- Sewing For Dummies
0-7645-6847-7
- Singing For Dummies
0-7645-2475-5

ERNET & DIGITAL MEDIA

0-470-04529-9

0-470-04894-8

Also available:

- Blogging For Dummies
0-471-77084-1
- Digital Photography For Dummies
0-7645-9802-3
- Digital Photography All-in-One Desk Reference For Dummies
0-470-03743-1
- Digital SLR Cameras and Photography For Dummies
0-7645-9803-1
- eBay Business All-in-One Desk Reference For Dummies
0-7645-8438-3
- HDTV For Dummies
0-470-09673-X

- Home Entertainment PCs For Dummies
0-470-05523-5
- MySpace For Dummies
0-470-09529-6
- Search Engine Optimization For Dummies
0-471-97998-8
- Skype For Dummies
0-470-04891-3
- The Internet For Dummies
0-7645-8996-2
- Wiring Your Digital Home For Dummies
0-471-91830-X

WILEY

SPORTS, FITNESS, PARENTING, RELIGION & SPIRITUALITY

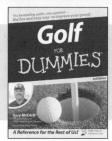

0-471-76871-5

0-7645-7841-3

Also available:

- Catholicism For Dummies
  0-7645-5391-7
- Exercise Balls For Dummies
  0-7645-5623-1
- Fitness For Dummies
  0-7645-7851-0
- Football For Dummies
  0-7645-3936-1
- Judaism For Dummies
  0-7645-5299-6
- Potty Training For Dummies
  0-7645-5417-4
- Buddhism For Dummies
  0-7645-5359-3

- Pregnancy For Dummies
  0-7645-4483-7 †
- Ten Minute Tone-Ups For Dummie
  0-7645-7207-5
- NASCAR For Dummies
  0-7645-7681-X
- Religion For Dummies
  0-7645-5264-3
- Soccer For Dummies
  0-7645-5229-5
- Women in the Bible For Dummies
  0-7645-8475-8

TRAVEL

0-7645-7749-2

0-7645-6945-7

Also available:

- Alaska For Dummies
  0-7645-7746-8
- Cruise Vacations For Dummies
  0-7645-6941-4
- England For Dummies
  0-7645-4276-1
- Europe For Dummies
  0-7645-7529-5
- Germany For Dummies
  0-7645-7823-5
- Hawaii For Dummies
  0-7645-7402-7

- Italy For Dummies
  0-7645-7386-1
- Las Vegas For Dummies
  0-7645-7382-9
- London For Dummies
  0-7645-4277-X
- Paris For Dummies
  0-7645-7630-5
- RV Vacations For Dummies
  0-7645-4442-X
- Walt Disney World & Orlando
  For Dummies
  0-7645-9660-8

GRAPHICS, DESIGN & WEB DEVELOPMENT

0-7645-8815-X

0-7645-9571-7

Also available:

- 3D Game Animation For Dummies
  0-7645-8789-7
- AutoCAD 2006 For Dummies
  0-7645-8925-3
- Building a Web Site For Dummies
  0-7645-7144-3
- Creating Web Pages For Dummies
  0-470-08030-2
- Creating Web Pages All-in-One Desk
  Reference For Dummies
  0-7645-4345-8
- Dreamweaver 8 For Dummies
  0-7645-9649-7

- InDesign CS2 For Dummies
  0-7645-9572-5
- Macromedia Flash 8 For Dummies
  0-7645-9691-8
- Photoshop CS2 and Digital
  Photography For Dummies
  0-7645-9580-6
- Photoshop Elements 4 For Dummi
  0-471-77483-9
- Syndicating Web Sites with RSS Fe
  For Dummies
  0-7645-8848-6
- Yahoo! SiteBuilder For Dummies
  0-7645-9800-7

NETWORKING, SECURITY, PROGRAMMING & DATABASES

0-7645-7728-X

0-471-74940-0

Also available:

- Access 2007 For Dummies
  0-470-04612-0
- ASP.NET 2 For Dummies
  0-7645-7907-X
- C# 2005 For Dummies
  0-7645-9704-3
- Hacking For Dummies
  0-470-05235-X
- Hacking Wireless Networks
  For Dummies
  0-7645-9730-2
- Java For Dummies
  0-470-08716-1

- Microsoft SQL Server 2005 For Dum
  0-7645-7755-7
- Networking All-in-One Desk Refere
  For Dummies
  0-7645-9939-9
- Preventing Identity Theft For Dumm
  0-7645-7336-5
- Telecom For Dummies
  0-471-77085-X
- Visual Studio 2005 All-in-One Desk
  Reference For Dummies
  0-7645-9775-2
- XML For Dummies
  0-7645-8845-1

LTH & SELF-HELP

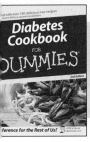

0-7645-8450-2

0-7645-4149-8

Also available:

Bipolar Disorder For Dummies
0-7645-8451-0

Chemotherapy and Radiation
For Dummies
0-7645-7832-4

Controlling Cholesterol For Dummies
0-7645-5440-9

Diabetes For Dummies
0-7645-6820-5* †

Divorce For Dummies
0-7645-8417-0 †

Fibromyalgia For Dummies
0-7645-5441-7

Low-Calorie Dieting For Dummies
0-7645-9905-4

Meditation For Dummies
0-471-77774-9

Osteoporosis For Dummies
0-7645-7621-6

Overcoming Anxiety For Dummies
0-7645-5447-6

Reiki For Dummies
0-7645-9907-0

Stress Management For Dummies
0-7645-5144-2

CATION, HISTORY, REFERENCE & TEST PREPARATION

0-7645-8381-6

0-7645-9554-7

Also available:

The ACT For Dummies
0-7645-9652-7

Algebra For Dummies
0-7645-5325-9

Algebra Workbook For Dummies
0-7645-8467-7

Astronomy For Dummies
0-7645-8465-0

Calculus For Dummies
0-7645-2498-4

Chemistry For Dummies
0-7645-5430-1

Forensics For Dummies
0-7645-5580-4

Freemasons For Dummies
0-7645-9796-5

French For Dummies
0-7645-5193-0

Geometry For Dummies
0-7645-5324-0

Organic Chemistry I For Dummies
0-7645-6902-3

The SAT I For Dummies
0-7645-7193-1

Spanish For Dummies
0-7645-5194-9

Statistics For Dummies
0-7645-5423-9

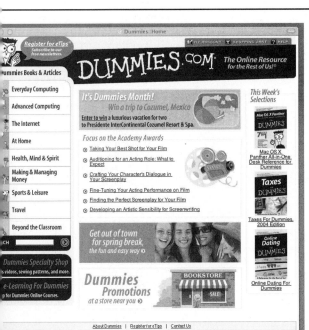

Get smart @ dummies.com®

- **Find a full list of Dummies titles**
- **Look into loads of FREE on-site articles**
- **Sign up for FREE eTips e-mailed to you weekly**
- **See what other products carry the Dummies name**
- **Shop directly from the Dummies bookstore**
- **Enter to win new prizes every month!**